Sucking SALT

Sucking SALT

Caribbean Women Writers,
Migration, and Survival

Meredith M. Gadsby

UNIVERSITY OF MISSOURI PRESS
COLUMBIA AND LONDON

University of Missouri Press, Columbia, Missouri 65201
Printed and bound in the United States of America
5 4 3 2 1   10 09 08 07 06

Library of Congress Cataloging-in-Publication Data

Gadsby, Meredith.
  Sucking salt : Caribbean women writers, migration, and survival /
Meredith M. Gadsby.
      p.   cm.
  Summary: "Examines the literature of black Caribbean emigrant and island
women including Dorothea Smartt, Edwidge Danticat, Paule Marshall, and others,
who use the terminology and imagery of "sucking salt" as an articulation of a New
World voice connoting adaptation, improvisation, and creativity, offering a new
understanding of diaspora, literature, and feminism"—Provided by publisher.
  Includes bibliographical references and index.
  ISBN-13: 978-0-8262-1665-6 (hardcover : alk. paper)
  ISBN-10: 0-8262-1665-X (hardcover : alk. paper)
  1. American literature—Women authors—History and criticism.
  2. American literature—Caribbean American authors—History and criticism.
  3. Canadian literature—Women authors—History and criticism.   4. English
literature—Women authors—History and criticism.   5. Women authors,
Caribbean—English-speaking countries.   6. Minority women in literature.
  7. Ethnicity in literature.   8. Culture in literature.   9. National characteristics,
Caribbean.   10. Caribbean Area—Social life and customs.   I. Title.
  PS153.C27G33   2006
  810.9'9287097291—dc22   2006013091

Designer: Kristie Lee
Typesetter: Phoenix Type, Inc.
Printer and binder: Thomson-Shore, Inc.
Typefaces: Minion, GillSans

For credits, see page 223.

This book is dedicated to the life and memory of

Millicent Eudora Gadsby

May 8, 1934–March 13, 2001

and to

Erma Loretta Gadsby Hinds

mother and friend

Contents

Acknowledgments

My mother was recently given a portrait of my maternal great grandmother, Millicent Gadsby. The photograph was taken in the early twentieth century, in Panama, where she lived with my great grandfather, William Gadsby, who helped to build the Panama Canal. Because no one in my family had ever seen it before, my mother quickly made copies for her siblings, nieces, and nephews. I have had my copy professionally framed; it sits on my fireplace mantle, amid photos of immediate family. Interestingly, the individual who did the framing for me told me that for the first time in his career, people asked to purchase this framed photo from him. Several people offered to buy it, remarking on what a striking and powerful photograph it is.

When I look at it, I see the faces of almost everyone in my family—aunts, uncles, cousins. We have inherited my great grandmother's small hands, hair, shape of eyes, and eyebrows. Her photograph is coded with loads of cultural information. Clearly taken in a photo studio, she is positioned with her left hand resting on a chair placed slightly in front of her. Her wedding band is evident, and the chair is positioned in a way that connotes her status as married. She is not smiling, and stares deep into the camera, as if commanding it to recognize her.

I do not believe that it is a coincidence that I received this photograph a year or so before the completion of this book. In fact, this makes perfect sense. My great grandmother shares the same name of the woman who is the inspiration for this book. That I should meet, on paper, the first Millicent Gadsby at this point in my life appears to be an act of fate, reminding me that in writing about the lives of Caribbean women, I must always remember those who created the space for me to do the work that I now do. It also reminds me to remember my investments; I am not writing for myself alone, but for my great grandmother, her mother, and so on, as well as my mother and my children after me.

I must thank the woman who was the primary inspiration for this book, Tantie, or Millicent Eudora Gadsby, who is the seed around which this study blossomed. Tantie was and is my mother's oldest sister. More than that, she is the person, besides my mother, whose life has had the most profound effect on me as a woman and scholar. Inspired by the brilliant portraits of Barbadian women captured by Paule Marshall, this book began as a creative writing project, in which I attempted to write about my family history as told from the vantage point of Tantie's kitchen. It is in this space that I felt most loved and cherished. My earliest memories exist there, and when I sit at her table in her chair with my son in my arms, I feel embraced by her presence, still.

To say that my mother, Erma Loretta Gadsby Hinds has been supportive of all my endeavors is an understatement, but it is true nonetheless. There is not a single thing or project that I have explored for which she has not offered wisdom, fabulous insights, and encouragement. She does not know this, but this book could not have been written without her calming, stabilizing energy and her quiet determination to see me do and see things she never even dreamed of. It is to her that I dedicate this book, and anything else of any consequence that I do in this life. I hope that I have made her proud.

This book is also the culmination of sleepless nights, missed deadlines, and triumphant trips to UPS and FedEx stores in the early morning hours. It is also the result of help from activists, scholars, and colleagues who offered constructive criticism at all stages of its development. I must thank the Oberlin College Department of African American Studies for constant encouragement to bring this work to fruition. My sisters and brothers in the department have given me valuable feedback on several sections of this manuscript. For this I will always be grateful. The Oberlin College Department of Gender and Women's Studies, specifically Frances Hasso and Wendy Kozol, have been true sisters in the struggle.

My colleagues at Oberlin College, specifically Pam Brooks, Caroline Jackson Smith, Gillian Johns, A. G. Miller, Gina Pérez, Pablo Mitchell, Anna Gade, and Sandra Zagarell, have provided much-needed feedback, encouragement, and advice. The Oberlin College Dean of Arts and Sciences award of the Grant in Aid provided funds necessary for the completion of this study.

I must also thank the membership of the Association of Caribbean Women Writers and Scholars for providing me a platform to share my work and a space to grow in the midst of a garden of fabulous scholars and writers. My professional development has been nurtured in this space. It is my goal to give to the organization more than I have received.

To all of my teachers, infinite thanks. Dr. Juliet Emanuel recognized my potential before I even knew I had any. She and Ms. Marilyn Beckford shielded me from those who sought to crush my intellectual curiosity before it saw the light of day. Ms. Keris Murray nurtured this curiosity and showed me that there was no limit to what I could achieve with proper diction and pronunciation! Thanks to Dr. G. Steven Moore for pushing me to realize my full potential as an intellectual, and for reminding me that this requires work, not platitudes. I must thank Dr. Gloria Wade Gayles, whose command to "claim my space" has inspired me to find my voice as a writer and intellectual. She and my sisters at Spelman College showed me that there is a space for Black women wherever we create it.

Most thanks to Dr. Carole Boyce Davies, who has seen more drafts of this book than anyone else. A mentor and friend, Dr. Boyce Davies encouraged me early on to give myself "the space to be brilliant." This is a space that many women, specifically women of color, have a difficult time claiming. Her work is a constant inspiration as an example of the possibilities for creating meaningful scholarship connected to the lives of Black women internationally. Thank you, Carole, for your friendship, love, and scholarship.

The African–New World Studies Program at Florida International University provided much-needed resources for research during the early stages of this project.

It goes without saying that my entire family has had a hand in the completion of this manuscript, whether they are aware of this or not. My family in Barbados housed me during trips to the island for archival and library research. They indulged me when I was a student collecting interviews, and they generously sat down with me to share experiences at home and abroad. Deirdre Gadsby shared her one-bedroom flat with me for many months as I conducted research in London. At key moments, Linda Gadsby offered and sent money to her broke cousin and offered to read drafts (which I never sent). Thank you to the entire Gadsby clan for sending me references, clipping articles, and supporting my work.

Thanks to Adrienne Blanding, Colette Stanford, Ladan Akbarnia, Gertrude James, Donna Weir-Soley—friends and colleagues who have helped take care of me and my need for loving and supportive sisters. I must thank the Peterson family for unwavering support and encouragement, especially my other parents, Gladys and Charles Frank Peterson Sr.

It is no small thing to have a partner with whom to share intellectual ideas, manuscript drafts, and scholarly interests. I am truly blessed to call Charles F. Peterson Jr. my partner and friend. His calming presence in the midst of the stress of manuscript submissions, late-night drives to FedEx Kinkos, afternoon walks with the baby (to give me time to work), and quiet conversations over glasses of wine help remind me of what is truly important in life. Most of all, thanks to (and for) our beautiful son, Caleb Cabral, who, in his first year of life, seems to have a sense of his mother's need for space to write.

Thanks as well to Millicent Gadsby (the first one) for gifts unknown.

Sucking SALT

One Introduction

Little Salt Won't Kill You

* *

*My aunt's kitchen smells of peppers, of stews, and mostly of saltfish. Tantie
loves saltfish, usually on days when she is undecided on what to eat for
dinner. "I don't feel like any meat today," she says. She beats back questions
and concerns about the effect this amount of salt will have on her diabetes
with the irrefutable "Eh, people that don't eat salt die too. People die everyday. I guess I'm just old-fashioned." She walks back and forth, then leans
against the counter, arms crossed on her ample breasts. Though she has no
children, she feeds her younger siblings, nieces, and nephews with mother
wit, wisdom, and life lessons, and with saltfish and cou-cou. Sometimes
she goes a bit overboard, both with salt and advice. Nonetheless, hungry
mouths, hearts, and minds continue to eat, washing down the salty meal
with mauby spiced with "old talkin'." "Little salt won't kill yuh." Tantie
speaks of people she knows, people she once knew. "Them people came up
hard, with nuthin'. But sometimes you just have to suck salt until you can
do better." It is in this space, this kitchen, that I learned most of what I
know about my family history. I found myself drawn to the histories of my
mother and three aunts and the lives that they have created for themselves.
Each woman has her own story to tell—four sisters: two in New York City,
two in Barbados. All but one left Barbados at some point, taking with them
literally "a little chunk of salt" to suck on when the situation demanded it.
They spin and have spun webs in the corners of a number of home spaces,
in Canada, the United States, and England, always connected to persistent
memories of "home." On their backs they carry their children, nieces,*

1

*nephews, cousins, and "the old people" from web to web. And they hold on
to that "little chunk of salt," breaking off pieces to give to their children to
sustain them when they have nothing else.*

*Aunt Muriel left Barbados in the late 1960s aboard a ship bound for
London. She went to take advantage of an opportunity to study nursing.
The "Little England" of her birth was dwarfed in comparison to the great
island called the "motherland." She knew the names of every English town
and hamlet by heart after having sat through hours of British geography in
primary school. But after a few years on the great island, following the
birth of her baby girl, she decided to return home. England was just too
cold: the people were cold, the air was cold, and the work was hard. Deciding
that it was better to suck salt in the sun than in the freezing cold, she returned
to Barbados.*

For my mother and my aunts, to "suck salt" is to survive on the bare
minimum, when one has nothing but salt, sweat, and tears to feed
oneself and one's children—no meat, no bread, no water, no food.
When asked what the term means to her, Tantie immediately responds,
"Hardship! Hard times." To elaborate, she references her own mother's
similar phrase, "picking peas out of shit." Implied in both is a determination to survive, to live to see another day, to pull something decent
out of nastiness. I deduced that the hardship Tantie describes can be
overcome with strength and resourcefulness.

The *Dictionary of Caribbean English Usage* provides the following
definition for *sucking salt*, which has Dominican, Guyanese, Tobagon-
ian, and Trinidadian origins: "To suffer much hardship; to have a rough
time of it, as in 'You're right boy, we have good luck or we would have
been *sucking salt* by now, like this bunch of paupers.'" Linda Spears-
Bunton suggests a similar connotation among African Americans in
Louisiana, taken from her recollection of the phrase as used by the
women in her family. In her words, one popular usage could be, "I said
hello to her and she looked like she was *sucking salt*," meaning that the
woman had a soured, disgusted look on her face.[1] Although both defini-

---

1. Richard Allsopp, *Dictionary of Caribbean English Usage,* 485. Spears-Bunton,
Associate Professor of English Education at Florida International University, shared

tions connote desperation and hopelessness, for the purposes of my study, *sucking salt* carries a simultaneously doubled linguistic sign of adversity *and* survival. It carries with it the will to overcome hardship, take stock of the situation, and rebuild. In a sense, then, "sucking salt" becomes more than the act of overcoming hardship. G. Addinton Forde supports this interpretation: "Even if I *suck salt*, [meaning] 'Even if I suffer.' With nothing to eat, *sucking salt* causes one to get thirsty and drink water, which makes the stomach feel full."[2] In my view, "sucking salt" is also a strategy for preparing oneself for impending hardship, often in an environment marked by constant upheaval, transition, and economic impossibility. It is a survival skill passed on from generation to generation of Caribbean women.

Although this study is inspired by the context of my own family history, the history serves as a point of departure that moves outward toward a critical reading of the meanings of *sucking salt* represented in Caribbean literature. It begins with the context in which I locate myself—within a history of extra-Caribbean migration and a larger history of African migration—and then examines the ways in which these forms of movement are experienced and written of by Caribbean women writers internationally. Fluid migration from the Caribbean to the United States, Canada, England, and back to the Caribbean is an integral part of my family's experience.[3] My aim is to examine the ways in which

---

this bit of cultural information with me during the discussion following my presentation of a paper (on the diasporic resonance of salt) for the African–New World Studies Works in Progress Series on Thursday, April 8, 1999, at Florida International University.

2. G. Addinton Forde, *De Mortar-Pestle: A Collection of Barbadian Proverbs*, 41. Other variations of the "sucking salt" theme include "Hungry mek cat eat salt" (Necessity causes people to do things they wouldn't normally do) (4); and "Crapaud have no right in salt water" (2).

3. Although many of the men in my family migrated freely throughout their lives for economic and personal reasons, in this study I will focus on the migrations of the women in my family. My grandfather's father worked on the Panama Canal. As a result, two of my great uncles were born in Panama. My grandmother's brother moved to Cuba for work and never returned to Barbados. In 1945, my maternal grandfather traveled to upstate New York to work for General Foods/Birdseye Schneider in a canning factory. During the seven months he spent in the United States, he traveled up and down the east coast and in California. He decided not to stay in the United States because "it was too busy."

Caribbean women construct and reconstruct communities and parallel worlds in migration.

The notion of salt as a metaphor for hardship and the symbolic meanings of "sucking salt" provide the unifying thread for this work. Each component contains a discussion of hardship coupled with a simultaneous narrative of transcendence or a strategic negotiation out of difficulty in the literature examined. "Sucking salt" then becomes a cultural/linguistic code signifying such theorizations. My work searches for these theorizations within the literary production of Caribbean women writers writing of migration to Great Britain, Canada, and the United States. Simultaneously, I will examine the strategies employed by Caribbean women writers, activists, and laborers for surviving hardship and adversity.

My work, therefore, has two components. First, it examines the cultural and historical significance of salt in the Caribbean. The recent proliferation of salt and salt imagery in works by Caribbean writers such as Earl Lovelace, Edouard Glissant, Fred D'Aguiar, Nalo Hopkinson, and others who are referenced in this study exemplify the persistence of salt imagery in the Caribbean literary imagination.[4] Second, this study explores creative resistance to systems of oppression as expressed in the novels of Black women writers in Britain, employing the same approach in a similar analysis of writings by Caribbean women and women of Caribbean descent who write about migration to New York City and Canada. Each component will examine the strategies with which Caribbean women writers articulate the conceptual meanings of *sucking salt* as they live, work, and write.

Since I am approaching this study of Caribbean women's writing through the lines of my maternal history, I deal specifically (though not exclusively) with migration to Canada, the United Kingdom, and the United States.

My work focuses on gender and Caribbean women's writing, examining the ways in which "sucking salt" is employed as a survival strategy in the literature discussed. I have found that allusions to numerous and unaccounted for representations of "sucking salt" exist in the culture

---

4. Earl Lovelace, *Salt: A Novel;* Edouard Glissant, *Black Salt;* Fred D'Aguiar, *Feeding the Ghosts,* 3–5; Nalo Hopkinson, *The Salt Roads.*

and creative work of peoples of African descent throughout the diaspora. Toni Cade Bambara's *The Salteaters* (in which the character Velma seeks out the healing and restorative powers of salt) and Earl Lovelace's novel *Salt* are but two examples which directly use salt in their titles, but the work of Edwidge Danticat contains several literal and figurative examples of "sucking salt," particularly in discussions of women's space and struggles for survival in Haiti and the United States (particularly in New York City). The creative artistry of Paule Marshall, in her novels as well as in her autobiographical essays, has had a profound influence on my critical approach to the study of Caribbean women's writing and the development of my understanding of Caribbean symbolic, cultural, and practical expressions.[5] Though salt is not identified practically, the celebration of Black women's language, space, and lives is an important contribution to theorizations in feminist studies, Black women's writing, cultural studies, migration, and diaspora studies. Honored by Edwidge Danticat as "the greatest kitchen poet of all," Marshall's influence on her contemporaries and on younger generations of writers and scholars is tremendous.[6] In my own case, reading *Brown Girl, Brownstones* was an important step in my intellectual development, as it provided me with the first literary example of the creative, political, and instructive qualities of the kitchen spaces in which I was raised. As such, Marshall introduced me to the possibility of recognizing theoretical spaces that exist outside of the academy.

The work of many feminist scholars and literary and cultural theorists have greatly contributed to my research.[7] Dionne Brand's work has been helpful to me in teasing out my own conceptual meanings of *sucking salt*. Brand's essay collection *Bread Out of Stone* is a creative and critical exploration of issues of power, race, gender, sexuality, global exploitation, and resistance. The chapter "Water More Than Flour" is a wonderful discussion of the ways that Caribbean Women resist hardship, even in

5. See the following works by Paule Marshall: *Brown Girl, Brownstones; The Chosen Place, the Timeless People; Praisesong for the Widow; Reena and Other Stories; Soul Clap Hands and Sing; Daughters;* and "The Making of a Writer: From the Poets in the Kitchen," in *Merle: A Novella and Other Stories.*

6. Edwidge Danticat, *Krik? Krak!* 227.

7. Please see the Literature Review at the end of this book for a discussion of extant literature.

the face of impossibility. She privileges women's space (here located in the kitchen) as a space in which Caribbean women can speak freely and gracefully of the pain, economic adversity, and racial and gender oppression that confronts them on a daily basis. Brand describes the artistry of their language, saying it is "more poetic, more expressive than any statement they could produce to say 'we are hungry and going to stay that way, and there are those out there who want us to be hungry, and we don't know when this is going to end, but it ain't right, and if we ever catch their ass it's going to be the big payback, but don't worry, god is going to take care of them.'"[8] Even in the midst of great hardship, Caribbean women use language to resist, to challenge, and to mobilize for retaliation. As a metaphor, "sucking salt" carries a conceptual challenge similar to "water more than flour," implying the same preparedness to persevere and fight.

Black feminist theorists such as Barbara Smith have already reclaimed the kitchen as a space of women's power and creativity. As part of a praxis that theorized away from discussions of domestic work as enslavement, Smith and the Kitchen Table Women of Color Press Collective founded a publishing company of the same name in 1983. In this context, the kitchen space can be read as a storehouse of creativity; a space in which women, while creating works of culinary art, feed their children and one another with a language of resistance. Novelist Paule Marshall submits that this "kitchen table talk" infuses its participants as well as the little girls who linger in the corners of the room and at the doorway listening in on "big women's talk" with much-needed communal support and spiritual sustenance.[9] Marshall and Brand create pictures of the kitchen space that remove it from the realm of the merely domestic prison as it is often described in mainstream feminism. From the perspective of the kitchen, "sucking salt" signals creativity—creative responses to difficult circumstances via language and culinary ingenuity.

Within the context of migration, then, both metaphors recall a culture of communal support that manifests in the determination of Caribbean women to confront oppressions in the new spaces they enter, to re-create

8. Dionne Brand, *Bread Out of Stone: Recollections, Sex, Recognitions, Race, Dreaming, Politics*, 124.

9. 'Molara Ogundipe-Leslie, "Re-creating Ourselves All Over the World: A Conversation with Paule Marshall," 21.

communities, and, in their literature and creative writing, to continue a tradition of social, political, economic, and cultural critique. Inherent in both formulations is a critique of dominant institutions and a commitment to survive.

Black Like Who? Converging Black Realities

Definitions of Blackness are often quite complex, especially in relationship to the shared multilayered histories of colonialism, neocolonialism, and imperialism of people of color in the West. For example, Reuel Rogers's essay "'Black Like Who?' Afro-Caribbean Immigrants, African Americans, and the Politics of Group Identity" offers valuable information on Caribbean patterns of outward migration and identity formation, particularly in relationship to the complex nature of negotiating Black and Caribbean identity in North America. Essays by Irma Watkins-Owens and Mary C. Rogers provide excellent insights into the immigration experiences and social networks created by Caribbean migrants in the early twentieth century and the resulting experiences of the second generation. Mary C. Waters, in *Black Identities: West Indian Immigrant Dreams and American Realities,* explores the history of twentieth-century Caribbean migration and the tension between expectation and opportunity for progress. Waters makes the brilliant point that the reality of racism in the United States "soon overwhelms the identities of the immigrants and their children," especially among the working class and poor. As a political concept, Blackness translates differently in different contexts. Whereas first-generation migrants to the United States from the English-speaking Caribbean arrive with their own experience with Blackness shaped by being reared in majority environments with Black peoples functioning successfully in multiple positions of power, for the second generation, "race as a master status in the United States soon overwhelms the identities of the immigrants and their children, and they are seen as black Americans. Many of the children of the immigrants develop 'oppositional identities' to deal with that status.... Over the course of one generation the structural realities of American race relations and the American economy undermine the cultures of the West Indian immigrant and create responses among the immigrants, and especially their children, that resemble the cultural

responses of African Americans to long histories of exclusion and discrimination."[10] Whereas, in the Caribbean, experiences with inequality
exist more at the level of socioeconomic class, the institutionalization of
racism in the United States creates another layer of Black identity in
which discrimination from a racial majority necessitates a reevaluation
of Black identity in the context of a long history of African American
struggles for equal treatment under the law. In response to this new reality, the children of Caribbean migrants often embrace a Black identity
that is simultaneously Caribbean and American.

In the United Kingdom, the term *Black British* at one point referred
to non-White populations in the same way *people of color* is used in the
United States, Canada, and Latin America. In the twenty-first century,
the term appears to refer most explicitly to people of African descent
born in England. The *Charting the Journey* editorial group explains the
development of Black British identity as the process of "transforming
transplanted ways of being, seeing and living—ways of life both determined by, and opposed to, colonial domination," into a way of existing
and surviving whole within the belly of the colonial beast. Black British
identity was thus a product of racism, as it was resistance to racist treatment, institutional and social exclusion, and persecution. The *Charting
the Journey* editorial group, writers, activists, and scholars have extended
notions of "Black" and "British" as subsequent generations struggled
against racism and social, sexual, and cultural repression.[11]

Kobena Mercer's discussion of Blackness in Britain is quite useful.
According to Mercer, understanding the notion of "translation," or the
"identity formations which cut across and intersect natural frontiers,

10. Mary C. Waters, *Black Identities: West Indian Immigrant Dreams and American Realities*, 8.
11. The subtitle of their anthology and the various nationalities and ethnicities
represented within its pages exemplify the fact that in the United Kingdom, the idea
of "Blackness" is incredibly complicated. The authors and editors in the text are
united by a common struggle against imperialism and racism and by their commitment to resist what the editors identify as "State-created fissures of ethnicity [that]
threaten to engulf and overwhelm us in islands of cultural exclusivity." Thus they
are continuing the process of migration "into a better, more comfortable place where
we are made in our own, ever-changing image" (Shabnam Grewal, Jackie Kay, Liliane
Landor, Gail Lewis, and Pratibha Parmar, eds., *Charting the Journey: Writings by Black
and Third World Women*, 1, 5).

and which are composed of people who have been dispersed forever from their homelands . . . [who] belong at one and the same time to several homes (and to no one particular 'home')," as articulated by Stuart Hall and Salman Rushdie, is central to comprehension of the particular meanings of Blackness in Britain.[12] For the people whose national identity has been completely reconfigured as a result of the convergence of Asian, African, and African Caribbean peoples and cultures living together on the small island that is England, the lines previously demarcating British identity (White British) have been blurred, if not almost completely eroded. To complicate things further, those whose racial history had already integrated both the Asian and African diasporas in the pre-emancipation Caribbean must be rearticulated in the United Kingdom as African, Indian, Caribbean, and British simultaneously. This means that the profile of the "Englishman" has been completely transformed, particularly in the wake of a generation of Black peoples who are English by birth.

I must also account for the increasing use of the term *African Caribbean* among Caribbeans in England. The reality of racist violence and discrimination has caused many to reject the notion of Britain as a mother country. Edward Pilkington writes that the Notting Hill Riots in 1958, in which Whites rioted against Black people for four days, forced Caribbeans to reevaluate their own colonial notions of citizenship and to begin a search for self-identity.[13] This search has resulted in the desire of Caribbeans and people of Caribbean descent to emphasize their historical and cultural connections to Africa and the Caribbean, and therefore to reject the erasure of that connection that British identity implies. Many Caribbeans in the United States have attempted to make this connection obvious as well by embracing the term *Caribbean American*. According to Grosfougel's work, the 1990 census in the United

12. Kobena Mercer, *Welcome to the Jungle: New Positions in Black Cultural Studies*, 27; Stuart Hall, "The Question of Cultural Identity," 308. Again, I challenge this notion of permanent separation, which seems to be more a result of the particular experiences of Rushdie, Hall, and V. S. Naipaul than that of many migrants from the Caribbean, who move between "home" and "home" with fluidity—that is, the expatriate set who travel constantly between their newly constructed homes in the Caribbean nations of their birth and England, Canada, and the United States.

13. Edward Pilkington, *Beyond the Mother Country: West Indians and the Notting Hill White Riots*.

Kingdom for the first time used "African Caribbean" as a category other
than "West Indian." It is interesting to note here that in scholarship on
migration from the Caribbean, specifically from the English-speaking
Caribbean, there persists an insistence upon using "West Indian" as opposed to "Caribbean" or "Caribbean American." For the purposes of this
study, I will use *Caribbean, Caribbean American,* and *African Caribbean*
in an effort to move beyond the legacies of colonial designations for
cultural identity. I do so in spite of the fact that many people from the
Caribbean continue to use this term.

Identity, then, must be characterized as fluidly ever-changing. In the
context of my work, it is inextricably linked to notions of diaspora,
migration, race, sexuality, and gender. History, gender, class, race, and
social conditions mediate articulations of identity. Stuart Hall argues
that Black Caribbean identities are "'framed' by two axes or vectors,
simultaneously operative: the vector of similarity and continuity; and
the vector of difference and rupture. Caribbean identities always have to
be thought of in terms of the dialogic relationship between these two
axes."[14] In my reading, however, this "framing" of African Caribbean
identities is far too confining. Rather than locate them amid a tired binary of "difference" and "rupture," it might be more useful to move away
from any type of "framing" and instead use the language and concept of
multiple locations. This clears plenty of space for looking at and experiencing Caribbean identities (as we who identify as Caribbean always
are) with all of its historical and cultural complexity. To "frame" binds
an object or idea in rigidly defined barriers, with very little room for
growth. It is precisely because Caribbean identities are constantly growing and changing, as a result of the experience of diaspora and migration, that they must be understood within the context of space. Caribbean identities redefine space, and although they do involve notions of
difference and similarity, they also involve notions of revolution, resistance, and change.[15]

14. Stuart Hall, "Cultural Identity and Diaspora," 395.
15. Although Hall does submit that the concept of difference with which he works
is always shifting, its boundaries extended in myriad ways, particularly as represented in African Caribbean film and visual arts, I find the location of Caribbean
identities within any binary—even those with flexible boundaries—stifling.

This study examines the ways in which Caribbean women effect this change in literatures and narratives of resistance. My work focuses on the identities these Caribbean women have created for themselves as writers, mothers, daughters, activists, and scholars. I read these identities through the lenses of Black feminism, cultural studies, history, critical race theory, sexuality, and gender.

My understanding of *Caribbean* is not limited to geographical location. I find myself more in agreement with authors, such as Michelle Cliff, who argue that Caribbeanness as a concept cannot be narrowed down to a particular space. Cliff asserts that "the Caribbean doesn't exist as an entity; it exists all over the world. It started in diaspora and continues in diaspora." With all of the migrations, forced and otherwise, that have historically been important elements of Caribbean experience, it seems ludicrous to force Caribbean identity to adhere to exclusive criteria that afford any one person or group the right to be "inside." Such a practice would reinscribe in the field of Caribbean women's writing the institutionalized exclusion and canonization that force it to the periphery in Western academia. "As Caribbean writers," Cliff submits, "we need to recognize the extremes we were brought up under, have internalized, which may charge our work as well as censor us."[16] In addition, considering the size of Caribbean communities outside of the Caribbean (especially Brooklyn, New York, which contains the highest concentration of Caribbeans outside of the Caribbean), limiting Caribbean identity as something that only those living in or born in the islands can possess seems ridiculous. Clearly those born to Caribbean parents outside of the Caribbean are shaped by their experiences in their places of birth; identity does not just fall away or disappear when one leaves home. Identities are constantly shifting and adapting to new encounters. Therefore it is quite common to find young people who, though they have never been to the Caribbean, speak with heavy Caribbean accents, eat only Caribbean food, listen to Caribbean music only, and who culturally have a complex identification with mainstream or Black American identity.

16. Cited in Meryl F. Schwartz, "An Interview with Michelle Cliff," 597; Michelle Cliff, "Caliban's Daughter: The Tempest and the Teapot," 38.

This speaks to the transitional nature of diaspora. By *diaspora* I mean specifically the African diaspora, or the massive forced migration for the purpose of enslavement of continental Africans with the advent of the Atlantic slave trade, and the resulting dispersal of Africans all over the world.[17]

With all of these discourses in mind, I use the term *diaspora* as a rope linking the histories of those who are the descendants of enslaved continental Africans in a cultural and historical continuum. Viewed in this way, the notion of peoples of African descent does not limit identity to phenotypic identity. Instead, it lends itself to a comparative approach to the study of these peoples that examines various articulations of subjectivity by those who, though sharing a common history, experience their realities in different ways. "Diaspora" is now understood as existing in multiple contexts. Both African and Asian diasporas shape the history of the Caribbean.[18]

Often, the return to ancestral homelands has symbolically occurred via re-creation of homeland in new home space, fusing past with present. East Indians and Chinese descendants of indentured laborers re-create

17. The term *diaspora* had historically been used by scholars of Jewish history to describe the experience of forced removal of Jews from a homeland to various parts of the world. What distinguishes the African diaspora is that it is grounded in an unequal hierarchical economic, political, and institutional relationship in which Black peoples are relegated to the bottom.

18. Scholars must be careful when using the term *diaspora* in regard to Asians. According to Wang Gungwu, director of the East Asian Institute at the National Institute at the National University of Singapore, "Scholars are applying the concept of a diaspora to the Chinese people living outside China, often for all sorts of reasons that I don't completely understand." He continued, "Now I'm adopting the word— but with a great deal of reluctance. . . . The problem is that, until the 20th century, the Chinese did not even have a word for diaspora." Karen J. Winkler, who interviewed Gungwu, explains that the Chinese had instead "used three different terms. First, imperial rulers—who discouraged peasants from leaving the land, and sanctioned relocations primarily to defend military outposts or because of such disasters as plague or famine—coined a term meaning 'moving people.' It almost always implied movement instigated by the government. . . . As Chinese merchants spread out, the word for 'sojourning' appeared: It applied mainly to elites, and was based on the assumption that people could, and would, return shortly to China. The word for 'flow people' applied to drifters, usually single men who were looked upon with disapproval." Thus, at the level of the academy, *diaspora* continues to be a controversial term that must be used carefully (Karen J. Winkler, "Historians Explore Questions of How People and Cultures Disperse across the Globe," A12).

India and China in religious practices and rituals, as is evidenced in the novel *The Last English Plantation* by Janice Shinebourne and *The Pagoda* by Patricia Powell. Similarly, people of African descent "return" via New World religious beliefs, including Myalism, Santería, Candomble, Obeah, Shango, Vodun, and so on, and with songs, mythology, and language.

Migration thus takes many shapes in this context—physical, metaphorical, and figurative. It embodies several states of being, including disruption, recollection, regeneration, and moving from confining spaces into open ones (and vice versa). The tie that binds each of these articulations in this study is the notion of migration. One must be careful not to conflate the terms *diaspora* and *migration*. As Colin Palmer has reminded us, "There is in the scholarly imagination too much conflation of the two terms."[19]

Migration refers to the movement and dislocation, whether voluntary or involuntary, of peoples of African descent from one place to another. I examine migration within the context of the Caribbean during the eras of colonization, decolonization, and independence. The shifts in global international relationships during these periods provide foundational information on the impetus for the Caribbean diaspora. As a concept, "sucking salt" is a web connecting the particular forms of hardship confronted by Caribbean women as they encounter these relationships. I argue that in their lives, writing, and the decision to move out of oppressive social, political, geographical, and economic spaces, Caribbean women have turned the notion of "sucking salt" into a battle cry. It connotes a commitment to overcome and transcend adversity.

Give Me Room! Clearing New Theoretical Spaces

My use of the phrase "give me room," or what Carole Boyce Davies refers to as "taking space" (in the context of dance and Carnival), is designed to take this discourse into the realm of the performative. It is my contention that theoretical interventions are as much performative as they are ideological. The exhortation "give me room" is directly connected to dance—to soca, calypso, and dance hall—and gently warns fellow revelers that someone will soon be moving in ways that cannot

19. Ibid., A11.

be contained, motivated by one's own personal relationship with the music being played. This movement is encouraged by the music, which tells the body how to move. Boyce Davies describes this process as one of constant negotiation:

> Taking space ... means moving out into areas not allowed. ... These areas include ... the basic sentence of Carnival parading that one sees versions of in New Orleans, Trinidad and Brazil, in which the dancer negotiates the road, creating space, as in the Trinidad verbalized "give me room." ... In this particular context, the dancer is able to negotiate among a variety of other dancers, his/her own particular dance space. Another example is limbo in which the space metaphor is graphically expressed in terms of a before and after with either side of the limbo bar or pole a space of physical freedom. The pole which has to be negotiated in the language of dance represents slavery and/the slave ship and the physical gesture of Middle Passage piled on with fire, lowered to the ultimate, necessitates physical dexterity and finally transcendence.[20]

Without using the explicit language of "sucking salt," the notion of creating new space is implicit here, particular in reference to transcendence. This conceptual intervention, then, seeks to contribute to scholarship on Caribbean women's literature that necessarily move, not in a self-consciously academic pattern of theorizing, with its limitations and attempts at recolonization, but in directions initiated by the writings themselves. This is where this book locates itself.

I will here borrow Carole Boyce Davies's discussion of journeying or "going a piece of the way with them." Referencing Zora Neale Hurston's discussion of greeting visitors to her town and engaging them with discussion as she went a "piece of the way with them," Boyce Davies likens her negotiations with theory as traveling with visitors whom she must engage only up to a point, lest she run the danger of being inevitably placed "in the 'homes' of people where [she], as a Black woman, will have to function either as maid or exotic, silenced courtesan, but definitely not as a theoretical equal." She uses what she refers to as "visitor theory"

---

20. Carole Boyce Davies, "Carnivalised Caribbean Female Bodies: Taking Space/ Making Space," 341.

to interrogate a variety of theoretical approaches for their usefulness to the study of Black women's literature.[21]

I would like to take this "visitor theory" in another direction, this time locating myself as the visitor, a Black second-generation Caribbean American woman with a working middle-class background, traveling through the academy, picking up bits of theory along the way, and discarding those that are counterproductive to hearing and understanding the complex subjectivities and theories that emerge out of Black women's lives and writings internationally.

Since the publication of Barbara Smith's "Towards a Black Feminist Literary Criticism" in 1970 and subsequent struggles for the existence and development of Black women's studies as a legitimate academic field, scholars have built a rich critical body of theory with which to analyze Black women's writing. Black feminist literary criticism has struggled with and continues to engage issues of silence and voicelessness, sexuality, race and racism, gender, and theories of migration (especially in recent debates around gender and migration in history). My work is informed by the work of Black feminist scholars and theorists such as Audre Lorde, Carole Boyce Davies, Dionne Brand, bell hooks, Barbara Christian, and Barbara Smith, particularly their discussions of silence, voicelessness, and resistance.

Barbara Christian's essay "The Race for Theory" is instructive here. Arguing against the co-optation of literary critics into the exclusivity of postmodern theory, she critiques what she sees as the academic gangsterism of postmodern theorists. Christian argues that "some of our most daring and potentially radical critics (and by *our* I mean black, women, third world) have been influenced . . . into speaking a language and defining their discussion in terms alien to and opposed to our needs and orientation."[22] For Christian, the issue of audience is crucial. For whom are we theorists writing? If the creative writers with whom we work resist oppression and silencing in all its forms, than we must refrain from creating theoretical categories that reinscribe such oppression. As Christian

---

21. Carole Boyce Davies, "Negotiating Theories or 'Going a Piece of the Way With Them,'" in Boyce Davies, *Black Women, Writing and Identity: Migrations of the Subject,* 46.

22. Barbara Christian, "The Race for Theory," 457. Christian's essay originally appeared in *Cultural Critique* in 1987.

explains, the "race for theory," then, "with its 1980's linguistic jargon, its emphasis on quoting its prophets, its tendency towards 'Biblical' exegesis, its refusal even to mention specific works of creative writers, . . . its pre-occupations with mechanical analyses of language, graphs, algebraic equations, its gross generalizations about culture," can silence us as theorists, if we let it, just as it can silence the creative texts themselves. This "race" is counterproductive to the work of such pioneering scholars as Gloria T. Hull, Patricia Bell Scott, and Barbara Smith, in their volume *All the Women Are White, All the Blacks Are Men, but Some of Us Are Brave*, in which the editors called for the development of a praxis within Black women's studies that was simultaneously academic and activist.

In the activist tradition of Audre Lorde, my work incorporates the notion of "the personal as political." Ethnographic research constitutes a large part of this study. The personal interviews conducted with Caribbean women and women of Caribbean descent in the United Kingdom, Canada, and the United States provide a wide range of migration experiences across generations. I also use oral histories, recorded and in print where available.

Cultural studies and critical race theory inform this study as well. Stuart Hall's discussions of diaspora and migration provide insight into the ways in which identity is constructed in relationship to race, culture, and history. In addition, to form useful conceptualizations on race, I study the literary output of numerous writers, along with the critical work done on their works.

Christian asserts that Black women writers and scholars of Black women's writing struggle with academic co-optation, even as they reside within academia, refusing to be confined by the boundaries created by various theories that attempt to lock their work inside narrow academic categories, and this position undergirds my work. My approach moves away from and "shakes off" limited understandings of Black women's writing and subjectivity that are fixed within geographical, national, or ethnic "categories" of writing.

Boyce Davies's work introduces a new way of imagining migrations by situating one's own family history as a point of departure for theoretical work instead of those of dominant discourses (such as postcoloniality, postmodernism, masculinist Western theorizations of "third world" peoples, and deconstruction). In my own work, I have discarded these discourses as confining, as they fall short of articulating Black women's subjectivities. Boyce Davies advocates a movement beyond the various "posts" to look at the resistant spaces created by Black women outside of and with no interest in academic discourses: "If we see Black women's subjectivity as a migratory subjectivity existing in multiple locations, then we can see how their work, their presences traverse all of the geographical/national boundaries instituted to keep our dislocations in place. This ability to locate in a variety of geographical and literary constituencies is peculiar to the migration that is fundamental to African experience as it is specific to the human experience as a whole."[23] Therefore, "going a piece of the way" with Black women writers translates into physical and historical journeys across international boundaries and through consciousness.

The works of Marlene Nourbese Philip provide a theoretical example; they carry us backward to the experience of slavery and forward into the present linguistic, cultural, and psychic legacies of the Middle Passage. In a reading held at Florida International University on January 20, 1999, she spoke of attempting to create a language in which to efficiently communicate the experience of the Middle Passage, its results, and its legacies for Black peoples. She also attempts to create what Gayle Jones, in her novel *Corregidora*, refers to as "a new world song," the creation of a language capable of expressing the experience of Africans in the West. Like Philip, she grapples with issues of silence and voicelessness, breaking silence with an implosion of the Black woman's lyric voice.[24]

"Sucking salt" is an articulation of this "new world voice," connoting adaptation, improvisation, and creativity. With its many manifestations,

23. Boyce Davies, *Black Women, Writing,* 4.

24. Jones's protagonist Ursa tries to develop a new language, a new song, borne out to the specific experience of Black women with enslavement, sexual abuse, incest, and psychological abuse experienced in the "new world." Out of this experience comes very particular theorizations about race, Black women's sexuality, issues of power directly out of a history of slavery, Black women's textuality, working-class Black culture, blues culture, as well as issues of performativity; see Gayle Jones, *Corregidora,* 59. See also the following works by Marlene Nourbese Philip: *She Tries Her Tongue, Her Silence Softly Breaks; Looking for Livingstone: An Odyssey of Silence;* and *Genealogy of Resistance and Other Essays.*

it lends itself perfectly to multiple readings of diaspora, literature, and feminism. Attached to migration is a type of exile that at the same time separates one from place of birth as well from the new society encountered. For example, according to Tantie, having left Barbados in 1952, when she was just eighteen, she was more of a New Yorker than a Barbadian.[25] This exile necessitates the creation of a new space, born specifically out of the experience of migration, that constantly confronts the challenges that such an existence entails. Thus Tantie's home became a new space in which one of her sisters and all four of her brothers were received and harbored until they were able to create new spaces of their own. Therefore, I deliberately attempt to move away from discussing only the alienating aspects of migration and instead focus on the ways Caribbean women theorize and work against such alienation. I also avoid representing Caribbean women as psychologically fragmented.

The women in my family around whom I built this study left Barbados for a number of reasons, but the primary impetus for leaving home was the desire to create new spaces for economic and intellectual growth. As they moved, settled, and resettled, their identities have undergone inevitable change. Notions of exile and return have shaped their lives as well as those of the children they raised in each of the spaces they have moved in and through. Growing up in the homes of my mother and aunt in Caribbean New York and making constant visits to Barbados throughout my childhood and adolescence have had a definite effect on my identity. In addition, constant migration and return has historically affected both the nations to which they migrated and the nations they left behind. In my reading of their literature, Caribbean women express the complex identities born out of migration and various practical approaches not only to theorize, but also to negotiate themselves out of difficulty.

My grandmother's legacy to her daughters is her determination to challenge, resist, and overcome. Hardship, according to Tantie, builds character and substance. While listening to my mother and my aunts talk about my grandmother and other women they left behind, I learned much about what it meant to be a Barbadian woman. I also learned much about language. Similar to Paule Marshall, listening to my maternal

25. Millicent Gadsby, interview with the author, September 10, 1998.

relatives "taught me how one uses language in a creative and vital way."[26] Sunday afternoons in Tantie's kitchen became a time and a space in which she, my mother, and my female sisters and friends could (re)claim a language of resistance against an outside world of patriarchal dominance (within and across racial lines), economic exploitation, and racist oppression. In infusing my work with the "kitchen table talk"—words, speech patterns, and wisdom of the women in my family—I am attempting to create a new conceptual space for critical examination of Caribbean women's literature that is directly informed by the lives and experiences of women as they "re-create themselves all over the world."[27]

26. Cited in Ogundipe-Leslie, "Re-creating Ourselves," 21. Marshall speaks in great detail of the kitchen poets of her childhood and their contributions to her development as a writer in "Making of a Writer."

27. Ibid., 22.

Two The Salience of Memory

The Cultural and Historical Significance
of Salt in the Caribbean

* *

*Master was frustrated with the recalcitrance and rebelliousness of his
slaves. They ran away constantly. He punished them, beat them, all to no
avail. Finally he turned to one of his most prized house slaves, Uncle Tom,
for advice. He asked him what he could do to stop the slaves from escaping.
The house slave told his master to feed them salt, for salt would make their
spirits heavy and weigh them down. The master then ordered that the slaves
be rationed salted cod, salted pork, and salted beef each month. From then
on, the slaves were forever bound to the plantation, unable to escape again.*

*When the slaves discovered Uncle Tom's betrayal, they beat him. In order
to guard against future betrayal from Uncle Tom or anyone else, they
used drums to communicate information from the hills to the plantation.
This way, no one would ever be able to inform the master of their plans or
secrets again.*

The tale above is an adaptation of one told to me by Sadner Con-
nell, a Grenadian woman poet I met at the Sixth International
Conference of Caribbean Women Writers and Scholars on May 21, 1998,
in Grenada. The tale functions in a number of ways. It rationalizes the
widespread use of salted foods among people of the Caribbean, a practice that originated in the days of slavery, when plantation owners purchased large portions of inexpensive dried and salt-cured meats and

fish for slaves from England.[1] These foods traveled well on the long journey from England to the Americas.

The tale also provides a historical example of the ways in which many enslaved Africans, psychologically damaged by the experience of enslavement, betrayed fellow slaves who had made the decision to free themselves from bondage and reject the brutalization and abuse experienced on the plantation. Last and equally important, the tale recollects the spiritual as well as physical rejection of the system of slavery. It recalls the body of tales and stories of slaves who "flew away" from bondage over cliffs, over seas, and home to Africa.

Frost provides an example of the diasporic currency of the "flying Africans" tale, linking it to the Surinamese legend of "Sjaki and the Flying Slaves." The tale has political significance, as it resonates with the July 1, 1863, abolition of slavery in Suriname. According to the legend, the flying slaves visit their descendants to celebrate their liberation annually on that day. Sjaki, a young boy, is wandering through the forest when he meets Liba, a witch woman who feeds him a drug that induces sleep and fantastic dreams. He dreams that Liba honors his request to turn him into a bird so that he can soar with the flying slaves. He soon

---

1. Barry Higman, in *Slave Populations of the British Caribbean, 1807–1834,* explains that slave owners in the British Caribbean fed slaves with products rationed from abroad until 1807. Rationing was rarely practiced after 1807 because of several subsistence crises (occurring after the American Revolution and the Napoleonic Wars) that resulted in the deaths of thousands of slaves. After these crises, slave owners depended less on external food sources and focused instead on internal crop cultivation and allocation of provision grounds to slaves: "All rural slave owners possessing land permitted their slaves to cultivate garden plots around their houses and to raise small livestock" (204). Slaves then depended on plantation owners for rations of imported saltfish and salted meat. Ground provisions (yams, potatoes, eddoes, tanias, and other roots) were grown locally and rationed out to slaves on a weekly or daily basis. Thus plantation owners continued to import salt products, which they distributed to slaves along with locally cultivated produce. Higman continues, "In Barbados, where the dependence on rations was greatest, the 'usual allowances' described by planters match quite closely those prescribed by the abolition act of 1834 and are corroborated by the evidence of actual practice on the large plantations. In 1824 the planter Forster Clarke claimed that 'grown' Barbadian slaves received daily allowances of 1½ pt of Guinea corn (sorghum) or 2 pt of Indian corn (maize), making 4.4–5.0 lb when dressed, or the same weight in roots, and weekly allowances of 1 lb of salt fish, 1 pt molasses, 2 pt of salt" (204–5).

discovers the flying Africans just as the men are making their ascent up the highest hill to subsequently jump off to escape slavery. However, the children of these men, in an effort to make their fathers stay with them, had put salt in their food, which would prevent them from flying. Here, salt represents enslavement, or a hindrance to physical transcendence of enslavement.

Fortunately, Sjaki is only dreaming, and the men do not fall to their deaths. In his dream, he is able to recall the history of the flying slave men, and they are able to relive the experience. They tell the boy, "We're glad you came. . . . It was the first time since it happened that we had a chance to relive it properly." They tell Sjaki how they had survived their dive:

> It was a long time ago, many years before Emancipation, that word had gone round that those of us who could stop eating salt would be able to fly back to Africa. So we all went on a salt-free diet. But our wives and children were forced to eat food in the houses where they worked. So it became clear that it would be mostly us men who would fly back. Our children did not want to lose us.[2]

The flying slaves return every year to caution those left behind not to attempt flight, for they have been tainted by the ingestion of salt. Instead, they must stay behind and construct lives for themselves in resistance to slavery and persecution. I would also argue that the flying slaves come to their descendants to remind them of the positive possibilities of resistance and of building transformative New World communities as they maintain the spiritual connection between the living and the ancestors.[3]

The Ibo Landing story is also important to examine, for although it has no direct reference to salt as discussed here, it is one of the most popular tales of slaves who returned home to Africa. Floyd White, an

2. In Eleanor W. Traylor, Alphonso Frost, and Leota S. Lawrence, eds., *Broad Sympathy: The Howard University Oral Traditions Reader*, 110.

3. Hopkinson's novel *Salt Roads* contains an excellent use of this narrative of salt avoidance. The character Makandal is fictionalized as a shape-shifting revolutionary Haitian leader who avoids salt for fear that it will hinder his ability to effectively communicate with the loa.

elderly man interviewed for the Georgia Writer's Project in the 1930s, told a tale of flying Africans that explicitly identifies Ibo Landing, located at Dunbar Creek on Saint Simons Island, off the coast of Georgia:

> Heahd bout duh Ibo's Landing? Das duh place weah dey bring duh Ibos obuh in a slabe ship an wen dey git yuh, dey ain lak it an so dey all staht singin an dey mahch right down in duh ribbuh tuh mahch back tuh Africa, but dey ain able tuh git deah. Dey gits drown.[4]

Frankie and Doug Quimby, professional storytellers, or griots, also from the Sea Islands, tell the tale a bit differently.

> During the time of slavery they would load and unload slaves at Dunbar Creek, on the north end of St. Simon's Island on the east coast of Georgia. On one particular trip a ship went to Africa to get more people to bring them here to America to sell them for slaves.
>
> While the slave traders were in Africa, they went by the Ibo tribe, and they found eighteen grown people. They fooled them. They told them, "We want you to go to America to work."
>
> When these people got to St. Simon's Island, they found out that they had been tricked and they were going to be sold as slaves. Then all eighteen of these people agreed together. They all said, "No! Rather than be a slave here in America, we would rather be dead."
>
> They linked themselves together with chains and they said a prayer. They said, "Water brought us here, and water is going to carry us away." They backed themselves out into Dunbar Creek and drowned themselves.
>
> As they were going down, they were singing a song in their African language. We continue to sing the same song today using English words.
>
> Today, Dunbar Creek on St. Simon's Island is a historical spot visited by throngs of people who have heard the story. Some visitors

---

4. Savannah Unit, Georgia Writers' Project, Work Projects Administration, *Drums and Shadows: Survival Studies among the Georgia Coastal Negroes,* 185 (hereinafter cited as *Drums and Shadows*).

who have gone to Dunbar Creek on nights when the moon shines a certain way say they have heard the muffled sounds of voices talking, people wailing, and chains clinking.

The Quimbys close their recounting with "The Ibo Landing Song," preserving the legend of the Ibos in the spiritual "Oh Freedom" with the chorus,

> Oh freedom, oh freedom, oh freedom over me
> And before I'd be a slave I'll be buried in my grave
> And go home to my Lord and be free.[5]

Paule Marshall uses a version of the Ibo Landing story modeled on White's recollection in her novel *Praisesong for the Widow*. Julie Dash, in turn, modifies Marshall's fictional account and uses it in her film *Daughters of the Dust*, which is set in the Georgia Sea Islands. Dash's cinematic representation of the story fuses the visual with the written, bringing the recollection to life in the history of the Pazant family. However, the slaves do not drown in either Marshall's or Dash's versions; they succeed on the journey home. It is interesting that Floyd White's account definitively states that the slaves drowned. Although Frankie and Doug Quimby make the same argument, they contend that in death, the Ibo made a spiritual journey back to Africa and out of bondage. This is the point at which the story makes the leap between history and mythology.[6]

Two African American tales of flight come to us from Wallace Quarterman. Quarterman, an elderly man living in Darien in the 1930s, told WPA interviewers that he remembered the following version of the "flying Africans" tale:

> Well, at dat time Mr. Blue he wuz duh obuhseeuh an Mr. Blue put um in duh fiel, but he coundn do nuttn wid um. Dey gabble, gabble, gabble, and nobody coudn unduhstan um an dey didn know how tuh wuk right. Mr. Blue he go down one mawnin wid a long whip fuh tuh whip um good. . . . He got tuh whip um, Mr. Blue, he ain hab no choice. Anyways, he whip um good an dey gits tuhgedduh

---

5. Traylor, Frost, and Lawrence, *Broad Sympathy*, 110.

6. Another variation of the theme of flight is told by Josie Snead, in Patricia Liggins Hill, ed., *Call and Response: The Riverside Anthology of the African American Literary Tradition*, 64.

an stick duh hoe in duh fiel an den say "quack, quack, quack," an
dey riz up in duh sky an tun thesef intuh buzzuds an fly right back
tuh Africa.

According to Alphonso Frost, although Quarterman had not actually
witnessed the event, he knew many slaves who saw the hoes left behind
by the Africans stuck in the ground.[7]

Other versions of this tale appear in Toni Morrison's *Song of Solomon*,
Earl Lovelace's *Salt*, and Paule Marshall's *Praisesong for the Widow*. Grace
Nichols references a bit of it in her poem "Ala", in which an African
rebel woman,

> who with a pin
> stick the soft mould
> of her own child's head
> sending the little new-born
> soul winging its way back
> to Africa—free ... [8]

is covered with molasses and left in the hot Caribbean sun, legs and
arms tethered to the ground, for ants to feast upon, as punishment and
warning to the other enslaved women. Here, flight in the form of bodily
death exists as resistant alternative to persecution—against all odds.
The body symbolizes a prison over which the enslaved have little physical control. In this context, transcending enslavement must take the
form of death, allowing the spirit to fly free.

In tales of flying Africans, the consumption of salt prevents the
enslaved from escaping bondage by making their spirits too heavy.
"Sjaki and the Flying Africans" provides one example. Earl Lovelace
uses a version of the tale in the beginning of his recent novel *Salt*. And
Lorna McDaniel, an ethnomusicologist who has conducted extensive
and invaluable research on the Big Drum Ritual of Grenada and Carriacou, was told by an "old head," or elder, in his late eighties (who identified
as African) on the island of Carriacou an almost identical story of the
inability of Africans who had eaten salt to fly home. She was told: "The

7. *Drums and Shadows*, 150–51; 96.
8. Grace Nichols, *I Is a Long Memoried Woman*, 23.

Africans who were brought here didn't like it. They just walked to the sea. They all began to sing as they spread their arms. And a few rose to the sky. Only those who did not eat salt left the ground. The Africans flew home."[9] Forever bound to the land to which they were now held hostage, the enslaved, in body and spirit, could not (except under specific circumstances, such as the founding of Liberia and Sierra Leone, for example) physically return home to Africa.

McDaniel provides an example of a discussion of salt as hindrance to spiritual transcendence and/or persecution in her study *The Big Drum Ritual of Carriacou: Praisesongs for Rememory of Flight.* In the various rituals connected with the Big Drum, food offerings to ancestors and to river and sea orisas are not prepared with salt. Participants can consume salt, but only in small amounts. McDaniel argues that overconsumption of salt is as much a part of African diasporic physical history and consciousness as is the insistence on avoidance of it. Again, salt makes the spirit too heavy to fly. Although the consumption of salt would be necessary under the conditions of slavery (for the purpose of water retention in the hot sun), overconsumption also leads to hypertension and various other health problems.[10]

The issue of salt, then, is very important for African diasporic representations of flight. According to McDaniel, when the body is heavy, levitation is impossible. In African diasporic mythology, spirits are the only beings that can travel all over the world, and they do not eat salt. In several belief systems, (Shango, Condomble, Santería) foods prepared for the ancestors never contain salt. McDaniel's explanation for this is that "We know from our physical experience that salt holds us down, so we are not going to [serve it] to the spirits."[11]

This belief in the spiritual benefits of the avoidance of salt is also held by Rastafarians and participants in the Kumina tradition. According to Clinton Hutton and Nathaniel Samuel Murrell,

9. Recorded at the roundtable on *Praisesong for the Widow* by Paule Marshall at the Sixth International Conference on Caribbean Women Writers and Scholars in Grand Anse, Grenada, on May 20, 1998. The culmination of McDaniel's work is *The Big Drum Ritual of Carriacou: Praisesongs in Rememory of Flight.*

10. Ibid.

11. Ibid.

A commonly held view among Kuminists and many Jamaicans is that the ancestral spirits do not eat salt. Within Kumina tradition, Africans who do not consume salt are able to develop the power to "interpret all things," as well as the ability to "fly from Jamaica back to Africa." The strongly salt-based diet introduced on the estates by the "plantocracy" is thus viewed by some Rastafarians as a European plan to thwart their desire to repatriate to Africa and to corrupt their minds with colonial thoughts. It is not hard to see why, within the context of communal life at Pinnacle [Hill, a plantation house purchased in the early period of the Rastafarian movement for meetings and services], where Kumina people constituted the core, cooking without salt—now an essential feature of Rasta menu—fit with [Leonard Percival] Howell's [one of the early founders of Rastafari, credited with being the first to preach the divinity of Haile Selassie] ideas of knowledge, repatriation, anticolonialism, and the rejection of European values. While eating unsalted food may not have any religious value in and of itself, in Rasta communes, psychologically this practice engenders hope, self-preservation, and identity with African roots.[12]

In Howell's pamphlet *The Promised Key,* an early text that explained Rastafari teachings, tenets, and rituals, instructions for fasting included placing a basin of fine or coarse salt on the table to be used with water for hand washing after fasting. This ritual was used to wash away all evil. In later versions of *The Promised Key,* this recommendation was altered with the substitution of salt with "herb," signaling the rejection of salt and the greater integration of ganja (cannabis) into the rituals of Rastafari. Kevin O'Brien Chang and Wayne Chen contend that the Rastafarian avoidance of salt "has been linked to a belief among the indentured BaKongo, who came to Jamaica after emancipation, that eating salt prevented them from flying back to Africa." These multiple metaphors

12. Clinton Hutton and Nathaniel Samuel Murrell, "Rastas Psychology of Blackness, Resistance, and Somebodiness," in Nathaniel Samuel Murrell, William David Spencer, Adrian Anthony McFarlane, eds., *Chanting Down Babylon: The Rastafari Reader,* 46. Kumina is a Central African cultural and religious tradition linked to the Congo people. Many Rastafarian rituals have Kumina as their source (ibid.).

and narratives of flight and the usage or nonusage of salt unite African diasporic cultural traditions, mythology, and ritual.[13]

McDaniel develops several interpretations of the flying home narrative that she uses as an organizational metaphor for her *Big Drum Ritual of Carriacou,* in which she reads the narrative of flying Africans through an analysis of the nation songs sung by each of the nations represented (Coromantee, Ibo, Mende, and so on) during the Big Drum ritual. She has identified 120 different songs, and her text is divided using four ideals of flight. Chapter 1 interprets the oldest nation songs as the physical rebellion against slavery and the final spiritual flight of suicide. Chapter 2 deals with the artistic, dream-inspired aspect of flying home as represented through ritualistic dance. Chapter 3 concerns religious flight of spiritual ecstasy. Chapter 4 examines the composition and transformation of ritual songs into calypso. She identifies the metaphor in African American spirituals such as "I'll Fly Away." The metaphor is clearly an enduring symbol in African diasporic culture that represents resistance to historical, cultural, and spiritual oppression. The descendants of the first enslaved Africans in the Americas, then, returned to Africa by way of the foods they ate, the songs they sang, and their hairstyles, fashion, spiritual expression, kinship networks, and, most important, struggle against all forms of oppression.

The Mysteries of Flight: Recent Literary Reimaginings of Salt

Toni Cade Bambara's groundbreaking novel the *Salt Eaters* is the first and most obvious discussion of the literal, metaphorical, and spiritual dimensions of "sucking salt" found in Black women's writing. But at the time of this writing, Nalo Hopkinson's recent novel *The Salt Roads* provides the most explicit discussion of "sucking salt" in Caribbean women's fiction. *The Salt Roads* revolves around the lives of three women: Auntie Mer, a slave woman and healer on Sacre Coeur plantation in eighteenth-century Saint Domingue; Jeanne DuVal (LeMer), the biracial, French-

13. William David Spencer, "Leonard Howell's 'The Promised Key,'" in Murrell et al., *Chanting,* 365–76; Kevin O'Brien Chang and Wayne Chen, *Reggae Routes: The Story of Jamaican Music,* 243. See also McDaniel, *Praisesong* roundtable, May 20, 1998.

born mistress of Charles Baudelaire; and Meritet, a Nubian prostitute in Alexandria, Egypt, fifteen hundred years earlier. The women are bound spiritually by Ezili Fredo, a deity in the Haitian Vodun pantheon of loas, who is born from the spirit of a baby who was stillborn on Sacre Coeur plantation. Auntie Mer, a healer born in Benin, delivers this baby, born to Georgine, a very light-skinned woman (a griffone), and buries it with the help of her lover, Tipingee, at the mouth of the nearby river. Ezili Fredo arises out of the experience of enslavement and shuttles between the psyches of Auntie Mer, Jeanne, and Meritet. She moves through time and space, between Africa and Europe, growing in strength and consciousness until she is able to take her place among the pantheon of New World African loas.

Hopkinson has explained that the title fits her novel well, for "salt is so much in the book. The salt roads are literally a means of travel for the goddess Ezili from one place to another. Salt is also life, and although these women's lives are hard, they are also full of joy." Much is made in the novel of the strength of the women, especially in relation to the hardships suffered in enslavement. The salt roads bind these women in a braid, according to Ezili Fredo: "Like them, I feel like crying, like squeezing out that salt water of which I am so, so weary. These bodies that entrap me—they are nothing but brine bound about by flesh." She, like the women, attempt to transcend the entrapment, the drowning in the legacy of the Middle Passage, to remember from whence they came and find the courage to move forward, as they must. Lasiren, lwa of all the waters, laments the drying up of the sea roads: "The sea in the minds of my Ginen. The sea roads, the salt roads . . ." She implores Mer to do something about this, to keep the connection between the enslaved peoples in Sacre Coeur and Africa alive in their memories, as they foment rebellion, led by Makandal.[14]

From the very first page, Hopkinson weaves into her novel the metaphor of salt. The text opens with the smell of salt rising from the cliffs. She begins the tale with Auntie Mer and Makandal in a discussion of the latter's refusal eat salt. Every slave had been "baptized" in seawater upon arrival in Haiti, to "bind [them] in salt to [the] island. Maybe not

---

14. Hopkinson quoted in Wilda Williams, "Must-Reads for Fall"; Hopkinson, *Salt Roads*, 265.

Makandal, . . . [who was] never fed the salt of the bitter soil of this new
world to tie his earthly body down to it, never ate the salt fish and the
filthy haram." It is Makandal's refusal to eat salt that angers the lwa, for it
is an indication of hubris. When Auntie Mer asks him, "You eat salt, or you
eat fresh?" she accuses him of a desire to transform himself into a lwa.[15]

Several writers have recently utilized the cultural meanings of salt
and of flight in their work, particularly in relationship to resistance to
slavery. For example, Toni Morrison, although she does not make an
explicit reference to salt, in *Song of Solomon* uses the "flying home" metaphor as a device to bring climax to the story of Milkman Dead's quest
for his family history. He pieces together the puzzle of his ancestry by
deciphering the following ring game:

> Jake the only son of Solomon
> Come booba yalle, come booba tambee
> Whirled about and touched the sun
> Come konka yalle, come konka tambee
>
> Left that baby in a white man's house
> Come booba yalle, come booba tambee
> Heddy took him to a red man's house
> Come knonka yalle, come konka tambee
>
> Black lady fell down on the ground
> Come booba yalle, come booba tambee
> Threw her body all around
> Come konka yalle, come konka tambee
>
> Solomon and Ryna Belali Shalut
> Yaruba Medina Muhammet too.
> Nestor Kalina Saraka Cake.
> Twenty-one children, the last one Jake!
>
> O Solomon don't leave me here
> Cotton balls to choke me
> O Solomon don't leave me here Buckra's arms to yoke me
> Solomon done fly, Solomon done gone
> Solomon cut across the sky, Solomon gone home.[16]

15. Hopkinson, *Salt Roads,* 9.
16. Morrison, *Song of Solomon,* 303.

In the Georgia WPA folklore collection *Drums and Shadows,* an elder named Prince Sneed shares a similar myth; his version includes many of the same African-based words and phrases used to initiate flight as Morrison's:

> Muh gran say ole man Walburg down on St. Catherine own some slaves wut wuzn climatize an he wuk um hahd an one day dey wuz hoein in duh fiel an duh dribuh come out an two ub um wuz unuh a tree in duh shade, an duh hoes wuz wukin by demsef. Duh dribuh say "Wut dis?" an dey say, "Kum buba yali kum buba tambe, Kum kunka yali kum kunka tambe," quick like. Den dey rise off duy groun an fly away. Nobody ebuh see um no mo. Some say dey fly back tuh Africa. Muh gran see dat wid he own eye.[17]

In his novel *Salt,* Earl Lovelace begins his narrative with the discussion of slaves who, having tasted salt, were unable to fly home to Africa—unlike Guinea John, who makes the journey successfully:

> With his black jacket on and a price of two hundred pounds sterling on his head, [Guinea John] made his way to the East Coast, mounted the cliff at Manzanilla, put two corn cobs under his armpits and flew away to Africa, taking with him the mysteries of levitation and flight, leaving the rest of his family still in captivity mourning over his selfishness, everybody putting in their mouth an saying, "You see! That is why Black people children doomed to suffer: their own parents refuse to pass on the knowledge that they know to them...."... [Guinea John] really wasn't happy hearing his children cursing him. It wasn't a good sign. He knew they had a heavy load to carry; but when a people begin to curse their elders, the next step they take is to curse their gods. He loved his children. It was their living that would make him an ancestor. His wisdom was theirs to have; but they had eaten salt and made themselves too heavy to fly. So, because now their future would be in the islands, he preferred not to place temptation in their way by revealing to them the mysteries of flight.[18]

17. *Drums and Shadows,* 78–79.
18. Lovelace, *Salt,* 3.

Here, salt symbolizes the conditions of diaspora, or more specifically the new lives, cultures, and histories constructed by those whom Guinea John left behind. Although they are unable to return to Africa, the salt they had eaten—in the form of separation from homeland and the attempts of their enslavers to "season" them, to break their spirits through brutality and torture—created a culture of rebellion.

In this opening chapter, Lovelace also parodies British attempts at dominating the Africans they had chosen to enslave, chronicling the "hardships" suffered by the British in their failed attempts at forcing their captives to submit: "The heat, the diseases, the weight of the armour they had to carry in the hot sun, the imperial poses they had to strike, the powdered wigs to wear, the churches to build, the heathen to baptize, the illiterates to educate, the animals to tame, the numerous species of plants to name, history to write, flags to plant, parades to make, the militia to assemble, letters to write home . . ."[19]

"Tasting salt" does not merely signify eternal separation from Africa. Even the name "Africa" takes on multiple signification as homeland and the ancestral birthplace of a people with a history of resistance to Atlantic slavery. If return to the continent of Africa was no longer an option, the Africans left on the island of Trinidad would fight for freedom on their own terms. Lovelace continues:

> Four hundred years it take them to find out that you can't keep people in captivity. Four hundred years! And it didn't happen just so. People had to revolt. People had to poison people. Port-of-Spain had to burn down. A hurricane had to hit the island. Haiti had to defeat Napoleon. People had to run away up the mountains. People had to fight. And then they agree, yes. We can't hold people in captivity here.[20]

In his discussion of revolt and revolution, Lovelace writes of the synthesis of the pan-Caribbean consciousness that recalls "sucking salt" in the forms of suffering and rebellion.

In J. D. Elder's retelling of "The Legend of Ma Rose Point," "tasting salt" takes on a somewhat different meaning. Elder writes that it was be-

19. Ibid., 5.
20. Ibid., 7.

lieved in Trinidad and Tobago that slaves who had "tasted salt"—here meaning those who had diluted their Ibo blood by intermarriage with slaves of other ethnic groups (or Whites)—were forever bound to the New World. In beginning to create new relationships within the context of enslavement, they had made a spiritual and psychological break with homeland. Ma Rose, a Scotch-Ibo—the product of a union between a Scot and an Ibo woman—is the symbol of such a break. Although this "tasting of salt" results in the creation of a new life in slavery, thus making her physical return to Africa theoretically and mythologically impossible, her constant acts of resistance against both her condition and the violence inflicted on slaves connect her to her Ibo ancestors, known as the fiercest and most rebellious of the slaves brought to the New World.[21]

In *Salt,* Lovelace makes a specific reference to the rebellious nature of women on the plantation, harkening back to the legend of Ma Rose:

> And it wasn't just the men alone. It had women there that was even more terrible. They had to ban them from talking. They had to ban them from walking and from raising up their dresstail and shaking their melodious backsides. They wasn't easy. The plantation people couldn't handle them. They beat them. They hold them down and turn them over and do them whatever wickedness they could manage: but they couldn't break them.[22]

Despite the circumstances that resulted in her birth, Ma Rose reconnects to the legacy of those who flew home to Africa by jumping to her death into the sea to avoid being whipped to death for biting through the windpipe of an overseer. The sea and salt here become diasporic metaphors signifying both separation and reconnection with homeland.

Ma Rose's final act of resistance is spatially transformative, altering the landscape of the plantation by infusing the land with sacrificial blood of the dead overseer and the blood and sweat of her fellow slaves. First, the landscape of the plantation, particularly the cliff over which she jumped, had been previously noted as being the location of the "whipping tree," where recalcitrant slaves were whipped to death and

---

21. J. D. Elder, ed., *Ma Rose Point: An Anthology of Rare Legends and Folk Tales from Trinidad and Tobago,* 14.
22. Lovelace, *Salt,* 7.

left to rot for various crimes. Ma Rose transformed this space from a point of psychic and physical brutality into "Ma Rose Point," the spot where she chose to claim ownership of her body, her life and death, thus becoming a symbol of revolutionary rebellion for the other bodies enslaved on the plantation. Ma Rose defined the boundaries between Africa and the New World, hurling her body into the very same sea that carried her ancestors to the New World hell that was slavery.

Second, Ma Rose Point and the sea around it (which is said to roar up in anger that can only be appeased with a libation of rum before a sailor can continue onward) take on new meaning in spirit, baptized with the blood of Ma Rose. In *Salt*, Lovelace writes of the ways in which resistance is etched into the landscape of the Caribbean, specifically Trinidad and Tobago: "Watch the landscape of this island . . . and you know that they could never hold people here surrendered to unfreedom. The sky, the sea, every green leaf and tangle of vines sing freedom."[23] "Tasting salt" therefore takes on a new representation with Ma Rose, who joins the countless Africans entombed in the floor of the salt sea during the Middle Passage, simultaneously becoming landscape, seascape, and history.

The Middle Passage provides both text and subtext for Fred D'Aguiar's novel *Feeding the Ghosts*. This novel makes direct references to salt in relation to hardship and misery. In fact, salt permeates the text. The novel is the retelling of the true story of a ship's captain who orders his crew to throw elderly and sick slaves overboard to safeguard his investment:

> Soon all those bodies melt down to bones, then the sea begins to treat the bones like rock, there to be shaped over time or ground to dust. Sea does not stop at death. Salt wants to consume every morsel of those bodies until the sea becomes them, becomes their memory. So it is from the sea that all 131 souls are to be plucked. From a sea oblivious to time. One hundred and thirty-one dissipated bodies find breath in the wind skimming the surface of the sea and howl. Those bodies have their lives written on salt water. The sea current turns pages of memory. One hundred and thirty-one souls roam the Atlantic with countless others. When the wind is heard it is their breath, their speech. The sea is therefore home.[24]

23. Ibid., 5.
24. D'Aguiar, *Feeding*, 4.

Sea and salt conspire to devour bodies and destroy collective memories of slavery. They cannot however, devour the souls of these Africans, even as they claim them. The sea, then, consists of simultaneous narratives of exile, hardship, and home—for as it destroys and devours, murders, dismembers, and separates, it becomes home to those bodies and souls buried in its depths.

While the sea is a symbol of diaspora, as the vehicle separating Africans from homeland, at the same time it connects Africa to the New World in a chain of bodies. As Michael Hanchard reminds us, "If the notion of an African diaspora is anything it is a human necklace strung together by a thread known as the slave trade, a thread which made its way across a path of America with little regard for national boundaries."[25] The sea also bears witness to the experience of the Middle Passage, residing in the imaginations of those who traveled through it to the Americas.

I submit that the Middle Passage is where the African–New World preoccupation with salt found its beginnings. In D'Aguiar's text, salt becomes more than merely a seasoning or preservative for food or a preventative for dehydration. It seasons the experience of rootlessness, of separation, and exile:

> This sea was nowhere . . . [and] their destination was not a beginning but an end without an ending. . . . If the sea came to an end and another land suggested itself to them they would be lost forever but not dead, lost but never to be found. And love would be nowhere: behind them and impossible to recover; a flat line in the wake of the ship where the sky bowed down to the sea or the sea ascended to the sky. Love was lost somewhere in the very sea with its limitless capacity to swallow love, slaves, ships, memories.[26]

Salt and sea are inseparable here, as both deliverer and devourer, conveying these enslaved Africans to the unknown, all the while eating them alive, body and soul.

As both nowhere and everywhere, the salt sea conveys, contains, and connects bodies, memories, and, as Peter Linebaugh has shown us, cultural formations and transformations in a reciprocal exchange of the

25. Michael Hanchard, "Identity, Meaning, and the African-American," 40.
26. D'Aguiar, *Feeding*, 27.

same, yet constantly changing notions of diaspora.[27] As all of the Africans transported to the Atlantic world create diaspora literally and figuratively, so, too, did the Africans in the Caribbean left behind by Guinea John and Ma Rose. Both figures left behind an African identity in the New World that was tied to a past, present, and future of resistance. So if we follow the model presented by the Ghanaian Adinkra symbol Sankofa (the figure of a bird whose beak is turned backward as its body faces forward), New World Africans, with all of their various identities and "imagined communities," constantly "repeat" themselves—in dance, music, religious practices, art, and so on.[28] These repetitions coincide with a look backward at the legacies of slavery while moving forward in spite of it into an elsewhere, described by Boyce Davies as a conceptual and theoretical space that exists despite and outside of the various Eurocentric categorical identities assigned to peoples of African descent, policed by various immigration, naturalization, and externally imposed boundaries.[29] For if we understand all of these movements forward as challenges to a past and present struggle against colonial, neocolonial, postcolonial, capitalist domination, the "elsewhere" to which Boyce Davies refers is located everywhere, from the maroon colonies of Jamaica's Moretown to the Black streets of South Jamaica, Queens, and beyond.

As Hanchard suggests, this human thread strung across America also interconnects Africa, Europe, the Caribbean, Central and South America, and more, creating a complex web of identities. Caribbean identities are therefore subject to constant negotiation, and in an era in which both air and sea are easily navigated, the boundaries between African

27. Peter Linebaugh, "All the Atlantic Mountains Shook."

28. Boyce Davies references Benedict Anderson's notion of "imagined communities" in her discussion of the designation "third world" to describe the ways in which people of color build communities shaped by migration (*Black Women, Writing,* 13). Antonio Benitez-Rojo, in *The Repeating Island: The Caribbean and the Postmodern Perspective,* argues that Caribbean history and culture must be interpreted as a series of repetitions. Amid the various chaotic events—nature disasters, colonialism, slavery, the exploitations imperialism and capitalism, wars, etc.—is a narrative of continuity that repeats itself. This narrative is a metaphorical "island" of order that connects the Caribbean and North, South, and Central America in an exchange of cultures, histories, and identities.

29. Boyce Davies, *Black Women, Writing,* 13, 88–89.

diaspora peoples and continental territories have become more legal and bureaucratic than physical. They are imaginatively porous, passing cultural information back and forth over land and sea with ease. This is not to say that this passing exists without conflict, for it is also mediated by colonialism, imperialism, and capitalism. A historical example is the fear that seized plantation owners upon the knowledge of an emancipated Haiti and a defeated Napoleon.

On D'Aguiar's literary slave ship, the *Zong,* only one of the enslaved Africans successfully escapes death in the arms of the sea, a woman called Mintah. An African woman taught to speak and understand English in a Christian mission, Mintah recognizes Kelsal (the first mate on the *Zong*), whom she had nursed back to health while she was a student, as he and the crew are rounding up slaves to throw overboard. Mintah calls out to him and questions the rationale behind the murders, challenging him to end them. For this, she is also thrown overboard, with 131 other slaves. Mintah manages to climb back onto the ship by grabbing hold of a rope hanging over its side and by dragging herself up to a porthole leading into the kitchen. From her hiding place in the supply room, she leads a failed attempt at mutiny.

Mintah's experience aboard the *Zong* and in Jamaica exemplifies the practical and theoretical meanings of sucking salt. We see this first in her ability to stay alive after being thrown overboard and her successful attempt to reboard the *Zong:*

> She choked on salt and raised her head towards cloud. Wind whipped up the sea and poured it on her head. She threw her arms forward to swim, and hit wood. Opened her eyes and saw the ship's hull passing close by, some giant sea creature whose bulk was submerged, so close she could see that it was barnacled and mossy and sprouted what looked to her salted eyes like vines. She stretched out her arm and grabbed at the wood. . . . She grabbed at the plaited grain and held on to it, stopped swimming and found she was being dragged along with the ship. She pulled herself close to the hull and saw the rope she clung to stretching up to an air vent where several ropes dangled off boats used to supply the ship when anchored offshore and, higher up, to rigging that led up the side. . . . She swung against the hull with the sway of the ship, searched with her toes for a grip and managed to support her

weight a little by sticking her toenails into a small gap between two
caulked boards whose oakum had worked loose. Then she straight-
ened, suppressed an urge to cough and peered upwards through
the river of rain and climbed.... Her arms pulled her up about
eighteen inches while her feet steadied her and held her position
by clutching the rope between the big first toes and second toes,
then her arms would pull again and draw her up a little more and
again her toes would search for and find the rope and grip it and
anchor her. At last she gained the closest boat and rolled into it.
Her body burned with the effort.[30]

The sea that destroyed 131 others conveys Mintah back toward the *Zong*,
and she decides to fight it by resolving to live, even if it means returning
to the ship. But she does not merely resolve to live—she devises a plan
to free the other Africans and find a way home. She chokes on the salt
sea, but she does not drown. Nor will she be destroyed on board the
Zong or allow the *Zong* to destroy her or the Africans on board. Mintah
decides that if she must die, it will not be as a result of being discarded
by the ship's crew like spoiled cargo into the sea to secure a White man's
profit. Instead, she would die in an attempt to be free. Having already
tasted the salt that might have resulted in death, Mintah mobilizes for
the fight for her freedom.

Like D'Aguiar, Edouard Glissant connects the sea and salt at the level
of metaphor, where they conspire in the silence of human suffering
resulting from the Middle Passage. In *Black Salt*, Glissant focuses on
the salt of history, memory, birth, and the sea. This sea is seasoned and
salted with the bodies and histories of those buried in it. Salt is also
discussed in reference to war, punishment, and oppression. As poet and
literary architect, Glissant mines this salt, excavating sand and earth,
beneath a Western historical tradition that obscures the voices of those
upon whose backs this history is delicately balanced. He begins the dangerous work of digging up the already deteriorating foundations of the
development of the West.

Black Salt is in fact the title of the middle section of the text, a collection of poems written in 1960. Tunneling through the center of the text,
Glissant lights a path for the reader through this selection of poems:

---

30. D'Aguiar, *Feeding*, 53–54.

> to the sea
> For the salt it means.
> Brilliance and bitterness once again.
> Lights in distress on its expanse. Profusion. The theme,
>   knotted with foam and brine, is pure idea. Monotony: a
> tireless murmur
> cracked by a cry.
>   There—on the delta—is a river where the word piles
> up—the poem—and where salt is purified.[31]

The "word," or the voices of those unheard, is excavated in this poetic exploration of history, brought into the light of the sun of the poet and purified on his page.

In "The First Day," Glissant explains his role as storyteller or griot, navigating words as a sailor navigates the sea:

> Then, as this wise sailor, this measured speaker is finished
> by his song it begins him again. He enters, mere child,
> the first morning. He sees originary foam, the first salt
> sweat. History, waiting.[32]

Birth introduces the griot to the sea foam of his mother's birth water, the sweat of her efforts to push him out into the world, where history awaits him. The symbolism of the sea is also apparent here. Betsy Wing, the translator of the collection submits,

> "The First Day" deals with the salt of memory and birth, in which the first taste of salt came with mother's milk and lingers only in the imagination. In adulthood the poet, the reflective self who speaks and is spoken by the words, now confronts the sea, knowing he is both formed by it and contributing to it. The poem is full of the vocabulary of the sea, some of which is common enough Martinican French. For example, *héler*, "to hail" means simply "to cry out" in Martinique. Names of winds, boat parts, ropes, sailing techniques, all turn up in these poems, as part of Glissant's drive to particularize experience.[33]

31. Glissant, *Black Salt*, 61.
32. Ibid., 63.
33. Ibid., 10.

"Carthage" and "Africa" chronicle the history of salt and oppression in Europe and Africa. Glissant witnesses wars for control of salt, a symbol of wealth. In the former, he bears witness to the Punic Wars, which "determined that Europe would rule the Western world, rather than sharing this world with Africa."[34] "Carthage" provides a historical example for the savagery of Western civilization, the salt sprinkled on the fields of Carthage to render them infertile, symbolic of the cruelty of those who would so wound and offend the earth.

> Salt already on gravediggers' hands. The dregs of the sea, no longer aroma, is spread on the conquered city. Everyone forgets the first salt he tasted: now traffics in its essence. The world—and more countless the pillaged Carthages today—feeds this burning fire within him to conquer, to kill. The docile sea is his accomplice.
> A people comes; to be allotted its share of salt on digging wounds. Finally free it bemoans the ashes. Salt is forever mixed with the blood of victims and with the wounded stones that were men's work.[35]

Salt is both prize and punishment, trafficked for its essence and packed into "digging wounds." These themes of hardship and persecution continue in "Salt Taxes" and "Africa." The former resonates with D'Aguiar's discussion of the destruction of the sea within the context of the Middle Passage:

> Just as the salt in day's fortress escapes
> And as the salt dries in a hand where sea
> Left the foam of her breast
> As no one ever will exhaust the night, no one from this hand
> Will drink of love . . .[36]

The sea and its Middle Passage significations devour love, history, and family connections, which must all be rebuilt by those who live to testify. *Black Salt* and *Feeding the Ghosts* are the testimonies of survivors. The last line of the passage above recalls D'Aguiar: "love was lost

34. Ibid., 11.
35. Ibid., 71.
36. Ibid., 83.

somewhere in the very sea with its limitless capacity to swallow love, slaves, ships, memories." Survival has meant struggling against slavery, for the right for freedom, and against colonialism, capitalism, and imperialism. According to René Depestre, "The history of colonisation is the process of man's general zombification. It is also the quest for a revitalising *salt* capable of restoring to man the use of his imagination and culture." Here, Depestre makes a connection between salt and slavery that can also be read in discussions of Haitian Vodun and zombification.[37] Lizabeth Paravisini-Gebert points out,

> The accursed fate conjured by the myth of the zombie is that of the Haitian experience with slavery, of the disassociation of man from his will, his reduction to a beast of burden at the will of a master. It is a connection stressed by Haitian writers and scholars whenever the subject is raised, and is at the core of many theories of Haiti's socio-historic development. "It is not by chance that there exists in Haiti the myth of the zombie, that is, of the living-dead, the man whose mind and soul have been stolen and who has been left only the ability to work," René Depestre has argued.[38]

If a zombie is defined as a person who has lost all free will, whose body and labor are completely controlled by someone else, it can be argued that Uncle Tom, with whom I open this chapter, represents the zombie to whom René Depestre refers. Uncle Tom, a slave to both his master and the institution of slavery, has been made a zombie.

Paradoxically, while it is salt that chained the slaves to the plantation, it is salt that is believed to be the mythological antidote for zombification. The curative benefits of salt are explored in the *Salt Eaters*, by Toni Cade Bambara, in which she writes of one Black community's search for the healing properties of salt. Salt has the power to awaken the zombie, freeing him or her from enslavement. In this light, then, the various forms of return that are described above, especially the form of resistance, constitute the *salt* of restoration to which Depestre refers.

---

37. D'Aguiar, *Feeding*, 27; René Depestre, *Change*, 20.
38. Lizabeth Parvisini-Gebert, "Women Possessed: The Eroticism and Exoticism in the Representation of Woman as Zombie," 39.

Salt carries both metaphorical and practical significance. However, the African diasporic relationship to salt, historical and cultural, cannot be discussed without addressing the issue of power. Once forced down the throats of enslaved Africans, it has become a staple seasoning, a weapon against evil and even death as well as a continuing source of pain in the Caribbean.[39] As described above, it exists as both a tool of enslavement and a weapon against it.

Sydney Mintz's *Sweetness and Power* speaks to a related type of seasoning that exists in relationship to the ways in which consumption is linked to power and meaning. Although his text deals with the history of sugar in Europe and America and its rise from luxury item to highly prized commodity for mass popular consumption, his theoretical framework has been helpful in thinking through the concept of "sucking salt." Mintz argues, "In the wider historical process that concerns us—the diffusion of sugar to entire national populations—those who controlled the society held a commanding position not only in regard to the availability of sugar, but also in regard to a least some of the meanings that sugar products acquired."[40] Those who controlled European society during the period of slavery certainly also controlled the meaning of sugar to the populations of enslaved Africans. For these people, therefore, sugar "meant" exploitation, abuse, theft of bodies, and of course death. Whereas sugar had represented a luxury affordable only

---

39. Lawrence W. Levine writes of the importance of signs in slave communities in the nineteenth-century United States as "calls to action." "A screech owl's cry was a sign of death which could be countered by turning shoes upside down at your door, or turning your pockets inside out and tying a knot in your apron string or turning your pillow inside out, or putting salt on the fire." Slaves also used salt to protect themselves from punishment and to arm themselves against mistreatment. Levine continues, "If slaves heard a killdeer holler—the sign that white patrollers were approaching—the remedy was obvious, and if they received one of the signs of an impending whipping, such as an itching left eye, they could try to avoid it by chewing roots, which was supposed to soften the master's hard heart, or by walking backwards and throwing dirt over their left shoulder, though they undoubtedly supplemented such rituals by acting circumspectly until the crises had passed. Once again the lesson was clear: the environment did not have to be accepted docilely; it could be manipulated and controlled to some extent at least" (*Black Culture and Black Consciousness: Afro-American Folk Thought from Slavery to Freedom*, 66–67).

40. Sydney W. Mintz, *Sweetness and Power: The Place of Sugar in Modern History*, 152.

for the rich (prior to the abolition of slavery and the resulting drop in the price of sugar), it represented suffering and starvation for the enslaved, who were punished for sneaking so much as a sliver of cane to eat.

This exploitation did not cease after emancipation. The newly freed were prevented from gaining any foothold in the sugar industry by special legislation that prevented them from owning land, by economic situations that forced them to work sugar plantations, and by the importation of labor from Asia to prevent strikes and collective bargaining. Mintz describes the continuing unfairness: "Now free but almost entirely ignored by the metropolis, the West Indian people became invisible, until their migration to the center of empire brought them back into uneasy view more than a century later."[41] Once again, the meaning of sugar to those who cultivated it and those who profited from it are quite different. Meaning develops out of very specific historical and cultural contexts:

> We need to learn that rice "means" fertility, and though that association may seem commonsensical or "natural" once we learn it, actually it is neither. If there is any explanation, it is historical. When we pass on to our children the meanings of what we do, our explanations consist largely of instruction to do what we learned to do before them. In societies arranged in groups of division or layers, the learned meanings will differ from one group to another— just as the learned dialect, say, may differ. The supposed webs of signification ought to be interpretable in terms of such differences, particularly if some meanings diffuse from one group to another. Otherwise, the assumption of homogeneous web may mask, instead of reveal, how meanings are generated and transmitted. This is perhaps the point where meaning and power touch most clearly.[42]

In discussions of an African diasporic relationship with sugar and salt, the historical and cultural symbolism of both explain the way in which they seem to have permeated the African diasporic consciousness. "Sucking salt," then, assumes a transformative dimension, for despite the experience of abuse that is attached to it, Caribbean peoples have devised

41. Ibid., 176.
42. Ibid., 158.

ways to use the concept, both literally and metaphorically, as protection against future abuse. What was first used to further disempower has been used to empower with new significations and new meanings.

Saline Seasonings: Salt Consciousness, Linguistic Memory, and Historical Connections

According to the late novelist, poet, and educator Beryl Gilroy, babies in some West African cultures are symbolically introduced to the world with a little bit of sugar and then salt on the tip of the tongue. It is believed that the sugar will sweeten the child's disposition; the first taste of salt introduces the baby to the foods of its people and ensures its ability to recognize its relatives in the future. Gilroy also asserts that in eighteenth- and nineteenth-century England, nobility and kings were often seated at dinner tables in relationship to where the salt was placed. Those sitting above the salt were of a higher station than those seated below it, hence the saying "worth one's salt." The *American Heritage Dictionary* defines this phrase as meaning "efficient and capable."[43]

In Kenya, children are given salt as treats. In tropical climates as well as in the desert, salt helps prevent dehydration by inducing thirst and thereby encouraging consumption of beverages. During the Ewe custom of "outdooring" (a Ghanaian naming ceremony in which babies are officially introduced to their families and communities), as Kofi Anyidoho explains, babies are given a taste of salt, pepper, and water to begin the process of teaching the child about the importance of balance. The philosophical underpinnings of the ceremony are important. For instance, the convener of the ceremony may say, "Taste this bit of salt. Know that a little taste of salt is good; all good stews have salt in them. But remember not to use too much, or you will ruin the dish. Taste this bit of sugar..." Each substance is a metaphorical reference to the principles of living a spiritually, culturally, and socially well-balanced

43. Discussion with Dr. Beryl Gilroy at the Caribbean Women Writers and Scholars Conference held at Florida International University in Miami, April 27, 1996. The *American Heritage Dictionary* (2d ed., Boston: Houghton Mifflin, 1982) includes among its definitions for *salt:* "4. To add zest or liveliness to: salt a lecture with anecdotes; 5. To give an appearance of value to by fraudulent means, esp. To place valuable minerals in (a mine) for the purpose of deceiving."

life.[44] The notion of balance incorporated into the symbolism of the ceremony, and the use of salt as metaphor, sheds a bright light on the comparative New World obsession with salt.

Ambivalence to salt as an instrument of punishment—for example, in "seasoning," or the agony of a whipped slave whose bleeding wounds are rubbed in salt or washed with brine—and the simultaneous necessary dependence on salt for sufficient seasoning of foods speaks to notions of balance and excess. Salt can cause harm, as does the salt sea to the unsuspecting swimmer, or fisherman, hurricane survivor, refugee, or the rebellious African.[45]

Perhaps the first incident of "sucking salt" occurred on the Middle Passage, among enslaved Africans, male and female, who chose to "suck salt" by diving into the ocean rather than endure bondage in a foreign land, or for the children many threw overboard for the same reason. In this case, taking on the ocean and its salt sustains/preserves the spirit against degradation, as represented in *Feeding the Ghosts.* Mintah took on and took in the sea before climbing back aboard the *Zong;* she was ritually murdered by attempted drowning and was reborn from the belly of the sea a revolutionary leader. Salt can thus be seen as being used to preserve, heal, cleanse, balance, season, and strengthen. Further, the notions of balance and seasoning suggest the history of survival against all odds.

An examination of the history of the trade in salt in West Africa provides insight into the importance of salt among continental Africans. In his studies of the eighteenth-century history of the coastal states of West Central Africa and of the colony of Saint Domingue, Hein Vanhee noticed

44. Discussion with Dr. Kofi Anyidoho on March 24, 1996, in Legon, Ghana. Dr. Anyidoho was the director of the School for Performing Arts at the University of Ghana–Legon.

45. Fictional and historical discussions of the salt trade and salt as a tool of oppression are numerous. In *The History of Mary Prince: A West Indian Slave, Related by Herself,* Prince claims that she and other slaves lived in constant fear of being sent to mine salt in the salt bogs. And in "Jean-Michel Basquiat as Heroic Hunter: An Assertion of Identity," Andrea Frohme has submitted that the late artist Michel Basquiat makes reference to the links between the exploitation of slaves for the trade in salt in Africa and the historical experiences of Africans in the West in many of his paintings.

the use of salt for symbolic reasons. For instance, he writes that Capuchin missionaries traveling in the kingdom of Kongo often met people indigenous to the region who asked them for salt, or *anamungoa*. These people used salt in rituals (Vanhee calls them "baptisms") that were probably similar to the Ghanaian "outdooring" ceremonies. Often, after receiving the salt, participants would rush off before the missionaries could apply water. He contends that although the historical information is scarce, it can be presumed that salt was used in other non-Christian initiation ceremonies.[46] It could also be argued that they rushed off to hoard the valuable commodity, before the missionaries could dilute it.

Although Vanhee's research did not yield information on the uses of salt in Saint Domingue among the African-born slaves working on plantations toward the end of the eighteenth century, much has been written on the use of salt for symbolic reasons in Vodun ceremonies in Saint Domingue. Anthropologist Wade Davis's *The Serpent and the Rainbow,* although correctly critiqued for its racist and ethnocentric representation of Haitians and at the same time praised for its verification of the pharmacological basis of zombification, contains information on symbolic uses of salt in Vodun rituals in twentieth-century Haiti. Salt had played an important role in the baptism of children, for an unbaptized child, it was believed, could be taken by the devil. In order to release the child from the devil's grasp, a bit of salt is placed on its tongue. Salt is believed to be the antidote for tetrodotoxin, the poison that initiates the zombification process, although there is no pharmacological basis for this at all. The actual antidote is composed of a combination of very particular substances, including the dried and pulverized body of a puffer fish.[47] Additionally, Steven Buhnen submits that, as in Haiti, salt was used as an antitoxin during the eighteenth century in what is now the Republic of Guinea.[48]

46. Hein Vanhee, letter to author, March 20, 1998.

47. Wade Davis, *The Serpent and the Rainbow,* 180. Davis demonstrates that tetrodotoxin, a toxin obtained from the body of puffer fish, when combined with other substances, is used to turn individuals into zombies (thus the puffer fish yields both the poison and the antidote).

48. Steven Buhnen, letter to author, March 20, 1998 (referencing Jean-Baptiste Labat, *Nouvelle Relation de l'Afrique Occidentale* [Paris: Chez Pierre François Giffart, 1728, 5:258]). For the cosmological and other meanings of salt, Buhnen references Viviane Pâques, *L'Arbre cosmique dans la pensée populaire et dans la vie quotidienne du*

Still, salt has contradictory meanings across the diaspora. Although one can certainly point to historic beneficial uses of salt, much medical-historical work has been done on the damaging effects of salt on African American communities in the United States. In 1986, Thomas W. Wilson presented what has become known as the "slavery hypothesis" for explaining hypertension in African Americans. Wilson posited that the prevalence of high blood pressure among African American populations in the United States is the result of, first, a salt deficiency in West Africa, second, the physical trauma of the Middle Passage, and third, the conditions of slavery in the United States, specifically the high salt content of the foods slaves were forced to eat. Recent research has found that African American peoples born in the United States are more sensitive than White Americans to increases in dietary salt and that, when injected with saline solutions, African Americans retained intravenous sodium longer that White Americans did.[49]

Still, for historian Philip Curtin, it is these observations that caused the medical community to look to the African past for genetic evidence of hypertension. He contends, however, that this hypothesis is both inaccurate and ahistorical:

> From the historical point view, the slavery hypotheses to explain African-American hypertension not only lacks supporting evidence but also runs counter to what evidence we *do* have. West Africans had plenty of salt through most of their history. They do not have notably high rates of hypertension today. The mortality during the slave trade was not from salt-depleting causes. No evidence has ever been advanced that the African Americans experienced different conditions of diet and disease from those of poor southerners.

Nord-Ouest africain (Paris: Travaux et Mémoires de l'Instut d'Ethnologie de l'Université de Paris, 1964), 280 seq. See also B. Marie Perinbam, "The Salt-Gold Alchemy in the Eighteenth and Nineteenth Century Mande World: If Men Are Its Salt, Women Are Its Gold."

49. Thomas W. Wilson, "Africa, Afro-Americans, and Hypertensions: An Hypothesis." Other related studies are Thomas W. Wilson, "Salt Supplies in West Africa and Blood Pressures Today"; and Thomas W. Wilson and C. E. Grim, "Biohistory of Slavery and Blood Pressure Differences in Blacks Today: A Hypothesis." See also K. A. Fackelmann, "The African Gene? Searching through History for the Roots of Black Hypertension"; M. F. Goldsmith, "African Lineage, Hypertension Linked"; and J. Diamond, "The Saltshaker's Curse."

No evidence has been advanced that a dietary trauma experienced by 80% of one's ancestors over a period of less than 1 year, 220 years ago, would bring about a genetic change lasting to the present. Yet these hypotheses were published in the serious medical press and picked up by the popular medical literature late in 1991 as though they were possibly true. Perhaps we should try harder to close the gap between scientific and historical knowledge.[50]

Curtin's position answers and raises several questions. First, he provides ample evidence that one of the primary elements of Wilson's hypothesis, that Africans brought to the Americas during the Middle Passage came from salt-poor regions of Africa, is incorrect. Countering Wilson's claim that historically, in most of West Africa the only locally available salt "was produced from vegetable matter,"[51] Curtin responds,

But while some parts of West Africa did lack good local sources of salt, they made up for it through an elaborate set of trade networks. All tropical regions near the seacoast have a cheap source of salt in seawater. At high tide, that seawater can be guided into any shallow pan or salt pond, where evaporation will do the rest. Where the terrain is not suitable and fuel is cheap, seawater can also be boiled. From the Senegal River to Benguela in southern Angola, salt was manufactured and exported into the interior over regular trade routes.... Indeed any place in West Africa close enough to the coast to be linked to the Atlantic slave trade was close enough to be supplied with sea salt as well.[52]

Paul Lovejoy, who has researched the salt trade in the western Sudan extensively, asserts that in the region including the Lake Chad basin, the south-central Sahara Desert, the Benue River basin, and the Niger Valley, from the Benue northward to the Sahel, the salt trade extended into present-day Ethiopia, Chad, Benin, Nigeria, Mauritania, Ghana, Sierra Leone, and Senegambia. Imported and locally made sea salt has been traded in the region as early as the eighteenth century. Lovejoy has discovered that "the salts of the Central Sudan were used for a variety of culi-

50. Phillip D. Curtin, "The Slavery Hypothesis for Hypertension among African Americans: The Historical Evidence," 1686.
51. Wilson, "Africa, Afro-Americans, and Hypertensions," 258.
52. Curtin, "Slavery Hypothesis," 1682.

nary, medicinal, industrial, and other purposes." He traced sixteen different types of salt, each with very specific purposes and uses. These salts can be broken down into two major classifications: salt and natron. The former consisted predominately of sodium chloride. The latter was a combination (sometimes erroneously called "potash") that included high concentrations of sodium carbonate, sodium sulphate, and other chemicals.[53]

Of particular relevance to my study is Lovejoy's discussion of the culinary uses of salt in eighteenth- and nineteenth-century Central Africa. Whereas salt was used as a condiment, usually sprinkled on food after it was cooked, Africans also seasoned their foods with salt prior to cooking, using it to enhance the flavor of food: "West African recipes required specific salts, as if each type were a different spice. A Hausa proverb demonstrates the sophistication of the taste factor: 'hanci bai san dadin gishiri ba,' the nose does not know the flavour of the salt." Distinctions in flavor were important in selection of salts, for the wrong type could ruin the taste of a dish. Lovejoy includes a series of recipes that utilize very specific types of salt.[54]

Access to the various types of salt was mediated by economic condition. The purer salts, especially those that were imported back into the central Sudan from Europe, were available only to the wealthy. Poorer people used natron and other impure combinations when they were able. Poverty often prevented many from being able to afford salt.

> The common people, *talakawa*, make their soup [*miya*] without meat, and the destitute, *matsiyata*, are forced to make it without salt and it is called "tasteless," *lami*. Some people, due to poverty, cook beans and eat them with salt at night. Some even cook beans to eat at night without salt, and again, this is because of poverty. Perhaps there is no better measure of poverty than the inability of people to afford salt, particularly in a society in which the salts were impure mixtures that varied greatly in price.[55]

53. Paul Lovejoy, *Salt of the Desert Sun: A History of Salt Production and Trade in the Central Sudan*, 16–17, 15. For information on tropical Africa's contribution to world salt production and consumption, see E. A. McDougall, "Salts of the Western Sahara: Myths, Mysteries, and Historical Significance"; and Samuel Adrian Miles Adshead, *Salt and Civilization*, 15–26.

54. Lovejoy, *Salt of the Desert*, 18.

55. Ibid., 20.

Poorer people relied primarily on natron, which existed in different colors and various levels of quality. Some dishes required natron as an ingredient. "Bean dishes in particular were made with natron, rather than salt, because, it is said, 'natron takes the fart out of the beans.' "[56]

Although Curtin determines that slave mortality had little to do with salt (and water) depletion and more to do with respiratory illness,[57] it seems highly likely that slaves died from a combination of the two, along with the various other illnesses they were susceptible to. As Kenneth F. Kiple and Virginia H. Kiple point out,

> The standard menu for slaves making the passage was a boiled cereal (usually rice) with "sauce" made by boiling salted fish—a diet lacking in many important nutrients. Moreover, the dysentery and diarrhea, always rife aboard a slaver, would have leeched away many of those nutrients which such a diet could have provided.
> ...Thus many West Africans, badly nourished to begin with and then subjected to the disastrous nutritional circumstances of the Middle Passage, reached the New World in a malnourished condition. Doubtless some never recovered, which must count as an important reason for the high incidence of "seasoning" mortality.
> ...Malnutrition, in addition to its inherent destructiveness, also renders the body susceptible to pathogenic invasion and, in the case of slaves moving into a new disease environment, to pathogens and strains of pathogens against which they had inefficient defenses.[58]

It is important to note that Curtin's scholarship has come under attack by several historians for his gross underestimation of the number of slaves taken from Africa from the sixteenth to nineteenth centuries, and for his insistence that the trade in slaves from Africa to the Americas "had effectively ended in 1807."[59] Although 1807 is the year in which the trade ended officially, it persisted until well after the Civil War, as

56. Ibid., 19–20.

57. Curtin, "Slavery Hypothesis," 1685–86.

58. Kenneth F. Kiple and Virginia H. Kiple, "Deficiency Diseases in the Caribbean," in Verene Shepherd and Hilary Beckles, eds., *Caribbean Slave Society and Economy,* 174.

59. Curtin, "Slavery Hypothesis," 1682.

has been argued by scholars such as W. E. B. Du Bois as early as 1896.[60] Curtin's flawed numbers in this regard thus become a potential warning flag for the rest of his hypothesis.

Last, Curtin's assertion that there is no evidence that the dietary trauma experienced during the Middle Passage is the source of African Americans' inability to conserve or metabolize salt is also suspect. Although this assertion is logical, it is also logical to explore the possibility that dietary habits forced upon slaves during the period of slavery initiated dietary habits that, having persisted in the present day, account for the high incidence of hypertension among African Americans and some Caribbeans. Salted meats and fish continue to be a staple of African diasporic cuisine even though many are moving toward more healthful foods. In addition, the socioeconomic conditions of most Africans in the Americas limit us to the very types of food that are least healthful, precisely because they are inexpensive and thus often the only ones that we can afford. Fresh fruits and vegetables and unprocessed, low-sodium foods tend to be more expensive and are often not offered in large supply in the communities in which we live.[61]

60. In fact, most of Du Bois's text is about the slave trade after its "official" end. W. E. B. Du Bois made this point plain in his classic study *The Suppression of the African Slave Trade.*

61. Even though slaves may have "earned" or were given plots of land on which they could grow products that supplemented their rations and which they could sell at market, slaveholders policed and monitored independent slave activities so that, in the end, they could capitalize from them. Ira Berlin and Philip D. Morgan, in their introduction to *Cultivation and Culture: Labor and the Shaping of Slave Life in the Americas,* provide a discussion of the relationship between slave economy and that of the slaveholder: "Slaveholders . . . not only worked hard to curb the benefits that accrued to slaves as a result of their independent activity but to integrate the slaves' economy into their own. At every opportunity they tried to maximize the time slaves spent growing the great staples and to limit the time slaves worked their gardens and grounds. They determined which goods slaves could buy and sell freely, constrained the slaves' right to hire their own time and collect overwork, and—if given the opportunity—denied slaves the property they had earned on their own, thus enforcing their claim to a slave's entire being and its product. To the extent slaves succeeded in feeding themselves and earning a surplus, masters reduced rations and added to the slaves' responsibilities for supplying shelter, clothing, and medication. In short, slaveowners recognized the slaves' rights only to the extent that those rights affirmed their own domination" (41). Many slaves refused to participate in this and other aspects of the plantation economy.

Besides its relationship with health concerns, salt can also be read in connection with spiritual health and well-being at the level of protection from evil. The *Drums and Shadows* collection contains several accounts of salt by Black southerners used to prevent or dissipate evil, complete with the African origins of some of these beliefs. One example are the following methods for keeping witches away, provided by Nathaniel John Lewis, the first mayor of Tin City, Savannah, Georgia: "You can lay a bruhmstick cross the doe befo night an they can't come in. A little salt is good. They don't take to salt." Lewis also described the recipe for a "conjuh mixin" that includes one box of table salt:

> Eggs—2
> carisin [kerosene]—1 pint
> turpentine—1 pint
> vinegar
> cy pepper
> table salt—1 box[62]

Interestingly, the root of this belief is found among the Vai of Liberia: "There is a belief, among the Vais that witches come to your house and ride you at night,—that when the witch comes in the door he takes off his skin and lays it aside in the house. It is believed that he returns you to the bed where he found you, and that the witch may be killed by sprinkling salt and pepper in certain portions of the room, which will prevent the witch from putting on his skin. Just before they go to bed it is a common thing to see Vais people sprinkling salt and pepper about."[63] This is probably one of the roots of the mythology of the "soucouyant" of Trinidad, or the "witch women" of Jamaica, who slip out of their skins at night and travel about as glowing balls of flames, usually sucking the blood of unsuspecting men, women, and children. Zora Neale Hurston referenced Rebecca Fletcher in her essay "Hoodoo in America"; Fletcher told of a witch who "went into a good woman's house when that woman was in bed." After discovering the witch, the good woman

62. *Drums and Shadows*, 264.
63. Ibid.

waited until she took off her skin and left it lying on the floor. The good woman then sprinkled salt and pepper on the witch's skin.[64]

Despite the many health concerns associated with salt consumption, African diaspora peoples enjoy an intimate relationship with salt, at the levels of culture and consciousness. We navigate through the salt of hardship, developing philosophies of transcendence, applying philosophies of balance in all things. African diaspora experience is characterized by constant negotiation between a past marked by constant upheaval, adversity, and struggle with a present and future filled with the legacy of creative, practical, linguistic, and psychological resistance. For although we are aware of the "salt of hardship" in all of its forms, we have mastered the art of separating out of this hardship just what we need to survive. To use an analogy, we have taken the salt of history, that is, in the form of the salted cod, beef, and pork we were once forced to eat, and boiled them down into something appetizing and invigorating. We have effectively transformed what was once unpalatable into works of culinary, linguistic, and cultural art, extracting just enough hardship in order to retain what was necessary to rebuild and recreate. We season our language with the salt of resistance.

64. Zora Neale Hurston, "Hoodoo in America: Conjure Stories," 404–405 (cited in Hill, *Call and Response*, 66).

Three "It Sweeter Than Meat!"

Saltfish, Sexual Politics, and the
Caribbean Oral Imagination

* *

While disembarking from a flight from Miami to New York's Kennedy Airport in October 1997, passengers (including myself) detected a rancid, fishy smell emanating from the vents in the passenger cabin. Looking around and laughing, a male passenger shouted out, "Is who din' wash dey saltfish today?" accusing at least one of the women on board of improper vaginal hygiene. The men nearby squealed with laughter, while we women responded with expressions of horror and disgust, signifying with "suck teeth" and "cut eye."

The wordplay represented here exists at all levels of Caribbean oral culture. As discussed earlier, links between food and sexuality are not uncommon in Caribbean and African American popular culture. For example, a generous backside on a Black woman in an African American context is often referred to as an "onion" (because it's so big, beautiful and round that it brings men to tears). A piece of "sweet potato pie" refers to the buttocks as well. And love for "a fresh vegetable" is analogous to the Caribbean man's love for women's sexuality in Jamaican dance-hall lyrics. This flirtation, this sense of play, that permeates Caribbean culture is what I will explore in this chapter. In addition, I will explore the metaphor of "sucking salt" through the lens of folklore, specifically the narrative of "soucouyant" and calypso in the English-speaking Caribbean. "Sucking salt" manifested in different forms exem-

54

plifies a duality or ambivalence that speaks to the importance of balance. As a "philosophy of cultural improvisation" (as Austin Clarke would say), the term connotes the creative capacity for constant rearticulation.[1]

The linking of saltfish to the vagina is quite common in Caribbean oral culture, on the one hand as a metaphor for the smell and taste of the vagina, on the other a metaphor for poor personal hygiene. Merle Hodge has commented on the denigration and humiliation of women at the level of Caribbean street culture, in which young men compete at finding inventive ways to verbally harass women on the street.[2] This, according to Keith Warner, finds its way into Caribbean orature, here represented in Calypso. Warner references Merle Hodge, who contends, "the embarrassment of woman is part of the national ethos," stemming, I am convinced, from a deep-seated resentment of the strength of women."[3]

In "Woman Is a Nation: Women in Caribbean Oral Literature," Carole Boyce Davies references Hodge's discussion as well as J. D. Elder's research on pejorative representations of Caribbean women in calypsos from 1850–1960: "The folksingers have turned their castigation and ridicule upon other human figures—the females in the society.... All through the stages of the calypso evolution, the female moves progressively over the years, as a subject of male preoccupation much as the victim of his condemnation." Boyce Davies submits that by the time *Out of the Kumbla* was published (1988), in calypsos written by men, women were constructed as deadly to the male, and criticized as ugly or unhygienic, in a genre of calypso designed to "put woman in her place."[4] Elder identified the primary themes of calypsos written about women during the period between 1850 and 1960: the sacred mother who, because of her selfless sacrifices for her children, is beyond reproach; the conquest of woman via sexual prowess; female rejection of a man, despite his overtures; sexual envy in which a man must fight off a rival for a woman's affections; obeah, in which a love-struck woman consults an obeah man for medicine

1. Quoted in Merle Hodge, "The Shadow of the Whip," in Orde Coombs, ed., *Is Massa Day Dead*, 115.
2. Ibid.
3. Keith Warner, "The Shadow of the Whip," in Carole Boyce Davies and Elaine Savory Fido, *Out of the Kumbla: Caribbean Women and Literature;* 193.
4. Boyce Davies and Savory Fido, *Out of the Kumbla*, 180, 165.

to attract and keep a man (such as is seen in Sparrow's "Imelda"); derision of women; and rejection of the female.[5]

It must be noted here that calypso is rife with double entendre concerning a wide range of subjects—sex and sexuality, local and international politics, history, and culture—with humor and sarcasm. Hollis Liverpool shows us how calypsos in the nineteenth century functioned as the newsroom of the populace, so to speak, and also as the resistant voice of a people. From its birth among chantuelles of the pre-Emancipation period, to the first calypsonians of the nineteenth century into the present, calypso has represented the pantheon of Caribbean experience. Just as the "chantuelle of pre-Emancipation times analyzed the happenings of the day and informed the masses present of environmental changes and pressures," so too did the calypsonian keep the populace informed of political events, putting the emotions of the masses to songs that critiqued colonial abuses.[6] In the twentieth century and into the present, calypso was consistently used as a forum for an infinite range of issues. So although denigration of women is frequently pointed to in calypso music, other topics were discussed as well: women were glorified as mothers, political attacks and social commentary were issued, and world events were analyzed. It is not, therefore, my intention to represent calypso as entirely corrupted by misogyny. Instead, I will focus on the complexity of the representations of sexuality and women that reference salt or saltfish and thereby both praise and assault female fecundity.

An example that incorporates my overarching concern with representation of salt occurs in the link between saltiness and a lack of feminine hygiene in a calypso by Spoiler, who describes a woman named Clarabell. As she walks past, her personal odor, he says, could "chase the Devil from Hell / With the kind of way she does smell." Sparrow's "Jean Marabunta" describes another such character, a "disgraceful female" who "Smells like saltfish tail / . . . She won't bathe, she fraid water."[7]

5. J. D. Elder, "The Male/Female Conflict in Calypso," 28.

6. Hollis Liverpool, *Kaiso and Society*, 9.

7. Spoiler, "Clarabell," and Sparrow, "Jean Marabunta," quoted in Keith Q. Warner, *Kaiso! The Trinidad Calypso: A Study of the Calypso as Oral Culture,* 100. Hodge contends that this street-corner machismo results from the feelings of emasculation of many Trinidadian men during U.S. occupation and of the perception of the empowerment of women in this context.

7 from "Colt 45"

Jokes and anecdotal narratives in which the smell of saltfish is mistaken for the proximity of a woman abound. One such anecdote, this time in the form of an actual experience, occurs in which my aunt attempted to buy saltfish from a *bodega* in the Bronx. Since her Spanish was deplorable, and the store proprietor's English was equally bad, after much effort, she finally remembered that Latinos call saltfish *baccalao*. She told him that she wanted *baccalao*, and he quickly returned with it. The merchant held it up to his nose, inhaled deeply, and said to my aunt, "Ah, smells just like my wife!" My aunt sucked her teeth, pretended not to hear him, quickly paid for her saltfish, and left, never to return to this *bodega* again. In recounting this incident, she explained she was disgusted and offended, believing that what the merchant had said was a "terrible thing to say about a woman."

It could be argued that some people do find the "saltfish" smell seductive, at the level of food or woman. This play between the seductiveness/repulsiveness of female sexuality as represented in "saltfish" is nicely illustrated in "Saltfish Tongue" by Monarch. Monarch uses "saltfish tongue" as double entendre for both female and male treachery, and of course, the clitoris and vagina. In the fourth verse, he sings how a hapless friend of his, Hopalong, is strung along by a woman named Emily, who would have sex with everyone but him. Hopalong describes her "Saltfish Tongue / Which he neva see." He is well aware of it, however, for "when de win' blow / It does smell so strong." Emily is told, "Dah'lin, you have the sweetest saltfish in town!" Hopalong admits to being "always around," evidencing his lust for her, despite the disturbingly strong odor she bears.[8] As anyone familiar with salted codfish knows, it is nothing that any woman wants to smell like. In fact, to render it palatable, it has to be boiled, soaked, stripped, and seasoned. However, it is precisely Emily's aroma, functioning as a pheromone, which is driving Hopalong mad. The lyrics also point to a belief in the woman's promiscuity, but this belief is probably the result of her refusal to share her "saltfish tongue" with him.

In this example we see a play between the kitchen and the bedroom, a connection between consumption of sexuality and consumption of food, as "saltfish" can be found in both places. Also, these two spaces are a

8. Monarch, "Saltfish Tongue."

constant site of conflict and compromise between men and women. Although, as I argue in the introduction, the kitchen space is usually the domain of women, it is also a space in which, within the context of a patriarchal society permeated by machismo, men (husbands, fathers, and sons) are catered to and wooed. In addition, from the perspective of economics, many women are forced to manipulate men with food and sex in exchange for the money necessary to support themselves and their families. Much the same can be said for the bedroom. For women, then, the economics of the bedroom and the kitchen are often inter-twined. So, the "wicked" Emily is making a cuckold of Hopalong, who is obsessed with the prospect of a lick from her "saltfish tongue."

The Mighty Sparrow's song "Saltfish" contains the same type of double entendre. Keith Warner explains the importance of this wordplay: "The way around outright vulgarity or open embarrassment is the use of *double entendre,* stretched to the very furthest ends of the calypso to escape self-imposed censorship of the radio stations; in its more vicious form, it parallels the very vulgarity or eroticism it is seeking to mask." Hollis Liverpool reiterates this point, arguing that censorship was used as a way of coding and defending the creativity of the singer.[9] Sparrow skillfully straddles this fence. As Sparrow sings in the song itself, "Saltfish" usually "generate[s] a lot of excitement"; women in the audience "go wild with laughter," and the "men with the mustache always pull aside and blush."[10] People's response to his suggestive lyrics emphasizes the artistry of Sparrow's wordplay in a song extolling the virtues of saltfish — the food and the organ. He pokes fun at the listener, alluding to the sexual connotations of his lyrics. It is not the mere mention of salted codfish that makes "women go wild." Instead, it is what this cod repre-sents that incites such a response — from men as well as women. As Sparrow tells the listener, even the mustachioed man blushing knowingly in the corner identifies with Sparrow's love for saltfish. The sexual sym-bolism of the mustache in relationship to cunnilingus is not lost here.

The chorus to the song, quoted in this chapter's title, is legendary, as Sparrow chants the word *saltfish,* reminding the listener that "Nothing in the world is sweeter" and regardless of whether it comes from Trinidad

9. Warner, *Kaiso!* 107; Hollis Liverpool, lecture at Carnival and the Caribbean Diaspora Symposium, October 8, 1999, Florida International University.
10. The Mighty Sparrow, "Saltfish (Solfish)."

or Barbados, "All saltfish sweet!" The connection between eating the products of the kitchen and enjoying one another in the bedroom— and the sexual politics of the both—is apparent in verse 1 as well. Sparrow sings, "Saltfish stew is what I like / . . . I like your food." Then he declares knowingly, "I'm sure every man in here already eat it." Of course, this is a not-so-subtle allusion to cunnilingus. Sparrow then compares the smell and the taste of saltfish, referring again to cunnilingus: "I like de taste / Though de smell / Sometimes hard to take." Here, rather than denigrating woman at the level of hygiene as in the earlier examples, Sparrow vouches for the paradoxical sweetness of woman, represented as saltfish: "it extra sweet it smellin' so."[11]

Many women of my mother's generation who heard this calypso initially indicate that it was the first time that a man had publicly indicated his love of "saltfish" (women's bodies and intimate parts) when the larger culture appeared to disparage oral sex. The song arose within a culture in which women were taught by their mothers to constantly wash themselves with antiseptics, teaching many women to believe their own bodies to be dirty.[12]

In a more recent example, Machel Montano is mesmerized not by saltfish, but by a "Big Phat Fish." "Big Phat Fish" is code for "desirable woman," and as the woman objectified in this song dances, she tantalizes the singer with her movements. He does, of course, focus on his own sexual prowess. Much like the "fresh vegetable" described earlier, "Big Phat Fish" is personified as a woman, or women "raining from the sky, makin man dem cry," complete with voluptuous thighs beckoning him onto the dance floor.[13] The word *phat* is a term used in hip-hop culture to refer to something that is great, spectacular, or worthy of admiration. (The term has fallen out of currency at the time of this writing, except for its use in marketing and advertising.) Montano, true to his generation, makes full use of the wellspring of international Black popular culture, fusing hip-hop and dancehall stylistically and linguistically.

Carolyn Cooper's discussion of the cutting and mixing of African diasporic musical traditions is informative here, particularly her discussion of the cross-fertilization of musical and technological forms. In her essay

11. Ibid.
12. This point was made by Carole Boyce Davies at the Carnival and the Caribbean Diaspora Symposium, October 8, 1999, Florida International University.
13. Machel Montano, "Big Phat Fish."

"Slackness Hiding from Culture," Cooper discusses the importance of double meanings and double entendres, arguing that in Caribbean oral culture "sexual innuendo is not at all peculiar to the much maligned lyrics of the DJs, but is firmly established in Jamaican popular culture."[14]

"Slackness" or "smuttiness," as discussed by Warner, persist despite middle-class attempts to marginalize such behavior, because their significations transcend class distinctions at the level of everyday experience. I would argue that the policing of "slackness" does not occur only from the middle class. Many working-class, Christianized, morally prescriptive types of all classes have just as strong critiques of "smutty" behavior and language. "Slackness" or "smutty" language in Caribbean music breaks through walls of privacy, exposing already-circulating private discourses for public consumption. Just as middle-class and "Negro" listeners initially balked at the bawdiness of the blues in the 1920s, so, too, do middle-class preoccupations with dissemblance and decency in the Caribbean attempt to silence incidences of "jammin' and whinin'" and "slackness" in Caribbean popular music. Double entendre, then, functions as the artistic attempt to give voice to the private via communal experiential knowledge, to "out" members of the community, so to speak, just as it seeks to criticize.

Cooper continues that the skillful use of double entendre by many Jamaican artists is evidence that they have been schooled in "picong, that Trinidadian art of wicked wit."[15] It is precisely this "wickedness"— particularly in relationship to the saltiness of sexuality represented in Caribbean oral and musical culture—that leaves its listeners hungering for more.

Meanwhile, we must remember that women are not hapless victims of patriarchal violence in calypso. As noted above, calypso has traditionally been preoccupied with a wide range of issues, including politics, motherhood, sexuality, and issues of Caribbean identity.[16] Indeed,

14. Carolyn Cooper, *Noises in the Blood: Orality, Gender, and the "Vulgar" Body of Jamaican Popular Culture*, 137.

15. Cooper, *Noises*, 137.

16. Lynette Lashley of Florida Memorial College explained how political parties in Trinidad use popular Calypso songs to sway public opinion in her paper "Calypso and Politics: A Communications Approach," presented at the Carnival and the Caribbean Diaspora Symposium at Florida International University, October 8, 1999.

there is a strong argument for a female origin of calypso. Carole Nathalie Maison-Bishop has shown that women have always been active participants in the composition and performance of calypso. Although some scholars (such as Gordon Rohlehr) have argued that calypso has been "a predominately male mode, whose themes are manhood and the identity of the individual within the group," Maison-Bishop points out that scholars (such as J. D. Elder) have shown that

> calypso is originally a women's song which was not only sung exclusively by the women who were in the retinue of the early bands, but which was also composed solely by them. Elder's commitment to this viewpoint arises not exclusively from his scrutiny of the records but from the oral narrative of someone who had actually witnessed this phenomenon. Elder claims that according [to] the narrator "the women were supporters of the men, provided them with ammunition and stones to pelt the police, and when the men were tired after the stick-fighting, the women served them with food and would then they sing the kaiso while the men were eating and resting."[17]

Maison-Bishop continues that Gordon Rohlehr, Keith Warner, and other scholars have discovered women calypso singers in their research, such as Bodicea, whom Andrew Pearse describes as "a black female chantwell who loved singing, fighting and drinking."[18] E. Hill was informed by

17. Gordon Rohlehr, *Calypso and Society in Pre-Independence Trinidad*, 53; Carole Maison-Bishop, "Women in Calypso: Hearing the Voices," 113, 114. *Kaiso* is said to be of African, specifically Hausa (spoken among those in this ethnic group from Nigeria into Senegal) and Yoruba origin. Hill submits that, among these two ethnic groups, *kaiso* refers to songs of derision and praise, which are usually improvised. Maureen Warner Lewis's research on Yoruba and Trinidadian culture and language shows that the stanza structure of early calypsos reflects the Yoruba musical tradition of repeating first lines of songs. *Kaiso* and *calypso* are now used interchangeably. John Cowley, in *Carnival, Canboulay, and Calypso: Traditions in the Making*, adds that in nineteenth-century Trinidad and Tobago, the "cariso" or "caliso" would have been performed with accompaniment by a goatskin drum (98). They were sung in French Creole until 1898, when the "first full-scale experiments ... part in French Creole and part in English" occurred (138).

18. Andrew Pearse, "Carnival in Nineteenth Century Trinidad," quoted in Maison-Bishop, "Women," 98. The "chantwell" was the person responsible for the composition of songs for kalinda bands. Calypso is derived from the kalinda, which, according

"old veterans of the late nineteenth century carnival" that "cariso" was sung and danced by both men and women.[19] Carole Boyce Davies concurs that there is enough evidence to support that calypso may in fact have been a women's song.[20]

Maison-Bishop argues that the hypotheses presented to explain the disappearance of women from the calypso scene at the turn of the twentieth century do not adequately address the issues of race, culture, class, and color in Caribbean society, the rigid code of censorship, and, I would argue, compulsory masculinity. One hypothesis is that with the banning of stick-fighting in Trinidad, the main male outlet for aggression between groups that allowed men to claim physical space in a way that was forbidden by colonial authorities was lost. Thus music became a "repository of fierceness and hostility." Previously attached to music and fighting, this aggression could only be vented through music. The male ego could no longer make space for the female in the composition of music and singing, for her presence now constituted a challenge to manhood. Another hypothesis suggests

> the status of the women who were singing was prescribed and thus diminished, by their race and social class. As black women from the lower class, they were unable to participate in any of the activities outside of their social stratum and although their activities in the bands provided an outlet for their creativity, the manner in

---

to J. D. Elder, is "an ancient dueling song for the game called by the French *Bois-bataille* (stick fight), which the Negroes engaged in during the rest periods on the estates, at evenings in backyards, or publicly on holidays like Easter Monday and Christmas Day" (J. D. Elder, "The Calypso," 3; cited in Maison-Bishop, "Women," 98). The chantwell was much like a griot, except that he or she functioned as social commentator, critic of the state, and popular informant, keeping the recently emancipated masses aware of political affairs. In addition, the chantwell was afforded great respect as the political and spiritual voice of the people.

19. E. Hill, "On the Origin of the Term Calypso"; Maison-Bishop, "Women," 114. The term *calypso* is thought to have arisen from the French-Creole *cariso* (from the French for "carousing"), along with the Venezuelan-Spanish *calisto* (a local song sung "along the Spanish main") and the Carib Indian *carieto* (a "joyous song used to heal the sick, to embolden the warrior, and to seduce the fair" (D. Crowley, "Toward a Definition of Calypso," 59–601; see also Maison-Bishop, "Women," 95–96).

20. Carole Boyce Davies, "'Woman Is a Nation...': Women in Caribbean Oral Literature," in Boyce Davies and Savory Fido, *Out of the Kumbla*, 165.

which this was expressed, drew the disapprobation of the custodians of the society's morals.[21]

Rohlehr presents the following, published in the *Port of Spain Gazette* in 1884 as an example of this disapprobation:

> the obscenities, the bawdy languages and gestures of the women in the street have been pushed to a degree of wantonness which cannot be surpassed, and which must not be tolerated. Obscenities are no longer veiled under the cloak of words of doubtful meaning, but lechery in all its naked brutality is sung, spoken and represented by disgusting gestures in our public streets. The growing generation of young girls will become the curse of the country if these yearly *saturnalia* are allowed to continue.[22]

It is clear that women continued to sing calypso, even if pushed to the margins of public performance. It was not until the 1930s that two women reemerged as performers in calypso tents and bands. The number of women increased into the 1960s and 1970s, but it was not until the 1980s that women really began to constitute a major presence in the art form, across social classes and ethnicities.

In our discussion of sex and sexuality and Caribbean orality, it is crucial to examine how female Calypso performers have represented themselves in their music. Although I have not encountered any overt references to salt in my research, many female calypsonians, such as Shirlene Hendrickson and Denyse Plummer, have been just as bawdy as men, bragging about their own sexual sophistication. Rudolph Ottley has compiled a collection of interviews with women calypsonians in which they discuss their professional experiences. The struggle of many of these women to excel in a predominantly male environment, however, speaks volumes to the symbolic meanings of "sucking salt." As Joslynne L. Sealey writes in her introduction to Ottley's book, "No one can dispute that at one time the 'tent' was the exclusive domain of the male singer." Female singers, including Calypso Rose, Singing Francine, Twiggy, Lady Wonder, and Denyse Plummer, faced an uphill battle as they took the

21. Maison-Bishop, "Women," 115.
22. Quoted in Rohlehr, *Calypso and Society*, 53.

stage and articulated their ideas and beliefs. Sealey points out that despite the obstacles, some women "have excelled in the Soca, giving superb presentation on stage, not only of phrasing and sweet rhythms, but also of their dancing ability.... However, I have observed that it is the more sensitive and nurturing calypsoes dealing with social problems, nation building, advice to the youth and personal relationships that are the forte of the female singers today."[23]

Calypso Rose, who, according to Ottley, is "to female calypsonians what Sparrow is to calypso in general," argues that it was her determination to excel as a woman in a field dominated by men, despite the criticism of her church and the popular presses in Trinidad and Tobago, that spurred her on. When Ottley interviewed her, she admitted, "When I started singing calypso, it was very, very hard." She was criticized for some of the suggestive calypsoes she demonstrated on stage: "There are certain lyrics that you have to project.... [And] they would say 'Oh Boy! Look at she, man' as the *Guardian* and the *Evening News* once deemed me the 'Queen of Smut.'" Nevertheless, she refused to supress her own culture and showed, instead, "that whatever a man could do, a woman can do too, this is a human being's world and is not segregated alone to man." She made it a point of saying that in the 1950s, Spoiler had been her inspiration and mentor—not the Mighty Sparrow.[24]

Unfortunately, Ottley emphasizes Calypso Rose's importance to female calypsonians over her importance to the field in general. But male calypsonians, recognizing her talents and creativity, mentored her, and they also performed songs that Calypso Rose composed in the 1950s. Eric Williams, upon hearing one of her compositions in 1956, encouraged her to sing calypsos in the tents of Trinidad and Tobago. Although she maintained that calypso was "not a woman's world" at that time, she was composing songs for men until she began singing professionally in 1964. According to Boyce Davies, Calypso Rose, who broke ground as the first female calypso monarch, struggled against rumors of lesbianism for years. Her performance style "had a distinctly androgynous appearance; her stage performance was similar to some male calypso-

23. Joslynne L. Sealey, introduction to Rudolph Ottley, *Women in Calypso,* part 1, vii.
24. Ottley, *Women in Calypso,* 2, 5.

nians like the Mighty Sparrow, including dancing and projecting the microphone as phallus."[25]

Rose has stated that she is convinced that women must write their own calypsos, so as to give voice to their creative energies in the art form. She believes that calypso is an African-based art form that each generation of Caribbeans must be taught to enjoy as part of their cultural heritage. As such, participation is open to all who love it. Encouraging women to write their own lyrics in order to maintain creative and professional independence, she submits, "You have to be productive and if you are not productive you would be lacking, instead of going forward, you would be reversing." When engaging in artistic pursuits, such as music, she says, "you are creating things that you are seeing, the other person would not see. You are creating things from within you and by doing so the creativity is more powerful."[26]

Rose was honored for her contributions to calypso and the rise of women calypsonians in 1991 by Marvelous Marva, in "The Woman of Calypso," in which she calls for greater acknowledgment of pioneers such as Calypso Rose. She reminds her listeners of the days when "it was shameful / If a woman sing Calypso" or even dared to "just make a try." Reciting the names of numerous female Calypso singers, past and present, Marva concludes, "Tell me who is responsible, I say / Calypso Rose, Calypso Rose."[27]

Praise of women pioneers and response to abuse are two common themes in calypsos sung by women. This is not to say that women do not also extol feminine sexuality in their music. Women's lyrics also openly challenge patriarchal attitudes toward women. Calypso Rose challenged the idea of "putting woman in her place" represented in most early calypsos by men. Boyce Davies identifies a shift from merely cataloging abuse to outright challenges to masculine violence, in, for example, the 1980 song "Ah done Wid Dat," by Singing Francine and Singing Diane. Women have continued to gain prominence in calypso, including, more recently, Barbadian Allison Hinds. And in 1999, Sennel Dempster won road march queen in Trinidad and Tobago for her song "The River."

25. Boyce Davies, "Woman Is a Nation," 183.
26. Ottley, *Women in Calypso*, 10.
27. Marvelous Marva, "The Woman of Calypso," in ibid., 3.

Calypsos written and performed by women trouble the waters of male dominance and shatter a master narrative of masculinity that permeates Caribbean culture. The increasing independence of women of the region has made it more difficult for men to keep women "in their place," for Caribbean women are reclaiming all areas of public space as their own. This independence has precedents in postslavery culture, in which women, Boyce Davies submits, were able to enjoy an equal "freedom to develop [their] finances independently," as men were freed from familial obligations in the polygamous "friending" relationships. Self-sufficient females posed a threat to men, however, as they could reject them at will.[28] This independence presents itself at the level of many calypsos by women, representing the changing face of Caribbean oral literature.

Much of this oral literature is based in folklore that portrays women in complex ways. Often designed to "put woman in her place," this folklore begs reconsideration, as it could very well provide an alternative narrative of resistance. In the eastern Caribbean, the mythical Mammy Water, for instance, lures greedy male suitors to live with her with the promise of treasures below the sea; the men inevitably die by drowning. Here, salt is represented both at the level of the sea and as the enchanting woman who resides within it, lying in wait for gullible men. Boyce Davies places the tales of soucouyant and Mammy Water (or mamma d' l'eau) (a Medusa-like figure with snakes for hair) in a Caribbean oral tradition that is often quite misogynist. Boyce Davies argues that these tales belong to a whole genre of "evil woman" tales that are symbolic of Caribbean society's response to slavery and racism.[29] For the purposes of this discussion, I will focus on the tales of the mythological soucouyant, who, as a symbol of female sexual identity and independence, is constantly punished (via the poisoning of her skin with salt or pepper) for challenging patriarchal control of women's bodies, not unlike those previously discussed in calypso.[30]

28. Boyce Davies, "Woman Is a Nation," 185.
29. Boyce Davies and Savory Fido, *Out of the Kumbla,* 171. Mammy Water should not be confused with Mammy Wata, who, in the Vodun pantheon of orisas worshipped in Benin, is the orisa of sweet water, of fertility.
30. It should be noted that salt has also been described as the tool for trapping bloodsucking duppies, who travel about at night draining the life from babies. Salt

In the tales of the soucouyant, succubus, or female spirit, the soucouyant sheds her skin at night and flies about sucking the blood of children and of careless travelers, usually men who are attracted to her. She can be killed by sprinkling salt and/or pepper onto her skin, so that when she returns to it, it burns and eventually kill her. Giselle Anatol provides an excellent genealogy of the soucouyant, locating the figure as a construction based on both Victorian-era vampire mythology of nocturnal, bloodsucking creatures and on preexisting Akan folklore of the obayfo, "which also turns into a ball of fire after leaving its skin behind."[31] The monstrous vampiric image was transposed onto the liberation-minded "New Woman" of the late 1800s:

> Independent *and* sexualized, the New Woman was a reaction against Victorian sensibilities. Intellectual women were viewed as "psychic sponges," sucking emotional and cerebral resources out of their companions. Doctors linked "nymphomaniacal" patients of the 1890s with blood fetishism: these women were believed to desire to drain their sexual partners of all vital fluids. European prostitutes, identified as vampires because they sapped men of money as well as bodily fluids, became associated with sexually transmitted diseases and were thus also blamed for depleting men of their physical, sexual health.[32]

More than likely, European travelers to the Caribbean who recorded and commented on the folklore of the region were reading the tales of soucouyants and bloodsucking women through their own misogynist cultural lens. Interestingly, Akan folklore on the "obayfo," who also "delights in sucking the blood of children," does not gender the figure as male or female. In fact, the obayfo could be either:

> Similarly, [Maureen] Warner-Lewis traces the term "soucouyant" to the Fula/Soninke words *sukunyadyo* (male) and *sukunya* (female),

---

(or rice grains), when sprinkled around the room, thwarts them, for they must pick up every grain before proceeding with their intended goal. Anatol cites Maureen Warner Lewis, *Guinea's Other Suns: The African Dynamic in Trinidad Culture,* as the source for information on the etymological origins of the word *soucoyant* (49).

31. Giselle Liza Anatol, "Transforming the Skin-Shedding Soucouyant: Using Folklore to Reclaim Female Agency in the Caribbean," 49.

32. Ibid., 48.

both of which mean "man-eating witch.". . . In the New World, the strict gender hierarchy of British society displaced the more equally valued gender roles of the West African cultures from which people were abducted during slavery. Strikingly, the demonization shifts to fall on women only.[33]

In all of the representations of the soucouyant encountered in my research, all have been female.[34] Marcia Douglas uses a version of this legend of the soucouyant, "Old Higue," or witch woman, in her novel *Madam Fate*, as does Opal Palmer Adisa in *It Begins with Tears*. In each case, the woman is robbed of her sensuality and sexuality via the violence done to her skin.[35] In Douglas's novel, the "witch woman" is betrayed by her husband, who salts and peppers her skin in an act of jealous revenge. Douglas focuses on the legacy of this violence, building a story around this woman that explains her pain and suffering.

The soucouyant in the folklore of Saint D'eau Island is an old woman who slips out of her wrinkled skin at night, stowing it in a mortar that she hides in a safe place before traveling about as a ball of flame. She moves through the night, sucking the blood of those she encounters. One morning, just before dawn, she returns home to put on her skin as usual. Much to her horror, she realizes that the village boys and men

33. Ibid., 49, 50.

34. Anatol has identified one allusion to a male soucouyant in folklore of the English-speaking Caribbean. He is a child of a soucouyant, who is killed along with his mother. She has also identified two male soucouyants in recent fiction, including Maryse Conde, *Crossing the Mangrove*, and Ernest Pepin's *L'homme au Baton*. See Anatol, "Transforming," 46.

35. Anatol identifies fictional discussions of soucouyant that include the use of salt and/or pepper to poison the witch-woman's skin. Lorene Cary, *Black Ice*, uses one narrative in which the soucouyant returns to her salted skin, attempts to slip into it, and is burned by it. In agony she cries out, "Skin, skin, ya na no me?" This version is recorded in Gérard Besson, *Folklore and Legends of Trinidad and Tobago;* in it, the soucouyant cries, "Skin, kin, kin, you na no me, you na no me. You na no me, old skin" (31, 46, 55). Anatol cites an example of the soucouyant tale, (recorded in C. R. Ottley, ed., *Tall Tales of Trinidad and Tobago*), in which the soucouyant is not murdered. Portrayed as a sexton's wife, this soucouyant is beaten by her husband only after he experiences a change of heart. He does salt her skin but then decides to rinse out the salt once she returns home at sunrise and realizes that she has been found out. Because he receives neither thanks nor apology, he beats her for her seeming ingratitude (Anatol, "Transforming," 51.)

have sprinkled coarse salt and pepper into her old skin. Soon they will come to scald her with boiling tar, bringing the priest with them.[36]

In another version of the tale, the "witch woman" navigates the night as a tawny-colored cat. She is described as a tall, handsome, "yellow woman," who lures an unsuspecting, gluttonous man into her home with the promise of good food. After falling in love with her cooking, he marries her. He soon notices that when he wakes up in the middle of the night, her side of the bed is always empty, and when he calls for her, she does not answer. One night, he pretends that he is asleep, in order to discover what she has been doing:

> She jumped up and patted a juba dance in the middle of the floor. After that she took a big gridiron down from the wall and raked it full of hot coals and hauled her spinning wheel over close to it. Then she sat down on the gridiron. When it had grown red-hot she began to spin her skin right off her body with the spinning wheel, starting at the top of her head. As she did so she sang,
>
> > Turn and spin,
> > Come off skin,
> > Turn and spin,
> > Come off skin.
>
> As he watched, she spun her entire skin off her body as easy as the shucks off an ear of corn. When it was all off, she was revealed as a tawny-yellow cat. She took the skin and chucked it under the bed. "Lay there, skin," she told it, "with that fool husband of mine snorin' in de bed until I come back. I'm goin to have me some fun."[37]

Her jealous husband, true to the pattern in these tales, murders her by contaminating her skin with salt. Again, woman's mobility and sexuality are policed by a man.

In another form, salt can be used to thwart male sexuality. Saltpeter (potassium nitrate or sodium nitrate) is widely believed to cause impotence in men. A friend once related a story about a woman who, frustrated by her husband's pattern of infidelity, prepared a succulent feast for him complete with chocolate pudding. The meal was full of saltpeter,

36. Traylor, Frost, and Lawrence, *Broad Sympathy*, 151–52.
37. Ibid., 152.

except for the chocolate pudding, which was full of Ex-Lax. When the man went out later to meet his mistress, he was impotent and was plagued with violent diarrhea for days.

Taken together, these tales recount a contradictory relationship with salt in the Caribbean, as a tool for both oppression and liberation of women. Nowhere is this seen more than in the narrative of soucouyant. She persists in her desire to fly in spite of fearing the salty destruction of her skin. However, Anatol argues that "the soucouyant holds tremendous subversive potential for women of the Caribbean diaspora, but she does not, and cannot, provide answers to all the questions of gender, sexuality, race and class."[38] Whereas she has been used in folklore as a cautionary tale for women who disobey men, she can also be read as a woman who refuses to sacrifice her sexual or emotional independence for middle-class domestic stability. The price she pays for this is extreme violence. I contend that the folkloric narrative of persecution of women who choose independence over social convention easily translates to calypso, in form and function. Affirmations of sexual empowerment and freedom can easily be seen in many discussions of "saltfish" and sensuality in calypso. If it is true that misogyny designed to "keep women in their place" has historically existed in Caribbean oral culture at the level of folklore, it makes perfect sense that a similar level of malevolence could be molded into a particular genre of calypso designed to do the same. What is also evident is that there is and has always been a counternarrative of transcendence to combat this demonization of women, often coming from the women themselves. In an examination of the symbolic use of soucouyant in *Black Ice,* by Lorene Cary, *At the Bottom of the River,* by Jamaica Kincaid, and the short story "Nineteen Thirty-Seven," by Edwidge Danticat, Gisele Anatol shows us the possibilities for reading soucouyant as an affirmative symbol of female subjectivity, one that provides a narrative for transcendence.[39] It is the

---

38. Anatol, "Transforming," 59. Anatol advocates reimagining the soucouyant to locate her away from "the figure that has traditionally been aligned with the forces of evil" and instead to place her within a feminist discussion of women's sexual independence and spiritual freedom (ibid., 46).

39. Anatol, "Transforming," 52–59; Danticat's "Nineteen Thirty-Seven" is in *Krik? Krak!* 31–49.

ability to fly that takes center stage, not the price paid for it. Again, sucking salt is linked to both punishment and sexual/spiritual mobility.

Caribbean women clearly have played an integral part in the history and development of calypso and soca. The importance of play—with words, language, and sexuality—operate as an example of the limitless possibilities for creativity in Caribbean cultures. The fact that "sucking salt" can be used simultaneously as a metaphor for hardship and denigration, as well as for extreme pleasure in both folklore and popular culture shows the range of this flexibility. In this context, the term also involves the high levels of contradiction inherent in carnival culture—for women, this includes the liberating aspects of "taking space," on one hand, and oppression via misogyny and objectification on the other. Per the ideas of Boyce Davies on the carnivalization of Black women's bodies, I acknowledge the contradictions inherent in my own arguments about sexuality and Caribbean popular culture in relation to "sucking salt" and "taking space." I also acknowledge the logic of a philosophy of survival implied here. By bringing private discourse, including sexual discourse, outdoors with double entendre and unsubtle allusion, linguistic and musical expression crosses infinite boundaries. Boundaries constructed by assumptions regarding gender are also crossed in this context, for it is not only men who own discussions of sexuality in Caribbean public space: women have become a force to be reckoned with. J. D. Elder, Keith Warner, Hollis Liverpool, Carol Maison-Bishop, Carole Boyce Davies, and many other scholars have shown us that women were making calypsos as early as the nineteenth century.[40] In Trinidad and Tobago, it was the colonial government's fear of the revolutionary potential of calypso, stick fighting, and street culture that forced women calypsonians to the margins. Although Calypso Rose argues that by the time she began composing calypsos, the field had become predominately male, this phenomenon marked a step backward, as evidenced by the ways in which Rose's full participation greatly contributed to the development of both male and female calypsonians.

40. See also Andrew Pearse, "Mitto Sampson on Calypso Legends of the Nineteenth Century," 260–61; and Hodge, "Shadow of the Whip," in Coombs, *Is Massa*, 111–18.

Marlene Nourbese Philip's essay "Dis Place: The Space Between" is useful here in its discussion of public and private space in the Caribbean as existing via the Caribbean woman's body. My examination of salt, sexuality, and Caribbean culture resonates with Philip's representation of the "jamette," who is unruly and leads her band through the streets in direct challenge to men, the colonial elite, and colonial governments. Philip makes the argument that no discussion of space in the Caribbean can exist without the discussion of women and women's bodies. Bodicea challenged the notion that the streets of Trinidad were the domain of men and participated in behaviors that were considered masculine. As we study the language of survival used by Caribbean women in public space, we find that the discussion of salt in relation to Caribbean women's sexuality exemplifies the struggle of the contradictory notions of gender that rest on or in the body, metaphorical, and literal, of women at the level of orature. Thus I intend to move the preliminary questions presented in "dis place" into a new space, the "elsewhere" of "the space in between"—between folklore and music, metaphor and reality—where the soucouyant continues to fly, aware of the consequences of flight, but nonetheless free.

Four Harvesting Salt

Caribbean Women Writers in England and the Philosophy of Survival

. . . .

Black women came to [England] because we wanted to work. We have made a lasting contribution to the British economy and we have paid for it with our blood, our sweat and our tears. We worked hard and long so that our children would be assured of a better future, and we fought many a battle against racism and exploitation, to ensure that they would be spared a similar fate. Whatever the future holds and whatever the implications of the technological revolution, we have made it clear that we will settle for nothing less.[1]

The statement above speaks boldly of the sacrifices Caribbean women have made to create spaces for themselves and their families in the hostile and inhospitable "mother country." At the beginning of Chapter 1, I described how my Aunt Muriel had moved to England to pursue nursing as a career, but how she had finally returned home to Barbados, deciding that if she were to "suck salt," it was better to do so in the warm sun than in cold, gray Britain. Auntie Muriel's experience of migration to and from England is part of a larger exodus of many women who sought the economic opportunities they were unable to find at home. Very quickly, however, Auntie Muriel realized that the

---

1. Beverley Bryan, Stella Dadzie, and Suzanne Scafe, eds., *The Heart of the Race: Black Women's Lives in Britain*, 56–57.

myth of England was a farce, and if her labor was to be exploited, it was much better to return home, where there was family to help her raise her baby girl.

This chapter examines the ways in which Caribbean women migrants to England have articulated their migration experiences, and how these stories have created a context for the literary articulations of their daughter generation of Black women writers in Britain. The generational dimensions of this discourse of identity and migration speak to the continuing importance of "sucking salt" as a strategy for survival. The literature created by these women shows how they have navigated such obstacles as slavery, racism, sexism, and sexual abuse.

From the nineteenth century to the present, Black women writers in Britain have chronicled their survival—their experiences with "sucking salt"—in ways that clear new spaces for subsequent generations. Alice Walker, in her essay collection *In Search of Our Mothers' Gardens*, provided for us an example of accounting for the creativity of our literary and ancestral foremothers. In that vein, I will locate the spaces cleared by early generations of Black women writers in Britain for their "daughters," a new generation of Black women writers.

The trope of "mothering, motherhood, and motherlands" has been used extensively in discussions on critical theories of Black women's writings. Susheila Nasta's work in this area, specifically the anthology *Motherlands: Black Women's Writing from Africa, the Caribbean, and South Asia,* discusses the idea of "motherhood" as it has been debated in mainstream feminist criticism and adds: "Clearly mothers and motherlands have provided a potent symbolic force in the writings of African, Caribbean and Asian women with the need to demythologise the illusion of the colonial 'motherland' or 'mothercountry' and the parallel movement to rediscover, recreate and give birth to the genesis of new forms and languages of expression."[2]

If the idea of "mothering" has figured prominently in theoretical discussion of Black women's writing, the notion of the "daughter" is equally important. Consuelo López Springfield describes Caribbean women as "daughters of Caliban" in her study that "bears witness to the multiplic-

---

2. Susheila Nasta, ed. *Motherlands: Black Women's Writing from Africa, the Caribbean, and South Asia,* xix.

ity of Caribbean women's roles," as mothers, daughters, activists, laborers, and so on. Mindful of the largely male identification of Caliban in
discussions of Caribbean identity, she chooses to

> appropriate his legacy of struggle cognizant that identity is never
> fixed, but fluid. We add to this image a new dimension, one which
> women writers of the Caribbean remind us of consistently: that
> we are daughters, reweaving our mothers' stories into our own as
> we challenge convention. These collective memories help to frame
> perceptions of feminism and the ways in which race, ethnicity,
> economic status, and sexuality affect potential coalitions across
> class lines.[3]

It is this idea of creativity and reproduction of newness, in the form of
language, that I will examine in this chapter, particularly within the
context of migration and self-identity.

Previously we have discussed the notion of "Black British" identity as
developed by Paul Gilroy and Stuart Hall; building on this idea, Susheila
Nasta has posited a discussion of the usefulness of *Black* as a term
which, "in its broadest political sense," is utilized as a "means of drawing
links, despite important social and cultural differences, between the writings of women of colour who have suffered the effects of a double colonisation brought about by history and male-dominated social and political systems."[4] Carole Boyce Davies elucidates further on these labels:

> There is some debate about the designation Black British, with
> suggestions that these two conjoined are contradictions in terms.
> A number of these writers may not refer to themselves as Black
> British but as Afro-Caribbean, Guyanese, Trinidadian, Black Scot-
> tish, Asian and so on. Some feel they have no particular sets of
> identifications they need to claim. Dorothea Smartt would suggest
> that Black British often refers to the generation born in England
> as opposed to the ones who migrate. What many of these writers
> have in common, however, is that they define themselves as Black
> women writers.... Janice Shinebourne and other writers I talked

3. Consuelo López Springfield, ed., *Daughters of Caliban: Caribbean Women in
the Twentieth Century*, xii.

4. Nasta, *Motherlands*, xix.

to on several occasions would help clarify this point, particularly about making distinctions and not approaching this group as monolithic, but there are of course a variety of perspectives on this issue of naming.[5]

It is quite logical to assume that the term *African* is used in keeping with the rejection of any national connection to England. This move towards greater self-definition in relationship to Africa is an acknowledgment of Anglo-racism and a response to the refusal of the British to recognize non-White peoples born in the United Kingdom or foreign-born individuals as eligible for British citizenship. Kobena Mercer writes

> The development of "black" political discourse in Britain's post-war economy, polity and culture has brought about the proliferation of antagonistic struggles around the signifier of "race," which has entered the domain of hegemony as its effects involve "a recomposition of relations of power at all levels of society."... This space simultaneously circumscribes "the black community" as that domain of the social in which the policing of black life is exerted with particular brutality by forces of both market and state (employment, housing, education, policing, immigration), *and,* over and above the ability to resist and survive such forces, it is the domain of all sorts of practices that make up a culture, a whole way of life, which affects the landscape of the society as a whole, in what it is and what it could become.[6]

Blackness, then, marks one perpetually foreign and therefore not British. Some Black peoples in England then, choose not to embrace British identity, embracing instead an anticolonial identity in the midst of the "mother country." In this context, England no longer figures as motherland. For many Black peoples born in, during, and after the 1960s, and as a direct result of international Black Nationalist movements, "motherland" is located elsewhere: in Africa, in the nations from which their parents migrated, or both. For these reasons, I will use the terms "Black British" and "African Caribbean" where applicable, based on the distinctions posited by Black activists and cultural workers, for the sake of speci-

5. Boyce Davies, *Black Women, Writing,* 188n97.
6. Mercer, *Welcome,* 9.

ficity. *African Caribbean* refers to peoples from the Caribbean of African descent who migrated to Britain, whereas, *Black British* refers to Black peoples born in Britain.[7]

An examination of the writings of three generations of Black women in England illuminates the ways in which they have responded to the political and racial climate confronting them. Focusing on *The History of Mary Prince, a West Indian Slave,* edited by Moira Ferguson, *Black Teacher,* by Beryl Gilroy, *The Unbelonging,* by Joan Riley, and the poetry of Dorothea Smartt, I will discuss nineteenth- and twentieth-century articulations of Blackness, womanhood, and resistance.[8]

As the first Caribbean woman to leave behind a narrative, Mary Prince articulates one of the earliest testimonies of the experience of the female slave. As a Caribbean woman who engaged in both inter-island (having been born in Bermuda, lived in Antigua, and sent to Turk's Island) and international migration (to England) as an enslaved woman, her life speaks directly to issues of African diasporic migration, as well as to the thematics and realities of the meaning of "salt." One could argue that Prince was not a migrant at all and that because of her enslavement she was an involuntary migrant at best. However, there are significant

7. I am careful here not to equate *African American* with *African Caribbean* in terms of an analogous relationship. Joan Riley has already warned us against conflating the "Afro-American" and "Afro-Caribbean" experiences. "There has always been a tendency to confuse, rather than link, the historical developments within the Caribbean basin with that which exist [*sic*] in the United States. This has been foisted by the common experience of slavery and the traditional migratory tendencies of Caribbean peoples towards the United States. It has also been a comfortable cushioning reality with overtones of inevitability taking away responsibility for a range of injustices from the shoulders of the host community.... The writer of the black reality in Britain must of necessity challenge this perception." (Joan Riley, "Writing Reality in a Hostile Environment," 548–49). In addition, there remains a question regarding the class affiliations of the term *African Caribbean. African American,* a term that had been used since the middle twentieth century (possibly in the nineteenth as well) and used liberally in the press in the 1980s, has clear middle-class origins, in a way that *African Caribbean* seems not to. For *African American* flaunts a clear allegiance to the ideology of imperialism as represented by "American-ness" internationally. *African* and *Caribbean* still carry the anti-imperial, anticolonial connotation, specifically in relationship to "British" identity, which rejects it altogether.

8. Joan Riley's fourth novel, *A Kindness to the Children,* did not lend itself as well to the topic of my discussion as do her first three. The novel does, however, deal with migration and subjectivity as well as diaspora.

parallels between Prince's life and the lives of the women represented by Gilroy, Riley, and Smartt.

Mary Prince is the first of a generation of Caribbean women writers who actively challenged colonial exploitation, both within the Caribbean and in the "mother country." She is the first African Caribbean woman to escape slavery and to "write" of and publish her experiences. As a previously enslaved Black woman living in England, what exactly is Prince's "nation?"[9] Obviously denied citizenship in Bermuda, where she had lived as a slave, and with slavery not yet abolished in the British colonies (although she was free in England), how could she lay claim to a "British" identity, Black or otherwise, except in coloniality? Prince's eventual emancipation pushes the boundaries of discussions of slavery, freedom, and citizenship—specifically of freedom within the context of pre-emancipation. According to Ziggi Alexander, "Even those who enjoyed legal freedom could not exercise the right to all that word implied, because connected with a slave by origin they were vulnerable to sexual abuse and violence which [Euro-American] societies encouraged and condoned." Although Alexander is referring to a situation in which a free woman who, once brought to New Orleans by her "master," was threatened with enslavement by a local official and later saved from enslavement by her "owner," the culture of violence Alexander describes occurred in Europe as well.[10]

Prince never returned to her husband in Antigua, and by the time of her emancipation, she was extremely ill with rheumatoid arthritis. At the end of her history, she tells the reader, "I still live in the hope that God will find a way to give me my liberty, and give me back to my husband. I endeavour to keep down my fretting, and to leave all to Him, for He knows what is good for me better than I know myself. Yet, I must confess, I find it a hard and heavy task to do so."[11] Even after leaving the home of the Woods (after constant ill treatment and incessant entreaties

9. Interestingly, Ferguson calls Mary Prince "Black British" (*History of Mary Prince*, 1). I question whether this is an accurate racial and national category in which to place Prince, since "Black British" is clearly a late-twentieth-century term that comes with its own set of complications, discussed earlier.

10. Alexander, preface to *History of Mary Prince*, 8.

11. *History of Mary Prince*, 83.

to leave and fend for herself in the streets of London), Mr. Wood would not allow Prince to return to Antigua as a free woman. Although technically free in England, she was not afforded the opportunity to enjoy freedom where it most mattered, in Antigua with her husband. In poor health and suffering with several ailments exacerbated by the cold climate in London, her freedom was bittersweet.

I begin with Mary Prince because hers is an actual lived experience of harvesting salt. Out of the many hardships and sexual abuse endured by Prince at the hands of her owners, the time she spent on Turk's Island mining salt is most useful to my study, as it provides an explicit example of the material conditions of slavery. Also, her experience in Turk's Island moves the notion of "sucking salt" beyond metaphor to the literal personification of hardship. Salt, in this context, is much more than diasporic metaphor; it is a brutal reality that preyed upon the bodies and lives of the slaves forced to harvest it. Mary Prince detailed the oppressiveness of being forced to harvest salt:

> I was given a half barrel and a shovel, and had to stand up to my knees in the water, from four o'clock in the morning till nine, when we were given some Indian corn boiled in water, which we were obliged to swallow as fast as we could for fear the rain should come on and melt the salt. We were then called again to our tasks, and worked through the heat of the day; the sun flaming upon our heads like fire, and raising salt blisters in those parts which were not completely covered. Our feet and legs, from standing in the salt water for so many hours, soon became full of dreadful boils, which eat down in some cases to the very bone, afflicting the sufferers with great torment. We came home at twelve; ate our corn soup, called blawly, as fast as we could, and went back to our employment till dark at night. We then shoveled up the salt in large heaps, and went down to the sea, where we washed the pickle from our limbs, and cleaned the barrows and shovels from the salt. When we returned to the house, our master gave us each our allowance of raw Indian corn, which we pounded on mortar and boiled in water for our suppers.[12]

12. Ibid., 62.

All of the aspects of salt in relationship to hardship in the African diaspora culture come together here.

Claudia Jones's formulation "superexploitation" provides an excellent discussion of the ways in which Black women's labor—in this case exploited for the harvesting of salt—is stolen in an unequal system of exchange. Jones, born in Trinidad in 1915, spent her formative years in Harlem, New York, to which she and her family had migrated in 1924. Truly a diasporic subject, she had firsthand knowledge of poverty and racism in the United States, and later in Europe, and she used this knowledge to build bridges between revolutionary women worldwide. She personally experienced the exploitation of poor people when she was a child, when her mother died over a sewing machine in a sweatshop. All this, and exposure to Jim Crow racism, motivated Jones to struggle against racism and economic abuses of the poor. Jones was one of the first Black women activists to make a connection between capitalism and the exploitation of the working classes of non-White peoples internationally. Under the umbrella of communism, Jones developed a political praxis that fused antiracist politics and activism with anticapitalist activism. In so doing, she created what Carole Boyce Davies refers to as an "anti-imperialist feminism" that was "truly international in nature. She was able to make decided links because of her anti-imperialist posture with other women struggling for liberation."[13]

In a searing critique of twentieth-century capitalism published in 1949, Jones challenged the hypocrisy of American democracy and its claims of equal treatment of all peoples. Despite these claims, Black people, particularly Black women, remained (and still remain) among the most exploited by capitalism:

> The vaunted boast of the ideologist of Big business that American women possess "the greatest equality" in the world is exposed in all its hypocrisy when one sees that in many parts of the world, particularly in the Soviet Union, the New Democracies, and the formerly oppressed land of China, women are attaining new heights of equality. But above all else, Wall Street's boast stops at the water's

13. Carole Boyce Davies, "Claudia Jones, Anti-Imperialist, Black Feminist Politics," in Carole Boyce Davies, Meredith Gadsby, Charles Peterson, and Henrietta Williams, eds., *Decolonizing the Academy: African Diaspora Studies,* 47.

edge where Negro and working class women are concerned. Not equality, but degradation and super exploitation: this is the actual lot of Negro women![14]

In the context of superexploitation, the bodies of the oppressed have no value that the capitalist is required to acknowledge. Therefore, according the philosophy of Marxist-Leninism, the use value of a person's labor does not match the exchange value, meaning that the laborer is never adequately paid for the value of her work. She receives minimal profit for her labor, the balance of which goes back to her employer. Therefore, Mary Prince, as an enslaved African Caribbean woman, is superexploited, systematically destroyed by the labor and goods she is forced to produce.

Prince argues that her time spent on Turk's Island was among her worst experiences. In constant pain, malnourished, and on the verge of starvation, she and other slaves endured overwork and constant beatings in the name of the salt industry. If working in knee-high saltwater were not punishment enough, slaves on Turk's Island were forced to drink warm saltwater as "treatment" for illness. In addition, salt was also thrown upon the fresh wounds of recently beaten slaves.[15]

For ten years Mary Prince worked under these conditions, her health constantly deteriorating. It is significant that she chronicled the cruelty of "the Buckra men" to the people of England. Mindful that she was educating British people of the horrors of slavery, she essentially addressed them throughout the narrative:

> Oh the horrors of slavery!—How the thought of it pains my heart! But the truth ought to be told of it; and what my eyes have seen I think it is my duty to relate; for few people in England know what slavery is. I have been a slave—I have felt what a slave feels, and I know what a slave knows; and I would have all the good

14. Claudia Jones, "An End to the Neglect of the Problems of the Negro Woman!" in Beverly Guy-Sheftall, ed., *Words of Fire: An Anthology of African-American Feminist Thought.*

15. *History of Mary Prince,* 7, 63, 64. Salt had been Bermuda's primary export to America, London, and Newfoundland in exchange for food and clothing. By the time Prince was sent to work there, around 1805, the salt industry was declining. See ibid., 7, for more information and references on the history of Bermuda.

people in England to know it too, that they may break our chains, and set us free.[16]

Here, Prince appeals to antislavery sympathizers in the hopes that, upon hearing her testimony, they will be moved to action. In this context, her discussion of salt provides an example of the ill treatment of slaves for the procurement of salt, a commodity highly valued by the British.

Moira Ferguson and Ziggi Alexander write in depth about the spoken and unspoken sexual abuse suffered by Mary Prince during her enslavement, as well as the frequency of her resistance. I am particularly interested in Prince's antislavery activity after she escaped her enslavement by the Wood family. Prince was only free in England, not in Bermuda or Antigua. The Woods left her behind in England, unwilling to endure the criticism that would be the result of public knowledge of their ill treatment of Prince and their attempts to force her to return with them to Antigua. Prince used her knowledge of their hypocrisy and shame to her advantage.[17] Ferguson argues that Prince used the Woods' contradictions against them, first in Antigua, then in London. They constantly challenge her to leave and find her own way in the streets. But just as often as they taunted her, they used their lawful right as master and mistress to force her to return, so they could

> protect themselves from a moral judgement about the quality of servitude in their household. Thus the spiral built and collapsed.

16. Ibid., 67, 64.

17. An interesting parallel can be made between Prince's and Claudia Jones's experience, in relationship to forced deportation presented as a *choice*. According to Buzz Johnson, "For her work, Claudia was hounded, persecuted, incarcerated on the basis of false evidence and finally given the choice of leaving the U.S. (her home for 32 years; the place where she lived from the age of eight and where she received the experiences which formed her view of the world) or being deported. This was possible because the U.S. authorities, as part of their policy to harass Caribbean migrants, and in Claudia's case because of her important political work, held up her application for citizenship which was made since 1940. She came to Britain because she was a British Colonial subject, and the Colonial administration in the county of her birth, Trinidad and Tobago, did not relish the idea of her returning." Just as the Woods challenged Prince with the *choice* to leave or stay behind, the United States dangled the *choice* of deportation before Claudia Jones. Both women, after being released, so to speak, continued to challenge the oppressive systems under which they had been forced to live (Buzz Johnson, *"I Think of My Mother": Notes on the Life and Times of Claudia Jones,* vii).

The more the Woods taunted Mary Prince into leaving and the more she negotiated advantageously for a new owner, the more they forced her back, using the law, the only weapon at their disposal. They failed to recognize Mary Prince's goading of their vulnerability. The Woods entangled themselves in their own net of psychological-political necessity and social self-deception. Nor did the Pringle household [the household of Thomas Pringle, who wrote the preface and published the original edition], we suspect, recognize the implications of Mary Prince's discourse at this point; they had constructed Mary Prince as a victim and they were blind to her politics of conscious or unconscious subterranean resistance.[18]

Prince was far from a victim. At each stage of her life she waged war against the institution of slavery. Her first attempt at escape was made when she was twelve, when she ran to seek refuge with her parents. At various times in her history, she writes of confronting her master verbally, challenging his authority. While living free in England, she continued this insurgency, first in her narrative, and then within the anti-slavery movement.

Merle Collins challenges us to understand Prince's experience within the context of framing or the framing of the words of Black women writers by Europeans. Although Prince's narrative is the retelling of her experiences as a slave, it is dictated to Susanna Strickland, a Quaker and abolitionist:

The shape the word took was influenced by the type of frame fashioned by white women writers from Aphra Behn in the seventeenth century onward, by the expectations of the Quaker women missionaries, and by white British women's ideas on femininity [hence the extensive veiling of truth surrounding sexual abuse]. It is within this framework that the Caribbean woman first began to publish her story, concerned for her own survival and freedom, and about how it would be received by the British public.[19]

18. Ferguson, introduction to *History of Mary Prince*, 17.
19. Merle Collins, "Framing the Word: Caribbean Women's Writing," in Joan Anim-Addo, ed., *Framing the Word: Gender and Genre in Caribbean Women's Writing*, 5.

Issues of translation also figure prominently here, as Prince's words were probably translated from Creole speech. Given the sociopolitical condition of most Africans and African Caribbeans in the Atlantic world, Prince communicated her experience along the only channels available.

We Are Here Because You Were There:
Beryl Gilroy's *Black Teacher*

Beryl Gilroy's autobiographical narrative of her experiences as the first Black teacher in London provides a vivid picture of Black female experience with "sucking salt" in Britain in the twentieth century. Migrating from British Guiana (now Guyana) as a student, Gilroy's experience upon entering the United Kingdom was quite different from Mary Prince's in the previous century. She arrived already in a position of privilege, as a student living among other Black students from the Caribbean and Africa in university housing or with British families.[20] In an interview on April 7, 1997, she contended that because she arrived in England during the preindependence period as a student, she was taken care of by the government: "We were looked after in a particular way. We were students. I went in with two Jewish families which the British council

20. By the time Gilroy arrived in London, Black women writers and activists such as Una Marson had left their mark on British politics and culture. Before Gilroy left for England, Marson had already published two works of poetry, *Tropic Reveries* (1930) and *Heights and Depths* (1931). After arriving in England in 1937, Marson served as secretary of the League of Coloured Peoples, editor of their journal, and private secretary for Haile Selassie during his exile in Britain. She was also a member of the Women's International League for Peace and Freedom and the International Alliance of Women. Marson left for Jamaica in 1936 and stayed there until her return to London in 1938. From then until the end of World War II, she was a radio broadcaster for the BBC World Service, where she started the Caribbean Voices Programme. By 1966, the year of Gilroy's arrival, Marson had already returned to Jamaica to continue her career as a publisher, journalist, and social worker until her death in 1965. In addition to the contributions of Marson, British society was also being influenced by Sylvia Wynter, who published *The Hills of Hebron* in 1962, one year after Gilroy's arrival in Britain. See Margaret Busby, ed., *Daughters of Africa: An Interntaional Anthology of Words and Writings by Women of African Descent from the Ancient Egypt to the Present*, 221, 336.

arranged for me. The British council looked after students from the colonies."[21]

Arriving in England in 1961, under the protection of the British council, she was at first provided with housing and had access to education. Thus, she was shielded from much of the mistreatment that economic migrants experienced. Still, she did not escape hardship: "My problems started when I became a resident here and started looking for a job as a teacher. Then I shared the same amount of prejudice and rejection—maybe at a different level than the migrants."[22]

She tells more of the story in *Black Teacher:*

> Just after the war, teachers in other lands were becoming excited by the new techniques, especially those related to child development, that were being pioneered in Britain. I came over to England to study them and all went well until it was time to take off my student's scarf and try to be a teacher. From then on all was frustration. As the months went by, my applications for a teaching post in an Infants' School became "the matter." Time and again I was told that "the matter" was being considered. The fact was that, as a Guyanese, I simply could not get a teaching post.[23]

Gilroy's experience differed greatly from that of other migrants. Although she maintains that she was not an immigrant (eschewing the economic connotations of immigration) she was a migrant seeking educational opportunities that were not available in Guyana. In the introduction to *The Heart of the Race*, the editors contend that the majority of immigrants to Britain in the 1960s had no government assistance, even when they came as recruits: "With no formal government efforts to assist those who came to settle, we relied on friends and relatives for support and accommodation, and on our own resources to help us through the early traumas of adapting to a new and unfamiliar environment."[24] A participant in a survey conducted by the editors testified:

21. Gilroy, interview with the author, April 7, 1997.
22. Gilroy, interview with the author, April 10, 1997.
23. Beryl Gilroy, *Black Teacher,* 10.
24. Bryan, Dadzie, and Scafe, *Heart,* 25.

I found things really difficult at first, because at home I always had my mother to help me out, but here I had to stand on my own two feet. I didn't come to this country to join my family, I came to join my friend. I didn't like it when I came at first, leaving home and coming to a different country, where there was a different atmosphere. I missed my family terribly. It was such a strange way of life to me, and I had to learn all over again. Shopping was different, getting on the bus, going places on my own.... This was 1960.[25]

During this period, equal numbers of men and women migrated, most in search of employment. Prevented by racist employers from obtaining employment in skilled professions, they were forced to take jobs that most British people no longer desired, in semiskilled and unskilled fields such as institutionalized housework, daytime cleaners, canteen workers, laundry workers, and chambermaids.

Life for Caribbean students during this period was not without conflict. For example, Gilroy speaks of being ignored by one lecturer in particular who refused to acknowledge her in the classroom. After a while, she just stopped going to class, knowing that the racist lecturer would continue to erase her. Winston James quotes a Trinidadian female migrant interviewed in 1966, who, like Gilroy, came to Britain as a student:

The whole experience of living in England, though at first almost traumatic, is of extreme value for the West Indian student, particularly the light coloured student. I have no knowledge of what the experience does for the African or the Indian, but I cannot help feeling that the consequences for the light coloured West Indian student are more wide ranging. He had removed an incipient white-type colour prejudice; he has his position as a member of one of the coloured races clearly outlined for the first time; he has a whole series of class prejudices overturned; he has the colonial myth of his almost British personality completely destroyed. In the end realization of this makes it impossible to be bitter about his stay in England. The English have at last rendered him a service.[26]

25. Ibid.
26. Winston James and Clive Harris, eds., *Inside Babylon: The Caribbean Diaspora in Britain*, 240.

Although this woman's Caribbean-based color privilege locates her in a different position from Gilroy, class privilege does not exempt either of them from British racism. Bryan, Dadzie, and Scafe report that poor working conditions, racism from bosses and workers, racism in housing, and low pay made it incredibly difficult for many new immigrants from the Caribbean to survive on a daily basis. Legislation brought little or no relief:

> The Race Relations Act of 1966, far from outlawing such attitudes, merely entrenched them. The act outlawed individual acts of incitement to racial hatred in places of public resort, but left racism virtually unchallenged in every other area of our lives, such as housing, employment, etc. The unions believed that their role was to protect the rights of the indigenous British workforce, rather than to take up and defend the rights and working conditions of Black workers.[27]

In addition, many Caribbean immigrant women had children to support at home, in England, or in both places. As Bryan, Dadzie, and Scafe point out, "Most Black women who came to Britain in the fifties and early sixties were young women who had just begun or were about to begin families."[28] Those who could not afford to care for their children themselves, and those whose work schedule made child minding impossible, were forced to foster their children out. In the absence of government assistance, many women relied on support systems established at work and in their communities.

Beryl Gilroy's introduction to British society, while not without problems, was at least far less traumatic than that of many others. She continues, "I didn't have to change my job. Some of the migrants who were doctors, blue collar and white collar workers couldn't get jobs. But I could go out and get a job as a teacher." Although she obviously received initial rejection on "the matter" of getting hired, in school, she was also subjected to the racism that permeated British society and culture:

> If you were in an academic circle, discussion group, seminar, you were not allowed to ask a question; no one would stop you and say, "Not you." They just ignored your question, [claimed] they

27. Bryan, Dadzie, and Scafe, *Heart*, 27.
28. Ibid., 28.

didn't understand your question, or ignored you. So [I] found it a
waste of time to ask questions. But then in my own time I refused to
go to the seminar. . . . I was sent for by the crown agents who looked
after the students and was warned . . . that I must return to seminar. I told [the crown official] that it would be irrelevant to go.[29]

This disillusionment with the educational system and the blatant
racism of teachers continued throughout the years and has contributed
to a high rate of attrition among Black children in British schools that
persists to this day. According to Bryan, Scafe, and Dadzie,

> The British educational system made no effort to prepare for their
> arrival. Regarded as a temporary though unavoidable ill born of
> economic necessity, their growing presence in the schools in the
> early sixties was viewed with distasteful complacency. Black chil-
> dren were nothing more than a short-term phenomenon, which
> would eventually disappear of its own accord. From the outset, the
> educationalists with their colonialist superiority regarded Black
> children as a privileged minority, who should be grateful for any
> education they got.[30]

Although Gilroy entered the British educational system at an entirely
different level, the institutionalized racism in Britain effected all Black
students, even those under the alleged protection of the Crown.

Discrimination by teachers, via allocation of resources, and through
the establishment of ESN (educationally subnormal) classes and programs incited Black parents to establish Saturday and supplementary
schools "to challenge racist assumptions about the intelligence of [their]
children."[31] I myself have been told by many African Caribbean parents
in London (as recently as April 1996) that they and many of their friends
had sent, and would still send, their children back home to Barbados,
once they had discovered that not only were their children being mis-
treated and miseducated, but also they were being undereducated. In
their homeland, specifically Barbados, where some of their children had

29. Gilroy, interview with the author, April 17, 1997.
30. Bryan, Dadzie, and Scafe, *Heart*, 61.
31. Ibid., 71.

begun their primary school education, these parents were assured of experiencing high educational standards of teachers and students. Because educators in British schools expected nothing from Black children, they did little or nothing to stimulate them intellectually.

Black Teacher, Beryl Gilroy's account of her experiences as the first Black teacher in London, chronicles her struggle against unfair treatment of Black children in British schools and the racism of the British educational system. Reissued in 1994, eighteen years after the first edition was published, the book continues to be relevant; Morgan Dalphinis writes in the preface that Gilroy's text remains an important chronicle of the experience of Blacks in the British educational system: "At this time, Beryl Gilroy's book is an excellent reminder of struggles and strategies we have had to use in order to survive overtly hostile and racist environments. Beryl states unambiguously the racist drip-feed which some pupils experienced at home and in society at large."[32]

Gilroy gives testimony of her experiences with British racism "in society at large" as well as in the educational system. She worked in sweatshops, picked potatoes, addressed envelopes, was a ladies' maid and a filing and mail-order clerk. While working these jobs, she was able to "study" a wide variety of people at different class levels of British society. She learned that they all had a distinct view of empire and a specific view of Blacks, learned from racist propaganda in film, texts, and so forth: "If I was going to be a writer, I wanted to understand the society in which I was living. And a part of that was to go and work with people at different levels.... It took me some time, and while I was waiting I had to do different jobs, but a part of that was from choice."[33] She deduced from these experiences that, when the average British person came into contact with a well-dressed, articulate Black person, he or she attempted to retain feelings of privilege and superiority by silencing the Black person.

This systematic silencing was enforced in the classroom, as we have already established. In keeping with the cultural mandate of empire, all the immigrant, non-White, and working-class children in the schools Gilroy worked in were erased in a number of ways:

32. Morgan Dalphinis, introduction to Gilroy, *Black Teacher*, ix.
33. Gilroy, interview with the author, April 17, 1997.

So much ignorance, so much prejudice, seemed to be built into the school curriculum. Once a year, without fail, the children "saved Black Babies." They paid half-a-crown each, chose a name for the child, and were given a photograph as a token. They showed me the photographs, exulting, "Cor, look, Miss! I've saved a black baby."[34]

As usual, her White coworkers (with the exception of one or two) were confused by her, unable to make sense of an articulate Black woman who was not intimidated by them:

Once when we were alone, [Mrs. Burleigh] turned to me and said in low and serious tones, as if it were something that could no longer be left unsaid, "You're not one of us, are you?"

"No," I told her. "I'm not English and I'm not Catholic but I'm a cracking good teacher. And that's what it's all about. Isn't it? They're short, you know—the whole world over. Ask anyone who really knows."

I expect I aggravated her. She was middle-aged, and a bit of a fossil, and I refused to give her the satisfaction of showing any hurt or ill-feeling. I smiled at her most times. Always she looked for stereotyped "black" reactions. Where was my Negro volatility? Where were the angry whites of me eyes? She got no answers.[35]

Gilroy endured this and several other racist insinuations and attacks from children, parents, and teachers. Despite the society's low expectations, she persevered to become one of the best multicultural education teachers and administrators in London. She understood intimately the problems faced by non-White and other children in her classrooms, and as headmistress she devised effective ways to help and teach them. She relished the idea of working in multicultural schools. In 1969, just as she was about to begin her second term as headmistress at a North London infant's school in Camden, she remarked how she relished the challenges posed by multicultural education.

But it wasn't until after a seven-year break from teaching to raise her son and daughter that Gilroy was confronted with the particular chal-

34. Gilroy, *Black Teacher*, 52.
35. Ibid., 53.

lenges faced by African Caribbean children in the schools. After applying for admission to a diploma course, she returned to a profession that had changed profoundly. The narrow-mindedness and rabid adherence to British educational traditions had given way to a more liberal approach to teaching that examined the ways in which children learned. She learned of the existence of multiracial schools from a friend who was a headmaster at what he called "the worst one in the world."[36] Another friend told Gilroy stories of children who were

> "looking for new anchorages" and so they go around in gangs. . . .
> The parents are only really conscious of one thing—economic
> need. After all, that's why they came here and so they expect the
> kids to fend for themselves. It comes to the point were the parents
> just lose their grip and give up all responsibility for the children.[37]

Gilroy admits that, having lived in the suburbs, she was relatively unaware of the affects that mass Caribbean immigration was having on the British educational system. On a visit to Bob's school, she marvels, "Entering his school playground was like being transported back to the West Indies. So many black faces everywhere."[38] Gilroy's work in this multiracial school reveals much about her antiracist work in the British school system. In Bob's school, she was confronted with the most racially diverse student population of her career. Refusing to respond to the recalcitrance of the children with violence or hostility, she used instead a mixture of firmness and kindness:

> The secret was that the children had begun to realise that they were
> of more than passing interest to me. They no longer expected hos-
> tility in the adult voice. They began to be aware of my interest in,
> and my concern for their welfare. The ban on going into prayers
> was removed and, to the delight of the whole school, class 2Y told
> the story of "The Pied Piper of Hamlin" and showed the pictures
> they had painted.
>   Parents came to see their large friezes, which were hung in the
> hall. Class 2Y—miraculously, it seemed to the rest of the staff—

36. Ibid., 122.
37. Ibid., 123.
38. Ibid., 127.

had turned over a new leaf. All it proved to me was that children respond to love and decent treatment.[39]

Gilroy had worked hard to counteract the internalized racism of the children, White and Black. After doing so and gaining their trust, she encouraged them to vent their feelings of frustration in journals. Many children attempted to ape White middle-class culture to escape their own realities. African Caribbean and African children, under the pressure to assimilate, often rejected their own cultures and any relationship to Blackness. Gilroy provides numerous examples:

> The West Indian children seemed so ashamed of any music or, indeed, anything that was black or African. I suppose they felt they got no support from such things. Once I gave them a picture showing a group of people and asked them to pick the bad people. The Black children picked out all the blacks. The people they picked were well-dressed and smiling but it made no difference. "They look like bad people," the black children said.[40]

And as the editors of *Heart of the Race* submit, many children were scarred by the experience of "fostering out." But Gilroy continues: "The black children . . . had their very special problems—many due to fostering experiences in early childhood. 'I was white once,' said Roger, who had been fostered by white middle-class parents in Brighton. 'I got black when I came home.'"[41]

Gilroy tells how other students rejected Blackness altogether: "Tunde, from Nigeria, kept referring to his father as 'The man' or 'That Black Man.' He just couldn't relate to black people. He even disowned his own photograph. And when I persuaded him to paint his self-portrait and colour it, he wailed, 'Stop it! I don't want all that blackness on me.'"[42]

By the end of the text, Gilroy organizes parent and teacher assemblies at which the former observe their children at work and ask questions about their progress. Parents were also allowed to speak of their own interests and work, creating a sense of family and caring at the school. The school, then, functioned as an extended familial unit, where teach-

39. Ibid., 143.
40. Ibid., 183.
41. Bryan, Dadzie, and Scafe, *Heart;* Gilroy, *Black Teacher,* 182.
42. Gilroy, *Black Teacher,* 182–83.

ers, students, and parents were allowed to share and care for each other: "In our Parent-Teachers Association and in our Parents' Classes we discuss aspects of child development and produce our own infant school magazine, as well as information about our aims and purposes for parents who are considering sending their children to our school."[43] By earning the trust of teachers, parents, and children, Gilroy was able to transform the school from "the worst" to a shining example of the best a truly multicultural education had to offer, serving the needs of the communities in which its children lived. As an educator, psychologist, counselor, and writer, she provides an example of a Caribbean woman who, when confronted with the various challenges inherent in living and working in Britain, created a safe space for Black children and their parents to live and learn.

Joan Riley's Women

Joan Riley chronicles the experience of many of the children that Gilroy encountered throughout her teaching career at a much different historical period. Like Gilroy, Riley does not make direct reference to "sucking salt." In their works, however, both writers chronicle struggles with public institutions, and these difficulties, along with the potential for strategic negotiation beyond the hardship, are exemplified in the term *sucking salt*. Though published twelve years after Gilroy's *Black Teacher*, Riley's texts are among the most effective articulations of the social, economic, and political conditions of women in Britain, describing the lives of Caribbean female migrants and their struggles with institutional oppressions. A social worker with extensive experience handling cases concerning encounters between Black men, women, and children and the British social services, Riley has woven factual experiences of real individuals into the fabric of her fiction. Her novels capture the issues of displacement, hopelessness, and sexual and labor exploitation that are part of the multiple experiences of Black women in Britain as they have struggled to reshape the face of Britain, recreating and transforming the communities in which they live.[44]

43. Ibid., 191.
44. For an extensive discussion on issues of "unbelongingness," displacement, and homelessness in Riley's works, see Boyce Davies, *Black Women, Writing*, 100–104.

Riley's insistence on representing the lives of "ordinary black women" in her novels has made many in the Black British literary community uncomfortable.

> To be a black person and a woman, writing in Britain is to tread a thin line. Coming from the Caribbean, yet choosing to write about the lives of ordinary black women in Britain creates certain ambiguities. For many British-born black people it is seen as a marked failure, that much of what is written as a representation of their environment comes from what they would consider non-indigenous people.[45]

This assertion exposes a tension between African Caribbeans and Black British, specifically at the level of the representation of the "Black" experience in Britain. Riley's texts deal with taboo issues such as incest in the Black community. The hostile response to her work by the Black community, though causing her much pain, has inspired her, through introspection, to persist in writing the stories of "ordinary" Black peoples in Britain without apology. Not to do so allows readers "to retreat back to their comfortable world and not accept their collective part in solving the issues that did not go away with the final full stop." To allow this to happen would mean that she had "failed in achieving the purpose of the work."[46]

The background for Riley's work lay in her years of experience as a social worker and in the circumstances that brought Black women to Britain, along with the social conditions they encountered when they arrived. In *The Heart of the Race: Black Women's Lives in Britain,* the editors provide a detailed discussion of the "day-to-day struggles of Afro-Caribbean women in Britain over the past 40 years." The introduction to the text describes European colonization, slavery and the plantation system in the Caribbean, and the roots of African Caribbean resistance to institutional oppression. Throughout the nineteenth and early twentieth centuries, Britain maintained a firm hold on political and economic power in its Caribbean colonies. The legacy of imperial exploitation created the unemployment and poverty that laid the basis for mass

45. Riley, "Writing Reality," 549.
46. Ibid., 552.

emigration from the Caribbean to England and the United States after World War II. According to Gail Lewis, "One of the characteristics of the British economy in the immediate post-war period was the mobilization of two sources of relative surplus-population: the mass of workers in the Caribbean and Indian sub-continent, and indigenous working women. By drawing on these pools of labour British capital was in fact attempting to overcome the effects of its long-term comparative decline by intensifying the rate of exploitation."[47] Caribbean migrants heeded England's call for a cheap and ready supply of labor to fill the void in the labor force created by six years of war, as well as to help rebuild the nation in its aftermath.

By the 1950s, in order to meet the postwar demand for consumption of consumer goods, and to mediate "the tensions between production and reproduction," the British encouraged the notion of "dual roles for women." Women were encouraged to participate in the workforce, while maintaining primary responsibility for the effective organization of the home. The combination of the increased production of consumer goods and the provision of welfare services to augment family incomes (which could not support the needs of the average British family) resulted in the increase in the demand for labor in the postwar period. Lewis described what this meant for Black women: "Developments within the sexual division of labour have acted in concert with developments within the wider economy, which together with the ideology of racism and the practices of racialism have determined the place of black women workers in the British economy."[48]

Of course, Black women's experiences with labor exploitation did not begin once they arrived in England. The stranglehold that the colonizers had on Caribbean economies had created conditions under which Black women had been forced to scramble for work since emancipation. After the abolition of slavery, the majority of women performed agricultural labor, which differed little from plantation labor during slavery. Income from plantation and domestic work was sometimes

47. Bryan, Dadzie, and Scafe, *Heart*, 2. In reference to "the last 40 years," the editors are referring to the post–World War II era to 1985, when their text was published. Gail Lewis, "Black Women's Employment and the British Economy," in James and Harris, *Inside Babylon*, 74.

48. Lewis, "Black Women's Employment," 83.

supplemented with income generated from taking in washing and sewing. Those who were able to fled to find waged work in towns, where new forms of persecution in kitchens and brothels awaited them. Some were fortunate enough to secure positions as clerks in the sugar industry, as independent seamstresses, and as traders.[49]

The labor scene in the Caribbean during the twentieth century had little more to offer Black women. One woman who had emigrated to Britain said the following in an interview:

> Most women who were poor worked in the fields or as domestics in Jamaica. If not, you were out of a job. You had to have a certain amount of education, because for somebody who didn't go to the best of schools, there wasn't a lot of opportunity. There were a lot of people who were passing exams but not getting jobs. I found work sewing raffia for the tourist trade. We were all young girls between sixteen and eighteen, earning about four shillings a week.[50]

Bleak job opportunities such as the ones mentioned above spurred many to seek waged labor via intra- and interisland migration, as well as through migration to the United States and Canada.

My own family history parallels the accounts of others. Tantie, in the middle 1950s, was the first of my grandmother's children to "seek her fortune" in the United States. By the time my mother and Aunt Muriel decided to leave home in the 1960s to go the Canada and England respectively, economic conditions in Barbados had worsened. During the 1960s, Afro-Caribbean migrants to England were quickly initiated into the struggle of life in the "mother country." Expecting to find streets paved with gold, they instead found low-paying, menial jobs not unlike the ones they had tried to avoid by leaving home. Fortunately, my Aunt Muriel was able to navigate difficult labor conditions by enrolling in nursing school. Many migrants, however, had left family, children, and spouses in the Caribbean and had expected to make enough money to support both themselves and those they left behind. Instead, Black

---

49. Bryan, Dadzie, and Scafe, *Heart*, 20–21. For further discussion of economic opportunities for Black women after emancipation, see Filomina Chioma Steady, ed., *The Black Woman Cross-Culturally;* and Hilary Beckles, *Natural Rebels: A Social History of Enslaved Black Women in Barbados.*

50. Bryan, Dadzie, and Scafe, *Heart*, 21.

women were often unable even to support themselves. Lewis explains
how this situation became more complicated:

> Whatever the wider "economic" effects of the ideology of separate
> spheres, this notion gave rise to an additional assumption that all
> migrants who came to Britain with the primary purpose of finding
> paid work were men, since it is men who are universally deemed
> to be the main breadwinners. On the other hand to the extent that
> it was recognized that black women came seeking work in their
> own right, it was assumed that these women had no family/domestic
> responsibilities whose fulfillment required an "adequate" wage.
> Their very migrant status was assumed to mean that the problems
> associated with the "dual role" were absent as far as these women
> were concerned.[51]

Although this was true in the 1950s and early 1960s, the underlying
assumptions began to deteriorate as it became increasingly clear that
many migrants were going to remain in Britain:

> Whether or not the assumption about the lack of domestic respon-
> sibilities within Britain was true at that time, it was more often
> than not the case that early black women migrants had financial
> responsibilities for dependents in the Caribbean or elsewhere. The
> number of Caribbean-born young women and men who remem-
> ber the departure of their mothers for England while they were
> left with a grandmother or aunt, is eloquent testimony to this.[52]

Thus it was that many Caribbean women continued to struggle to earn
a living for themselves, for their families, and for their communities
back home. The poet Yvonne Weeks expressed the despair confronted
by generations of women:

> ...doors slammed in Granny's face,
> in my mother's
> now in mine.
> Full circle we three queens have come[53]

51. Lewis, "Black Women's Employment," 82.
52. Bryan, Dadzie, and Scafe, *Heart,* 21.
53. Excerpted from Yvonne Weeks, "Our Father," in Grewal et al., *Charting,* 46.

Riley's novels represent via fiction the lives of the women discussed by Lewis and others. Her novels tell the migration stories of these women, integrating the historical and the sociological with the literary. The second novel, *Waiting in the Twilight,* is the tragic story of Adella, a woman of my mother's generation. Adella came to England to escape the poverty and sexual exploitation suffered by many Jamaican women, who, with limited economic opportunities, fall into the trap of depending upon men to support them and their children. The father of these children, Beresford, forces her to have sex with him in exchange for money to feed their two children. Adella becomes linked to him in Kingston when, after having left a nurturing maternal community, she falls in love and has sex with him. Her first sexual experience results in pregnancy, and she is thrown out of her cousin's home. Now alone and with no prospects, Adella has no choice but to depend on Beresford to support her. Life for her becomes more desperate after the birth of their second child, upon which time she discovers that Beresford is married. Her dream of economic success prevents her from leaving town and returning to her family in the country, even after her grandmother comes to bring her home. Granny Dee attempts to give her granddaughter the skills necessary for survival on her own, independent of men. The old woman, well preserved with years of strength recycled from salt tears and sweat, is nevertheless unable to pass this skill on to her granddaughter.

In *Waiting in the Twilight* Joan Riley shows us how the expectation of success that migration to England is supposed to facilitate is shattered by the material reality of desperate poverty, physical abuse, racist oppression, and physical disability. The first lines of the novel plunge the reader into Adella's misery. Staring into a filthy mop bucket as she works as a cleaning woman, she comes to realize that like the dirt and rejected items of garbage, she, too, has been thrown away. The discarded rubbish and darkness reflect Adella's feelings of abandonment and rejection, both at home and in Britain. She is forced to endure the drudgery of working as a cleaning woman and being the sole provider for her five children for ten years without any help from her husband, Stanton.[54]

---

54. Joan Riley, *Waiting in the Twilight,* 1.

Her weariness, coupled with physical and emotional abuse from Stanton, cause her to have two strokes; the first, when she is only thirty-four, leaves the right side of her body paralyzed. In England, economic dependency is supplanted by an emotional dependency on her abusive husband. In the end, Stanton discards her. Although she acknowledges his mistreatment of her, she is doubly crippled by her inability to leave him.[55]

When Stanton leaves her, he takes up with Adella's cousin Gladys, who had moved in to ease her cousin's housework load after her first stroke. He and Gladys eventually go the United States, but not before Stanton informs Adella that she had failed him, blaming her for not taking adequate care of his children. She is unable to argue against him for fear of his probable violent response. Despite her knowledge of Stanton's wrongdoing, Adella holds fast to her hope that he will return to her, and that her children do not lose respect for him. She fears that this lack of respect is symptomatic of their disillusionment with social conditions in England. This generation of children has no idealized image of "home" to turn to for escape.[56]

Although she is unable to sustain a resistant consciousness of her own, Adella's two youngest daughters manage to "harvest" the salt—left behind from their mother's sweat and tears—for their own reserves. Where their mother refuses to critique her husband's callous disregard for his family, Audrey and Carol can and do critique his behavior. These two girls, both born in England, have developed a voice with which to demand the respect that their mother fought so hard to gain for them. Through her backbreaking labor and endurance, Adella created a space in which her daughters can raise up their own voices to protest the racism of British society. This is evident in their handling of encounters with British institutions. Both women boldly defend their mother, challenging police and health care officials who attempt to condescend to her. Even though Adella dies (after a second stroke) with her ill-founded dream of Stanton's return and an idealized vision of "back home" intact, Carol and Audrey have learned the skills necessary for survival in England.

55. Ibid., 30.
56. Ibid., 132.

In another of Riley's texts, *The Unbelonging,* Hyacinth Williams, who has migrated from Jamaica as a young girl, is part of a younger generation of Caribbean immigrants in the United Kingdom. The courage that Riley has spoken of has not yet developed in Hyacinth, and she has none of the skills needed to survive and be healthy in this alien space. Although Hyacinth herself is constructed by British society as "alien," it is Britain that, in Hyacinth's mind, is truly "alien" to anything she had anticipated. It is this "alien" identity that creates in the young girl a sense of "unbelonging" that she is unable to avoid. Unlike Adella, Hyacinth comes to England as a child, summoned by her father. She is taken from the loving, Jamaican home of her Aunt Joyce to the cold dinginess of London and her father's abusive household. Thus forcibly removed from Jamaica by her father, she falls victim to sexual and physical abuse. Her experiences in the metropolis mirror Adella's in that the combination of disorganization, brutality, and incest in the home and abuse by British social institutions manifests itself in physical and emotional degeneration. Where Adella suffers two strokes, Hyacinth suffers from chronic habitual bedwetting. The frightened child is pushed into silence, unable to speak of her pain. This spilling over, this loss of control over bodily functions, is symptomatic and emblematic of the young girl's loss of control of her body. The danger of sexual aggression and bodily harm exists outside the home as well. The physical colonization of her body and sexuality at home and in the external White society close in on her. Also—like young Nigerian student Tunde, whom Beryl Gilroy described as being completely horrified by any connection to his race—any exposure of her Blackness, in her mind, exposes her to further abuse. This is exemplified in two analogous scenes in which Hyacinth's body is exposed in the act of bathing. In one, a "large red-faced woman" supervises her bathing, and she feels ashamed and unable to explain the differences of her body, skin, and hair, and how, for example, she needs a "big enough comb" and "oil to rub into her scalp."[57]

Each time her body is exposed, Hyacinth identifies her Blackness as a source of displeasure, ugly to all who can see her. She thinks herself beautiful only in connection to the landscape of her island when she lived with her Aunt Joyce: "Her hair had been nice then, long and soft to

57. Joan Riley, *The Unbelonging,* 68.

the touch. She would have thrown that at the taunting children, but, once again, fear and shame at the response kept her quiet. It was awful being different."[58]

The physical exposure by the matrons in the youth hostel for young offenders to which she escapes from her father's final attempt at raping her does not much differ from the violation of her body performed by her father. The very social institutions that are supposed to protect her are permeated with the racism that transforms her father into an abuser, as he ordered her to scrub herself while he watched and grew aroused. The young girl is alienated from her body, hating the visibility that her Blackness and blossoming sexuality give her.[59]

Like Adella, migration from Jamaica for Hyacinth leads to great alienation from her island home. She resents having to leave the safe home of her Aunt Joyce and is frightened by the prospect of living in England. Upon arriving at Heathrow Airport, Hyacinth becomes immediately aware of her separateness, her "unbelonging," and the "threats and madness" of England.[60] She knows that her "unbelonging" is a result of her Blackness and British racism. In a desire to belong, she yearns for the "long hair" that would make her Blackness less visible, less alien. Here she has already begun to lose the communal sense of belonging that could strengthen and preserve her on the other side of the Atlantic.

Contrasted with Hyacinth's dreams of returning to Jamaica is the drab, lonely landscape of England. Like Adella, she is forced to live in a series of damp, gray places that intensify her feeling of unbelonging. Years of abuse cause her body to assume the ugliness around her. Jamaica represents freedom and safety, whereas life in England symbolizes isolation. Carole Boyce Davies has pointed out the connections between interior spaces and being separate from one's homeland: "Rooms in this context become metonymic references for reduced space and the references to home are therefore often within the context of alienation and outsideness."[61] Rooms and institutional homes are contrasted with Hyacinth's memory of "homeland." These memories are idealized images that ignore the destruction of the Jamaican landscape. By the time she returns

58. Ibid., 68.
59. Ibid., 52.
60. Ibid.
61. Boyce Davies, *Black Women, Writing,* 102.

to Jamaica, she witnesses firsthand the destruction and desolation that her friend Perlene tries to tell her about in university. Seeing her aunt's house for the first time in years, inside and outside conflate into an abyss of isolation. The home brings back memories as well as confusion; the house's dilapidated condition is unfamiliar to her, yet she recognizes pictures on the walls that she had drawn as a little girl, recognizes the table, the crucifix on the wall. Aunt Joyce's formerly immaculate home is now dirty, smelly, and abandoned, filled with trash. Hyacinth's dream of "back home" has now become a nightmare. Now completely rootless, Hyacinth's feelings of unbelonging engulf her.[62]

While harboring a romantic image of home for comfort throughout her miserable experience in England, the migrant has allowed her connection to those she left behind to erode; the tragedy manifests itself in a total alienation from any homeplace. The indictment by her school friend to "Go back whe yu come fram" resonates with the racism indoctrinated in her psyche by mainstream British society: "Go back where you belong."[63] In the end, Hyacinth realizes her mistake in not taking her friend Perlene's example to create a new home space for herself, one not based on fictitious constructions of her childhood home.

Winston James argues that return home is always impossible, because both the homeland and migrant have changed too much during the period of separation for "return," as it exists in the migrants' imagination, to ever be possible. Although he acknowledges that "thousands of migrants have returned from Britain to the Caribbean and have successfully re-adjusted to Caribbean life," he writes that return is impossible because the "home" that the migrant remembers no longer exists, for it has changed over time just as the migrant has. The exile can only return to his homeland by coming to terms with the fact that he is indeed a foreigner:

> The tragedy of the exile's return is that he/she forgets this and is reminded of it the hard and painful way. It is not that the returning Jamaican is "a foreigner in my own country" (Jamaica), it is that he has no country at all and is a foreigner everywhere—in Britain as well as in Jamaica. He is indeed "an eccentric at home and [an]

62. Riley, *Unbelonging,* 138.
63. Ibid., 142, 140.

exile abroad." Time and change have robbed him of his "country"—he is a citizen without a nation. He can only "return" to his homeland by coming to terms with the fact that he is indeed a foreigner: he and his country have both changed and they will both have to re-learn and learn about each other. This is the new relationship that each returning migrant has had to embark upon more or less consciously, more or less successfully. Sometimes the new relationship succeeds, sometimes it ends in failure.[64]

Despite the validity of James's argument in some respects, I must challenge what I see as a static notion of home and of return. Return can be effected in many forms, such as a constant movement between homes, or "back home" and the new homes that Caribbean migrants create continuously. Additionally, his assumption is that "home" is not changed or affected by the "foreign." In reality, many migrants have residences in both places, using money earned in the United States, Canada, and Britain to build houses "back home." Patricia Pessar has argued that there are several reasons for this:

The Janus-faced existences forged by immigrants and returnees are eminently appropriate and predictable in our contemporary times. First, changing forms of capital accumulation contribute to deteriorating social and economic conditions in both home and host societies with no locale being, necessarily, a secure site of permanent settlement. Second, many new immigrants are "people of color" who have relocated to countries where institutional racism exists. As such, they face the very real prospect of having their educational or economic achievements dismissed or devalued by inhabitants of the host society. Thus, many immigrants retain contacts with a home society whose members, they hope, will value their compatriots' sacrifices and achievements. And, third, the nation-building projects of both countries create political identities, loyalties, and interests that bind migrants to more than one nation-state.[65]

64. Winston James, "Migration, Racism, and Identity Formation: The Caribbean Experience in Britain," in James and Harris, Inside Babylon, 248–49.
65. Patricia Pessar, Caribbean Circuits: New Directions in the Study of Caribbean Migration, 4.

Many actually return repeatedly to this network of *homes*. Return can also be experienced in the form of cultural participation, such as through literature, music, and carnival.

Hyacinth and Adella's refusals to heed the attempts of friends and relatives to show them how to utilize the well of resistance that resides in them render them incapable of protecting themselves against the onslaught of racism and patriarchal oppression. Hyacinth's friend Perlene and Adella's friend Lisa provide examples of women who knew when to "suck salt" when necessary to create new realities and new, resistant spaces for themselves and their children. Whereas Adella was driven to an early grave in an abusive relationship, her crippled body saddled with the sole responsibility for five children, Lisa left her children in Jamaica, opting instead to build a nest for them independent of similar burdens. Lisa does everything short of beg Adella to leave the abusive and irresponsible Stanton, to tear away from false hopes of reconciliation. Yet despite her husband's cruelty, Adella feels obligated to wait for him because he married her with two children, rescuing her from the abject poverty of the yard. This obligation, coupled with dreams of home, cripples her mentally. Likewise, Hyacinth's desire to erase her racial identity and nostalgia for her Aunt Joyce in Jamaica, devoid of communication with her aunt, result in total estrangement. Here we see the importance of writing home, the importance of remembering the emotional and economical needs of the people left at home. Margaret Prescod-Roberts writes of the importance of remembering relatives and friends who could not leave home:

> Many of us remember seeing them, driving down the road to the airport, and neighbours—people that you've known all your life—just standing by the side of the road, waving, telling you to remember them. And you knew that was also mixed, when they said, "Remember me when you get to America. You're not going to forget me, you hear."
>
> Because you knew that meant two things, "Remember that we still have between us all the things we've shared," but also the other side of that was "When you get to that money, remember me, 'cause I'm still here."[66]

66. Margaret Prescod-Roberts and Norma Steele, eds., *Black Women: Bringing It All Back Home*, 25.

Hyacinth had not remembered. Her forgetfulness of the financial and emotional needs of her Aunt Joyce contributed to the woman's suffering. The artificial world Hyacinth had constructed for herself as protection against sexual, social, and psychic violence cripples her emotional growth. Denied a mother to teach her the skills necessary for survival against the world around her, Hyacinth wanders rootless and unprotected. She continues to "suck the coarse salt" of hardship. Instead of processing her experiences, learning from them, and moving beyond them, this hardship destroys her.

In Riley's third novel, *Romance*, sisters Verona and Desiree "receive a fresh supply of salt nuggets" from Desiree's grandmother-in-law, Granny Ruby, in the form of self-esteem and self-love. Both women suffer from disillusionment with their lives and are slowly losing the emotional strength to construct resistant spaces. Verona, at twenty-seven, is committed to overeating, romance novels, and avoidance of Black men. Her fear and distrust of Black men results from having been raped by one of her sister's boyfriends at the age of fourteen. This experience estranges her from her body and instills in her a paralyzing fear of Black men. Sweets, White men, and romance novels fill the void in her spirit. Verona lives vicariously through the White women in these novels, psychologically reenacting the stories. She imagines herself to be the White heroines with blue eyes and blond hair. The rape robbed her of a sense of self:

> What was herself anyway, she wondered unhappily? She never seemed to know from one day to the next who she was, and she sometimes thought her many lives would catch up on her, it might not be such a bad thing. Normally she would pretend Guy was one of the heroes in her novels and she was an innocent blonde-haired virgin. She would walk along feeling special, then she would catch a glimpse of their reflection in a shop window and depression would descend. It would be such a shock—the fat black woman looking squat and untidy, and the old leathery-skinned white man. But she would continue the charade, hiding her disillusionment.[67]

Like Hyacinth and Adella, Verona's body is a source of displeasure. And also like Hyacinth, Verona seeks to reconstruct an identity for herself in

---

67. Joan Riley, *Romance*, 74.

which she can erase her Blackness, locating beauty in "European features and physical characteristics." A parallel passage from Hyacinth's reflections illuminates this point: "She often wished that she had nice hair, that her skin was lighter. She was sure they would not pick on her then. The more she suffered, the more she clung to thoughts of Jamaica, sinking further into her world of dreams."[68] Instead of romantic image of home, Verona reimagines herself as a rich White woman in an effort to feel beautiful and powerful.

Verona's older sister, Desiree, is not afflicted with such self-hatred. However, she does find herself in an abusive relationship, which she refuses to leave. Women's inability to find the strength to break patterns of dependency with abusive men is a thread that runs through Riley's work. Stanford, Hyacinth's father, Lawrence, and Desiree's husband, John, are all abusers who could be called "new colonists." As such, they all suffer under the boot of colonial oppression, exploited for their labor potential in England and victimized by institutional racism. They each leave Jamaica for the mother country to escape economic and class oppression only to find more of the same in England. Angry, discouraged, and robbed of what the colonized is taught is his birthright as a loyal subject of the Crown, each man lashes out in frustration at his wife and children.

Frantz Fanon's discussion of the neocolonial as an extension of colonial domination is helpful here. The neocolonial is himself a victim of oppression by the state and terrorizes citizens of his own culture, thereby replicating the exploitative practices of the mother country to attain wealth, prestige, and, above all, power. Greed for the spoils of colonial privilege creates false hopes for the accumulation of wealth on par with that of the mother country. He is doomed to fail, lacking the insight to see that in exploiting his fellow citizens and expropriating the country's resources for use in foreign markets, he weakens his country, preventing any substantive economic development. Fanon observes,

> As we see it, the national bourgeoisie of certain underdeveloped countries has learned nothing from books. If they had looked closer at the Latin American countries they doubtless would have recognized the dangers which threaten them. We may thus conclude that

68. Riley, *Unbelonging,* 74.

this bourgeoisie in miniature that thrusts itself into the forefront is condemned to mark time, accomplishing nothing. In under-developed countries the bourgeois phase is impossibly arid. Certainly, there is a police dictatorship and a profiteering caste, but the construction of an elaborate bourgeois society seem to be condemned to failure. The ranks of decked-out profiteers whose grasping hands scrape up the bank notes from a poverty-stricken country will sooner or later be men of straw in the hands of the army, cleverly handled by foreign experts. In this way the former mother country practices indirect government, both by the bourgeoisie that it upholds and also by the national army led by its experts, an army that pins the people down, immobilizing and terrorizing them.[69]

Although far from bourgeois, Stanton, Lawrence, and John's initial hopes of economic advancement in England and subsequent disillusionment create a desire for control that manifests itself in the physical and sexual exploitation of their wives and children. Each lacks the money, social class, and racial identity that would guarantee access to higher social strata. And as the incestuous greed of the neocolonial bourgeoisie retards the home (is)land and the body's economic growth,[70] so, too, do the assaults on the bodies of Adella, Hyacinth, Verona, and Desiree's minds and bodies stunt their emotional growth and sexual development. Dispossessed in British society by institutional racism and class exploitation, the three men seek to reinscribe patriarchal control. Stanton, Lawrence, and John claim ownership of the bodies of the women and children in their households.

Albert Memmi writes that the institutional strategies designed to keep the colonized disempowered defines and establishes concrete situations that close in on the colonized, weighing on him until they bend his conduct and leave their marks on his face. This control, however, is a delusion:

The ideological aggression which tends to dehumanize and then deceive the colonized finally corresponds to concrete situations which led to the same result. To be deceived to some extent already,

69. Frantz Fanon, *The Wretched of the Earth*, 174.
70. Ibid., 176.

> to endorse the myth and then adapt to it, is to be acted upon by it. That myth is furthermore supported by solid organization, a government and a judicial system fed and renewed by the colonizer's historic, economic and cultural needs. Even if he shrugged his shoulders at insults and jostling, how could the colonized escape the low wages, the agony of his culture, the law which rules him from birth to death?[71]

Patriarchal control and racist abuse by public institutions converge in a vise around women's necks. Each man's body becomes "the memory which haunts all physical encounters in later life."[72]

John's abuse of Desiree is more emotional than physical. But as her friend Mara tells her, there is more than one way to oppress a woman. John is completely self-absorbed and is intimidated by Desiree's desire to return to school for a law degree. This fear resonates with his frustration with being constantly passed over for promotions that are instead given to White men. His self-obsession makes it impossible for her to tell him about her impending hysterectomy. When she does finally tell him, his response is less than comforting: "What happen if you don't come back? What you going to do about the children? Who's going to look after them while you gone?"[73] Instead of giving his wife the patient reassurance that she needs during a crisis, John worries about who is going to care for his children in case Desiree fails to survive her surgery. As always, his needs come first. He takes his frustration with his job out on her once again, and Desiree suffers in silence.

All this changes with the arrival of John's Granny Ruby and Grandpa Clifford. The couple comes to England from Jamaica for Granny's hip operation. Granny recognizes her granddaughter-in-law's loss of spunk and slips her a bit of salt to suck on: She quickly picks up on the problems in John and Desiree's marriage and observes, "Dis England mek [John] rude.... Doan pay ihm no mind, and 'member what I say 'bout no mek ihm step pon you neck back." She reiterates this point upon hearing of John's resistance to Desiree's return to school. She gives her the

---

71. Albert Memmi, *The Colonizer and the Colonized,* 91.

72. Gabriele Griffin, "'Writing the Body:' Reading Joan Riley, Grace Nichols, and Ntozake Shange," 22.

73. Riley, *Romance,* 85.

inspiration to go back to school by telling her own life story. In Jamaica, Granny had taken up with a man who tried to keep her dependent upon him, prohibiting her from opening a small business and forcing her into consecutive pregnancies to yield him a son. She eventually threw him out. When the pressure of supporting her children independently threatened to overtake her, Granny Ruby used her own mother's strength as a source of inspiration. Luckily, Grandpa Clifford came along and eased her burden. But she warns Desiree that if things don't work out with John, she should leave him: "If you caan 'gree wid de man, is best you fe lef him . . . like dat friend you have, de one Jahn complain 'bout and Clifford always a gi joke. Is aright inna England, you can find life fe lead when you lef dem."[74] Granny Ruby reminds Desiree that she can create a life for herself with or without men. If John cannot support her, if his insecurities prevent him from giving her the space that she needs to grow, she should end their relationship. Granny's own life experiences and the memory of her own mother provided her with the ability to harvest the salt from the blood, sweat, and tears shed for her loved ones. In her last days, she passes along the legacy of salt to the generations of women that come after her.

The gentle Grandpa Clifford imparts the same onto Desiree's daughters, Lyn and Carol, just before he dies. He revises the history that the girls learn in school, providing a discourse of Afro-Caribbean resistance that counters the racist colonial teachings they are forced to endure. His tales of the Maroons' fight for land and economic autonomy provide them with a historical context in which to cushion themselves against British institutional attempts to make them feel rootless. In the absence of a "back home" to point to for origins, Grandpa provides them with a history of resistance from which to draw strength.

Dorothea Smartt: Medusa—Muse(ings) on History

For a more recent generation of African Caribbeans, particularly those who were born in England, "back home" assumes a different significance. Here the notion of "sucking salt" is seen at its logical conclusion—the creation of a space of transcendence, in which new subjectivities emerge.

74. Ibid., 139, 164.

For those such as Dorothea Smartt, who refers to herself as Black British, born in south (or "sauf") London, the notion of home resides somewhere between London and Barbados. Smartt's poem "generations dreaming" points to the new identities formed in migration, specifically from the Caribbean to the United Kingdom:

> How many hundreds of thousand,
> Island voices.
> Mother   Father   Stories?
> Your coming made me. As I am,
> not a Clarendon girl, or a
> Bridgetown girl, but a
> Norf, sauf, west, east London
> Of a girl, even
> A different kinda Essex girl.
> The kinda Blackwoman the world ain't seen yet.[75]

This poem is taken from a performance piece, created and produced by Smartt and Sherlee Mitchell, entitled *From Me to You to Me,* a photographic and poetic representation of the experience of losing a parent. Smartt explains,

> In 1994–5 I was commissioned by the ICA [Institute of Contemporary Art], to do a piece on death and dying . . . as a way of acknowledging my father and Shirlee's mother, dealing with death and holding on and letting go. . . . We were struggling with issues of making sense of the things parents try to teach us, that might have been applicable to the 50s and 60s, but not in the 80s and 90s. The piece was a way to honor that generation of people who were so very important.[76]

Raised in London by Barbadian parents, Smartt is simultaneously British and Caribbean. Not a typical British young woman, she is something new: "A different kinda Essex girl," different by virtue of her immersion in both Barbadian and British culture, a British-born Caribbean. In Smartt's one-woman performance piece *Medusa,* she shares

---

75. Dorothea Smartt, "generations dreaming," in *Connecting Medium,* 14.
76. Dorothea Smartt, interview with the author, April 17, 1997.

with the audience various parts of herself—British, Caribbean, Black
British, woman, Zami, activist, storyteller, and muse of history—in a
show featuring visual images, movement, and poetry. Produced and presented in 1993 at the Institute for Contemporary Art in London, Smartt
reclaims the image of the mythically monstrous Medusa as an empowering historical symbol for Black women. In an interview on April 17,
1997, she asserted that her Medusa "is a Black British woman."[77] At the
time of that interview, Lizbeth Goodman had written the only critical
analysis of the performance piece:

> In *Medusa*, Smartt shows how expectations about black women's
> appearance are connected to a sense of self-definition in relation
> to the cultural values of (white) women's appearance. She draws
> on the figure of Medusa partly to connect with her status as a power-
> ful mythic figure, and partly for a more physical, and comically
> understandable, reason: children in her Brixton neighbourhood
> would see her hair and call her "Medusa"; in turn, Smartt not only
> looked at the children but looked at herself through their eyes, and
> took that title back as a comic claim of the mythic status, and also
> a powerful way to connect with a powerful figure.[78]

Making a symbolic connection between her own dreadlocks and the
snakes that extended from Medusa's scalp, Smartt claims the implicit
power that hair represents:

> To me, hair is an extension of your skin; yet what you put on your
> hair you wouldn't dream of putting on your face, your skin. I was
> sparked by a programme I heard on the radio in New York . . .
> about caring for African hair. It was raving about the importance
> of hair, on a spiritual level: hair as an antennae to the cosmos,
> power coil, circular imagery of matriarchal religious communities
> of women. If you think about the curl, the kink, the nappiness of
> black hair, then to straighten it is to unplug yourself from a power
> source. And then to perm it back is to uncoil the receiver and coil
> it back on itself the other way. I realized that when I changed my
> hair, people looked at me differently, got angry, mad, even scared.

77. Ibid.
78. Lizbeth Goodman, "Who's Looking at Who(m)? Re-Viewing Medusa," 197.

I would go home and look in the mirror and ask myself what had vexed them.[79]

Metaphorically, it is the notion of difference, and the desire by Black women to police other Black women who refuse to conform to European standards of beauty that turns others to stone. Exposing the Medusa unleashes the fear of being "outed," so to speak, as someone who— underneath the relaxer, fade cream, and corporate attire—*is* different, has African hair, darker skin, fuller lips, and a different culture. There is also the fearful power of Medusa to turn men into stone: Her hideousness, as signified by her difference, makes her a threat.

The actual text of the piece is divided into several sections. In the opening section, "Medusa Settle," Smartt likens herself to Medusa, reclaiming her as a positive goddess and internalizing the transformative power that the mythology surrounding her implies. The transformative power, represented as the ability to turn men into stone, is here recast as the power of self-transformation and creativity:

> THIS BLACKWOMAN IS A POET
> AMONG OTHER THINGS
> WEAVES PICTURES WITH HER WORDS
> FOR YOU, FOR ME
> OUR STORIES INFOLD
> IMAGING A 1,000 SCENES ACROSS HER MIND
> THIS BLACKWOMAN IS A LOVER
> OF LIFE
> THE EROTIC
> HER PEOPLE
> OUR SELVES
> IN LEAGUE WITH THE GODDESS
> THAT HIDES INSIDE
> ALLOWING HER THAT SPACE TO BE
> AS SHE RAISES HER HEAD
> COOL
> IN RECOGNITION
> TO FACE OUR MEDUSA-SELF
> AND NOT BE TURNED TO STONE!

79. Ibid., 200.

HAUNTING, CEASE!
MYTH, SETTLE!
LET OUR BEAUTY BE EXPOSED
LET OUR FURY BE RELEASED
THE MASK SHATTERED.[80]

Smartt's Black feminist inspirations, particularly the ideas of Audre Lorde, are evident here and throughout the piece. Goodman makes this connection in her own analysis: "In her 1980s essay 'Eye to Eye,' Audre Lorde offered figurative images of Medusa: looking at herself, and looking at other black women to see what they see, together and apart."[81] Smartt, as Medusa, figuratively uses the mirror, the tool that facilitated Medusa's demise, to challenge Black women to look upon themselves and other women and find beauty, instead of the monstrosity attributed to the goddess.

In the stage performance at the ICA in 1993,

> The opening slide shows Medusa's face, slightly out of focus, solid, as if carved in stone.... The second sequence ends with Smartt's embracing of her alienation and fearful presence in the line: "Medusa is my shield, impregnable." As the poetic sequences and images intertwine, the audience is drawn into a relationship with Smartt as Medusa, a powerful black woman making herself heard, even through the symbolic mask and the multiple layers of "otherness" she claims from her audience.[82]

This "otherness" emerges from her racial location as a Black woman, a wearer of dreadlocks, and her embrace of Zami consciousness. Audre Lorde, who, as "a forty-nine-year-old Black lesbian feminist mother of two, including one boy, and a member of an inter-racial couple,"[83] spoke

---

80. The full text of *Medusa* has not been published. An excerpt from the larger piece, "Part of Me Is a Stranger," has been anthologized in Black Womantalk Collective's *Black Women Talk Poetry*.

81. Goodman, "Who's Looking," 201. See also Audre Lorde, *Sister Outsider: Essays and Speeches*, 145–75.

82. Goodman, "Who's Looking," 194.

83. Lorde, "Age, Race, Class, and Sex: Women Redefining Difference," in *Sister Outsider*, 114.

strongly in the 1980s of the ways in which she was often identified as "other" in many of the political, organizational, and ideological spaces she inhabited, as a result of other women's refusal to acknowledge her identity in its entirety.

It is within a Zami community (one in which women "work together as friends and lovers"),[84] as a member of the Brixton Black Women's Group, that Smartt first received encouragement to write, publish, and perform her work. Artists and writers such as Jackie Kay, Bernadine Evaristo, Beverly Randall, Maude Sulter—all of whom worked with the Theatre of Black Women in Brixton in the later 1980s—provided great inspiration. In the tradition of many Black women who migrated to London from the Caribbean in the 1950s through the 1970s, Smartt had aspirations of entering the nursing profession. From the age of five and well into adulthood, she made plans in that direction. She enrolled in the extremely conservative Nightingale School of Nursing, where she spent four stress-filled months. It was during this experience that she realized that she had never really been interested in nursing; she had chosen the profession out of an obligation to do "the right thing." Despite the negative aspects of the experience, it was while she was in nursing school that she became politicized around issues of racism and gender and began to question her sexuality. Her critical education emerged out of her frustration with the mistreatment of patients with sickle-cell anaemia, and the hospitals' inability to adequately treat patients with the disorder.

> I didn't know about sickle cell while I was there, and we had a patient, a Black woman on the ward [who was struggling with the disease] . . . I wrote to a feminist magazine called *Spare Rib* expressing my outrage about how this woman was being treated and generally [about] the lack of information, and I was writing *Spare Rib* to say "You need to write an article about sickle cell and how it affects Black women." They responded to my letter, and the Black woman who was working there at the time . . . got really interested in the idea, and I was like, "Great, great so are you going to write about it," and she said, "Well why don't you write about it." So I spent the summer between having left St. Thomas [where I went]

---

84. Audre Lorde, *Zami: A New Spelling of My Name,* 255.

to study social sciences and sociology, writing this article, coming out as a lesbian, going to Amsterdam, and writing my first review of a Black women's theater company.[85]

The Black women's theater group from London, which Smartt met up with in Amsterdam, was a revelation to Smartt; she hadn't known of its existence. After returning to London, she continued writing, and she performed some of her poetry for the first time in Brixton at the Brixton Art Academy.

> Before then . . . I had been singing with this Black women's a cappella group. And then I got to perform my poetry with a group of women that included a woman called Pamela Mirage from California, who was in London, and she was a dancer and choreographer; she heard my poetry and said, "Well why don't you do this with it, or why don't you . . . stand up and perform it, choreograph it. . . . And we sort of did it together with other Black women writers and another Black British dancer and did this whole thing which was called "Coming Together as One in Spirit." We called ourselves "I Spirit." We did this one performance, and I really, really loved it. And I suppose that was a sort of significant point for me, when I thought, "Oh, I can perform my poetry." That sort of gave me the confidence . . . years later, to write *Medusa* and send my poetry out for publication and things like that. So then I just started performing my poetry mainly to other women . . . on the feminist circuit, doing women's festivals and women's events, and women's nights, and things like that, and getting a lot of support and encouragement from Black women, support and encouragement for seeing other Black women doing it as well.[86]

When she discovered the Theatre of Black Women, she was inspired by Bernadine Evaristo and Beverly Randall, early members of the theater group who went on to attain success in other creative literary endeavors. She met Maude Sulter before she went on to a career supporting Black women's creativity, when she was still an education worker. Another inspiration was Jackie Kay, the prizewinning author and playwright.

85. Dorothea Smartt, interview with the author, April 17, 1997.
86. Ibid.

The women in the arts with whom she came into contact, then, were workers and activists who had woven their personal and political lives into the fabric of their creative work.[87]

This Zami community was instrumental in providing an example of performance art for Smartt. She therefore rejects the label "lesbian" on a number of levels, arguing that it was within the context of a creative community of Black women that she was encouraged to "come out" and perform publicly:

> I like the term *Zami* very much, and am a lot more comfortable using it. I don't always use it as much as I might do because people don't always know what it means, but that's becoming less of the case as time goes on. What I like about Zami is that it's about being woman identified, a woman-identified woman, and it doesn't nec-essarily imply a sexual relationship, but it does imply the possibil-ity of that. And, it just seems more rooted in the ways of how Black women have related to each other in the Caribbean. So it's not about being a separatist ... but it's about prioritizing ...
>
> ...I wouldn't have come out in the same way if it wasn't for Black women, not just Black lesbians, but Black women in general, being a part of Brixton Black women's Group, and a whole sort of education I got politically, ... a political education that I got from them was really significant in terms of me ... claiming that part of myself and being comfortable with that. I wasn't "selling out of the race," or [didn't have] "some sort of disease." ... And anyway the whole Western conception of sexuality is very sort of ... "you is or you ain't," a "box" over here and a "box" over there. I think Zami is much more ... fluid, maybe that's why a lot of people don't like it, you know they still want to know, "Well, are you or aren't you?"[88]

Arguing against any historical connection to Sappho or the island of Lesbos, Smartt argues that her development as a writer is intertwined with her experience as a Black woman, Zami "performance poet, live artist," and activist, in a historical continuum of Black women warriors and artists from Medusa into the present. The need of some European

87. Ibid.
88. Ibid.

critics to relocate, contain, and label people, especially writers and other artists, is rejected by Smartt:

> Another reason why I don't like the term [*lesbian*] is generally in the popular culture it doesn't relate to me. I definitely don't like the term *queer;* it's a very sort of nineties term.... I don't see myself as being a sexual outlaw... I don't see myself as having any type of preferred alliance with gay men or transvestites, transsexuals, etc. I have a big problem with that.... I might guess that it's a term of currency among younger people.... The contexts in which they're coming out are different from the one I came out in.... And I guess the root of the word *lesbian* is kind of like Sappho,... and I don't have any relationship with white girls floating around—okay so I write poetry too—probably being serviced by Black women.[89]

In her research on Medusa, Smartt discovered that Medusa "was a Libyan Princess, a black woman, and outcast,"[90] silenced by a history of racism and misunderstanding.

> I thought to myself: Medusa was probably some black woman with nappy hair, and some white man saw her and cried: "A monster!," and feared her, and so told stories about her dangerous potential. To see her more clearly, I studied anthropology and thought about the first encounters of white men in Africa, and how they might have viewed and feared these strange and fantastic creatures: black women. What did early explorers see or think they saw? That's what I ask, in a sense, in performance.[91]

At the time of our 1997 interview, Smartt discussed an upcoming project in which she was developing *Medusa* into a piece with three voices. Medusa would exist with the muse of history (Clio), inspired by Maude Sulter's photo exhibition of the nine muses (in which Dorothea Smartt appeared, in a huge photo, as the muse of history). In the updated version,

89. Ibid. It is interesting that Goodman reads Smartt's work within the context of lesbian and/or queer performance and theater, for Smartt rejects both terms for lack of cultural relevance.

90. Goodman, "Who's Looking," 194.

91. Ibid., 200.

Medusa would be refigured as a Black British woman. As the muse of history and as Medusa, Smartt provides inspiration for generations of Black women as activists and storytellers. As such, Smartt is recording her family's history and stories: "I see story telling as active and intentionally healing."[92]

Telling Medusa's story, then, initiates healing both for Smartt and for those Black women who dare to see her as an extension of themselves. She challenges the audience with all of the negative images thrust upon Black women, which, when internalized as self-hatred, becomes projected onto other Black women as critique, mistrust, anger, and rejection.

> MEDUSA WAS A BLACKWOMAN
> AFRIKAN DREAD
> CUT SHE EYE AT A 'SISTAMIRROR
> TURN SHE SAME SELF T'STONE
> SHE LOOKS REALLY KILL?
> ASK SHE NUH, MEDUSA WOULD KNOW
> SHE TERRIBLE EYES
> LEAVE ME STONE
> COLD

Here, Smartt speaks of mistrust between Black women, each mirroring the other in stony silence. In the subsequent lines, she chronicles the voice behind each "cut eye," using what Marlene Nourbese Philip calls the "Caribbean demotic" or Edward Kamau Brathwaite's "nation language." Entering into another consciousness, that of the Caribbean woman in Britain, Smartt must claim and speak in a language of resistance. As she told Lizbeth Goodman,

> Performance has become a space where I can exercise my Bajan [Barbadian English] voice—at one point I thought I was losing it out of neglect, so to me performance is a place where I can make powerful use of that voice. Seeing [Kamau] Brathwaite's *Mother Poem* performed, and reading that aloud, hearing that voice, I suddenly realised that there were people who spoke like my parents— I read words I'd always known but never seen in print. Then I was inspired by Audre Lorde, Theatre of Black Women and Munirah,

92. Dorothea Smartt, interview with the author, April 17, 1997. Sulter's photo installation has been purchased by the Victoria and Albert Museum.

by Ntozake Shange's *for colored girls*...and Spell #7. Seeing what could be done with poetry, that it didn't have to be this flat thing on the page, and looking at and working with other black women allowed me to experience writing differently.[93]

The fusion of voice and the visual is central to Smartt's work, for it allows her to communicate with great flexibility. As a live artist, she is able to explore endless possibilities.

In performing *Medusa,* Smartt was able to give voice to all of her selves intertwined, in both a visual and poetic presentation. She claims Medusa as a dreadlocked woman warrior who fights against the pressure to

> MAKE IT GO AWAY
> THE NAPPIHEADED
> NASTINESS
> TOO TUFF/TOO UNRULY
> TOO UGLI' TOO BLACK...

Smartt embraces Medusa as a powerful Zami—righteous, strong, and capable of reclaiming all that centuries of hardship had sought to strip away:

> DREAD ANGER
> WELLING UP IN HER STARE
> NATURAL ROOTS BLACKWOMAN
> LOVING BLACKWOMEN
> SERIOUS...

Medusa assumes the identities of Nanny, Assata Shakur, Cherry Groce, and many other warrior women and Black women activists from antiquity to the present. She has been reclaimed and reimagined into a contemporary goddess for Black women, a muse teaching us a new version of Black women's history.

"Harvesting salt," both as a metaphor and as actual expression of hardship, provided the background for four generations of African Caribbean women writers in England. Mary Prince's experience mining salt on

93. Goodman, "Who's Looking," 198.

Turks Island provides a real example of the exploitation endured by enslaved women and the toll that this superexploitation had on their bodies and spirits. Claudia Jones defined *superexploitation* as the specific
type of capitalist exploitation intensified by racism and sexism experienced by Black women. Prince, though debilitated by the time she finally
obtained her freedom, nevertheless grasped her history as motivation
and as a tool for her antislavery work.

Beryl Gilroy, as the first Black teacher in London, challenged racism in
the British school system. By refusing to allow her employers to pigeon-
hole her and her students into racist assumptions of Black character,
she persists to become one of the best headmistresses in a multicultural
school. "Sucking salt" is manifested differently for her, as she came to
London as a student. But even though her economic background was
different from that of many other migrants, as an African Caribbean
woman, she still had to endure the hardships of institutional racism.

Joan Riley represents the experience of "sucking salt" at the level of
dealing with British social institutions in *The Unbelonging*. In her novels,
she shows what happens in the absence of a mother, or a mother culture,
to teach her daughters the survival skills necessary to challenge the
"mother country's" insults, inequalities, and injuries.

As a member of a younger generation, Dorothea Smartt writes of new
identities generated in migration. The spaces created by African Caribbean women in England through literature, activism, and hard work
are represented in Smartt's work. Claiming Caribbean and British identity simultaneously, she writes of a subjectivity that challenges all racist
and heterosexist constructions of Black womanhood. Her ability to do
so is the result of the creatively resistant spaces produced by earlier generations of African Caribbean women.

Five | Suck Coarse Salt

Caribbean Women Writers in Canada—Language,
Location, and the Politics of Transcendence

• •

*In the winter of 1967, Erma Loretta Gadsby took one last look around the
bedroom she shared with her sisters. It was a wonder that eight children, at
least five at any given time, had slept in this room, on this bed. She was the
third of her brothers and sisters to leave Barbados. Unlike many who left
home in search of jobs in England, Canada, and the United States, Erma
was moved by a severe case of wanderlust—she wanted to "see what the
world had to offer." So, when an opportunity to go to Canada presented
itself, she was up to the challenge. Once there, she would work as a domestic for two years, after which point she would be eligible for citizenship.
Although nervous and slightly reluctant to leave behind all that was familiar, Erma was excited by the possibility of newness.*

*It seemed as if the whole of St. George was at the airport to see her off.
Mrs. Bledman from next door, Mrs. Lashley from up the road, numerous
children, and of course her mother and father. Leaving was not supposed
to be so difficult. Erma said her goodbyes quickly, vowing to remember
everyone and forget nothing. She embraced her parents quickly and gin-
gerly before taking another long look at the faces that smiled before her,
lined up like rows and rows of sugarcane. She took a deep breath, turned
around, and walked quickly to the steel bird bound for Winnipeg.*

*When my mother arrived in Winnipeg, it was freezing. The frigid air
found every opening in her clothing and rushed into her nostrils before she
had a chance to brace herself. The wind pushed its way into her lungs,*

121

washing out the last residues of salt. The cold hit her hard—so hard that memories of home, of sunshine, of warmth flooded her mind. She remembered her last taste of Saturday afternoon sweetbread, roasted breadfruit, fried flying fish, and saltfish. As the cold dampness of Winnipeg encircled her, memories of home wrapped themselves tightly around, shielding her from the freezing temperatures. Warmed by her memories, she walked up the front steps of the building she would soon call home.

My mother's recollections of her first trip to the north are vivid. She still remembers, fondly, the names of all of the people who came to Seawell Airport (now Grantley Adams International) to see her off. She did not *have* to leave home; she had a job and could probably find another when she was ready. When she tells her story, she makes it clear that her decision to leave Barbados and participate in the program bringing Barbadian women to Winnipeg to work as domestics for two years (after which time their employers could sponsor them for citizenship) was motivated by her desire to travel. She was, however, acutely aware that greater economic opportunities existed for her overseas. So she traveled with her cousin Cynthia and other women to Winnipeg, nervous yet excited to see what lay ahead for them in Canada. My mother is also a part of that generation of Caribbean women who migrated from their homelands during the 1960s in search of economic opportunity and change. Although my mother's experience was a positive one, she does remember that many of her friends had radically different ones. Her narrative is one of many. She left Canada for New York City at the end of her two-year tenure.

When she speaks of living in Canada, there is no bitterness, no resentment. Instead she paints pictures of a place in which she stopped for just a short while before moving. She seldom talks about the White people she worked for or how she was treated. What she does talk about are the times shared with other Caribbean women; these women created a community for themselves that shielded them—at least for the time that they were alone together. When they embarked upon their early morning treks to the homes of the White households that employed them, racism, sexism, and economic adversity snapped at their heels. And for the women who were live-in domestics like my mother, weekends spent away from their employers were priceless. Free from the suspicious eyes of the White women they worked for and from the hungry eyes of these women's husbands, they could laugh, relax, and talk of home.

It is this "talk" that I want to focus on here. Paule Marshall, in her essay "From the Poets in the Kitchen" and in her novel *Brown Girl, Brownstones*, describes her memories of women she knew when she was growing up in Brooklyn, New York. Once these women were in the company of other Caribbean women, they could speak, in a language all their own, of the homes they had left behind and of the cruel trick played upon them by those who had promised a brighter future in the north. Marshall submits that this "kitchen table talk" infuses its participants— as well as the little girls who linger in the corners of rooms and in doorways listening to the "big women's talk"—with much-needed communal support and spiritual sustenance. It is also in this space, inhabited by working-class women of her mother's generation, that Marshall learned poetry, rhythm, and political critique. In recollections of her girlhood in New York City, she continues:

> One of the things that really prompted me to write was the fact that I came out of a family of poets. My mother and her friends spent endless afternoons talking when they came home from work. They worked as domestics. And their whole ability to convey the character of the women they worked for taught me about characterization. Their ability to tell stories in a colorful, exciting way taught me about the narrative art.... They were highly political people. They would sit around and talk about Marcus Garvey, the New Deal, the Depression, talking about Roosevelt so that they gave me a sense that women could be involved politically.... They were the main influences in terms of technique, because those women had taken a language imposed upon them, English, and had brought a new dimension to it. They made it into a language that reflected them, with their use of imagery and metaphor, making their points through story.[1]

Marshall creates pictures of the kitchen space that removes it from the realm of the merely domestic prison as it is often described in mainstream feminism. Black feminist theorists such as Barbara Smith have reclaimed the kitchen as a space of women's power and creativity. As

---

1. Paule Marshall, in Ogundipe-Leslie, "Re-creating Ourselves," 21.

part of a praxis that theorized away from discussions of domestic work as enslavement, Smith and a collective of like-minded women formed the publishing company Kitchen Table: Women of Color Press in 1983.[2] In this context, the kitchen space can be read as a storehouse of creativity; a space in which women, while creating works of culinary art, feed their children and one another with a language of resistance. So located, it is rooted in a series of experiences and identities that are in constant transition, constant movement across time and geographical location. Carole Boyce Davies has noted, "it is location which allows one to speak or not speak, to be affirmed in one's speech or rejected, to be heard or censored."[3]

For these women, resistance to economic hardship, racism, and patriarchal dominance is articulated in a language that refuses to be colonized by Standard English or the confinement of the page. Like their counterparts elsewhere, Caribbean women writers in Canada speak out against the hardships suffered in a hostile landscape, using mother tongue to give tongue to their rage and lash out against repression. Language connects us to our people and to our histories of resistance to physical, emotional, psychic, and linguistic conquest. For the writers discussed here, the coarse salt of hardship, communicated through language, conjures memories of resistant subjectivity. They continue this tradition of resistance, "spitting salt-filled bullets" at the page and into the air.

Caribbean women writers based in Canada paint vivid pictures of the lives of the women in these communities. Contemporary Caribbean women's writing is often preoccupied with a struggle with language. The Canadian-based writer Marlene Nourbese Philip writes that for the

---

2. Kitchen Table, Women of Color Press emerged out of a need for progressive, Black feminist publications. In October 1980, Audre Lorde told Barbara Smith, "We really need to do something about publishing." Smith and others spent the following three years establishing the "nation's only press founded and directed by women of color." Kitchen Table, Women of Color Press was one of the first to publish groundbreaking feminist work by scholars and activists such as Cherríe Moraga and Gloria Anzaldúa, editors of *This Bridge Called My Back: Writings by Radical Women of Color,* and Barbara Smith, editor of *Home Girls: A Black Feminist Anthology.* See Jaime M. Grant, "Building Community Based Coalitions from Academe: The Union Institute and the Kitchen Table: Women of Color Press Transition Coalition."

3. Carole Boyce Davies, "Other Tongues," in *Black Women, Writing,* 153.

African Caribbean creative writer, the struggle with language is the struggle to create powerful images for oneself using the language of the colonizer—the British, in this case:

> The progenitors of Caribbean society as it exists today created a situation such that the equation between i-mage and word was destroyed for the African. The African could still think and i-mage, she could still conceive of what was happening to her. But in stripping her of her language, in denying the voice power to make and, simultaneously, to express the i-mage—in denying the voice expression, in fact—the ability and power to use the voice was effectively stymied.[4]

And because being forced to speak another language is the same as being forced to "enter another consciousness, that of their masters, while simultaneously being excluded from their own," African women are forced to define themselves in a language that abuses them with every flick of the tongue: "Language . . . succeeded in pushing the African away from the expression of her experience and, consequently, the meaning of it." The project of the Caribbean woman writer then becomes to create her own language, which means, according to Michelle Cliff, "finding the artforms of these of our ancestors and speaking in the patois forbidden us."[5]

Patois, therefore, as a weapon, "wreaks havoc" on the English language, resisting the colonizer's attempt at suppressing African history and language. More important, patois, as a fusion of English and West African languages, is a creative subversive response to a linguistic system whose brutality mirrored the physical, social, and political situation of enslavement. Trapped within the prison that is English, African Caribbeans shook its walls with an English language that to the colonizer was unintelligible. They constructed a new language, the Caribbean demotic, which provided a tangible psychic and linguistic link to their histories while creating a new social/linguistic/symbolic order that would provide subsequent generations with the psychic power to resist the master.

4. Philip, *She Tries*, 14.
5. Ibid., 15; Michelle Cliff, *Land of Look Behind: Prose and Poetry*, 14.

Despite the destabilizing power of patois, it is often relegated to the private communal space for most Caribbeans. The admonition to "speak properly" and to avoid using "bad English" in public banishes patois to the realm of the homespace.[6] Makeda Silvera argues that although Jamaican "patwah" is her first language, she had to work at becoming literate in it. "We were taught Standard English in schools, and patwah was never recognized as anything but the language of the illiterate masses." Black British performance poet and activist Dorothea Smartt echoes this statement, admitting that when reading her own poetry she must reach back into her psyche and grab hold of Barbadian English in order to express herself in it during performances. As a child, "Bajan" was spoken in the confines of her home and never in school.[7] Standard English, then, becomes first language, best language, and above all the language that signifies education and civilization. The Caribbean woman writer must struggle with the problem of working in a foreign tongue that robs her of her ability to freely articulate her creative voice. She must also struggle with the presence of characters in her work who refuse to define or express themselves in English. Silvera writes that after months of attempting to write, in *Remembering G*, about her experience of being harassed and strip-searched by a racist Canadian immigration officer upon returning from Jamaica (despite her possession of a Canadian passport), the story would not come to her because she tried to tell it in Standard English:

> The characters would not have it. They were Jamaican. The woman was angry, and her anger could not be expressed in Standard English—it didn't have the words, and the story would not make sense unless I wrote it in patwah. After *Remembering G*, writing in Jamaican patwah became easier.[8]

6. By *homespace*, I refer to any space in which Caribbeans signify and communicate with each other in patois, oblivious to and separated from nonspeakers, and/or at times at which there is an explicit desire to make one's language unintelligible to others.

7. Makeda Silvera, ed., *The Other Woman: Women of Colour in Contemporary Canadian Literature*, 415; Dorothea Smartt, performance and lecture at SUNY Binghamton, March 15, 1994. Silvera continues that the relegation of Jamaican patois to the untutored speech of the illiterate masses has been challenged by the life and work of performance poet Louise Bennett and the emergence of dub poetry.

8. Silvera, *Other Woman*, 415.

As a writer, then, Silvera had a responsibility to write the story in the language that the characters demanded. Another example is provided in the following excerpt from the poem "Marriage" by Lillian Allen:

> When mi sidown
> Pon mi bombo claat
> ina calico dress
> under the gwango tree
> a suck coarse salt
> fi the night fi dun
> wen twist face joan
> and mi man mus come
> down those concrete steps
> from her tatch-roof house
> han in han an' smile
> pon them face.[9]

For Allen, the anger and rage experienced by the character in the poem cannot effectively be expressed in any other language. "Sucking coarse salt" here assumes the dimension of steeling oneself against the pain of rejection as she watches her lover boldly strut around with another woman. It also assumes another dimension—that of preparation for battle. The woman above sits quietly, waiting for the inevitable. When it comes, her actions are subject to limitless possibilities. She is clearly prepared for whatever situation approaches. Like Silvera, the characterizations of the actors involved demand the use of patois. For Allen, Standard English lacks the syntax, grammar, and idiom necessary for the expression of this Caribbean woman's experience.[10]

9. Lillian Allen, "Marriage," 33.

10. In his book *History of the Voice: The Development of Nation Language in Anglophone Caribbean Poetry,* Edward Kamau Brathwaite offers an excellent analysis of the structure of Caribbean English and provides examples of the complexities of what he calls "nation language" and the ways that it differs in form, diction, and syntax from Standard English. Brathwaite acknowledges work on the African influence on language in the Caribbean by scholars such as Maureen Warner Lewis, Beverley Hall, and Mervyn Alleyne. Many other works have emerged since Brathwaite's publication. In addition to the dictionaries he references (including Allsopp's *Dictionary of Caribbean English,* which has a French and Spanish supplement edited by Jeannette Allsopp), newer references include Kumar Mahabir, ed., *A Dictionary*

Here is a perfect example of what Philip calls the "foreign anguish" that is English in her poem "Discourse on the Logic of Language." In the poem, she strives to create a mother tongue that will save her from the foreign anguish of her "father tongue," English. Here, fatherhood symbolizes patriarchal dominance, enslavement, and linguistic violence perpetrated by the slave master and the master narrative: "therefore English is / a foreign language / not a mother tongue."[11]

In an adjacent column, Philip tells a creation myth that exhumes the history of mother tongue, passing it down orally from mother to daughter. "Margin" becomes "center" as the written word and its history becomes decentered by the rememoried language. This rememoried language "re-members" the tongues of all the African slaves who sacrificed their tongues as penalty for their determination to retain their languages. Writes Philip,

THE MOTHER THEN PUT HER FINGERS INTO HER CHILD'S MOUTH—GENTLY FORCING IT OPEN; SHE TOUCHES HER TONGUE TO THE CHILD'S TONGUE, AND HOLDING THE TINY MOUTH OPEN, SHE BLOWS INTO IT—HARD. SHE WAS BLOWING WORDS—HER WORDS, HER MOTHER'S WORDS, THOSE OF HER MOTHER'S MOTHER, AND ALL THEIR MOTHERS BEFORE—INTO HER DAUGHTER'S MOUTH.[12]

Mother('s) tongue reconnects the African woman in the New World to a history encoded in language. According to Philip, Caribbean women

---

of Common Trinidad Hindi; Velma Pollard, Dread Talk: The Language of Rastafari; and F. G. Cassidy and R. B. Le Page, eds., Dictionary of Jamaican English.

11. Philip, She Tries, 56. Scholarship in Black English and United States–based African American vernacular culture provides extensive examination of discursive strategies for resisting internalized racism and the legacies of enslavement. Geneva Smitherman's works Talkin and Testifyin: The Language of Black America; Black Talk: Words and Phrases from the Hood to the Amen Corner; and Talking That Talk: Language, Culture, and Education in African America provide thorough and detailed insights into the form, function, and political significance of African American vernacular and identify the origins of Black English. See also John R. Rickford's African American Vernacular English: Features, Evolution, Educational Implications and Spoken Soul: The Story of Black English. Also instructive are the discussions of Black English in Allan Dundes, ed., Mother Wit from the Laughing Barrel: Readings in the Interpretation of Afro-American Folklore.

12. Philip, She Tries, 56.

writers must meet the challenge to use language to rewrite or re-create history, to touch their tongues to those of subsequent generations of women and writers, enabling them to recognize their ancestors. In so doing she continues the linguistic tradition that connects Caribbean women to a history of resistance, waging a battle against the colonizer's language with words spat from the tip of centuries of mother tongue.

Read from a slightly different perspective, the previously discussed Ewe custom of "outdooring" is useful here. The context of the outdooring ceremony is important, for it is a ritual in which a baby is introduced to his or her family and community. Because the infant is introduced to its people through the tasting of bitter and sweet foods of particular significance to the community, taste and memory are connected to the collective consciousness of a people. Philip's discussion of mother tongue/father tongue could be seen as a permutation of the metaphor for sweetness and bitterness that is the writer's struggle with language. More important, as the vehicle for transmission of culture, the tongue becomes a tool with which this collective consciousness and experience is conveyed via language. The principles of balance and seasoning, linked to memory, are transmitted through the tongue, without which speech is impossible. It is only fitting that the tongue be identified here, in regard to language and resistance, as a fundamental tool, a weapon against the erasure of linguistic memory. The tongue is the site of confrontation, gagging on the bitterness of the battle against colonial control. According to Philip, the "Caribbean demotic," or the demotic version of English, is the

> Language of the people. Language for the people. Language by the people, honed and fashioned through a particular history of empire and savagery. A language also nurtured and cherished on the streets of Port-of-Spain, San Fernando, Boissiere Village and Sangre Grande in the look she dey and leh we go, in the mouths of the calypsonians, Jean and Dinah, Rosita and Clementina . . .[13]

As a writer, Philip finds excitement in the confrontation between Standard English and the Caribbean demotic within the text. It is left to the Caribbean woman writer to strike a balance between the two languages

13. Ibid., 18.

that adequately represents her experiences and those of the community of which she writes. Caribbean women's literature, then, is a form of verbal "outdooring," creating a situation in which the writer must reconcile herself with the bitter sweetness of the language at her disposal. This reconciliation is both symbolic and literal, as it exemplifies the complexities of Caribbean history and culture. As the mother in "Discourse on the Logic of Language" touches tongues with her daughter and blows her words into her mouth, she is sharing the sweetness of history and the legacy of resistance, both imparted through language. This language also contains the "i-mage" necessary for the African woman to find her voice. Outdooring can also become a metaphor for moving beyond the boundaries of enclosure as symbolized by the master narrative of English language and history. Furthermore, the balance struck between demotic and Standard English exemplifies the principle of balance, as taught during an outdooring ceremony, and the ability of peoples of African descent to constantly create strategies for survival that challenge a history of destruction.

Edward Kamau Brathwaite's discussion of "nation language" is particularly important to the discussion of mother tongue. *Nation language* refers to patois spoken by the slaves and proletariat that is largely composed of various languages brought to the Caribbean by African slaves. Brathwaite submits that the current forms of language found in the Caribbean today were preceded by an "underground language" that has evolved and continues to transform itself in the face of submersion by colonial powers. This resistance to submersion and proliferation (in various forms) throughout the Caribbean signals what poet Louise Bennett might refer to as "colonization in reverse."[14]

The language and culture of the enslaved resists and overthrows the authority of the master and the master narratives symbolized by language. Nation language, thus located within the culture of the enslaved, in fact recolonizes the plantation and island space at the level of culture. Language becomes the battleground for the continual struggle between colonizer and the colonized. Grace Nichols discusses the "struggle with language" that she, as a poet, has had to endure in the interest of preserving, recovering, remembering, and relegitimizing her Creole lan-

14. Brathwaite, *History*; Louise Bennett, *Jamaica Labrish*.

guage (and creating an empowering woman identity and consciousness) in the face of colonial domination.[15] Similarly, Dionne Brand
argues against the notion that any language is "neutral"; to illustrate her
point, she fuses language with the collective history of slavery, physical
violence, and linguistic violence:

> There it was anyway, some damn memory half-eaten and half-
> hungry. To hate this, they must have been dragged through the
> Manzinilla spitting out the last spun syllables for cruelty, new sound
> forming, pushing toward lips made to bubble blood. . . . Hard-bitten
> on mangrove and wild bush, the sea wind heaving any remnants
> of consonant curses into choking aspirate. No language is neutral
> seared in the spine's unraveling. Here is history too. A backbone
> bending and unbending without a word, heat, bellowing these lungs
> spongy, exhaled in humming, the ocean, a way out and not any-
> thing of beauty, tipping turquoise and scandalous. The malicious
> horizon made us the essential thinkers of technology. How to
> fly gravity, how to balance basket and prose reaching for murder.
> Silence done curse god and beauty here, people does hear things
> in this heliconia peace a morphology of rolling chain and copper
> gong now shape this twang, falsettos of whip and air rudiment
> this grammar. Take what I tell you. When these barracks held slaves
> between their stone halters, talking was left for night and hush
> was idiom and hot core.[16]

Brand represents the struggle with language as a battle between colonizer
and colonized. The enslaved fight to maintain language and culture in
spite of physical and linguistic brutality. Present-day nation language
contains the history of this battle in its syntax, structure, idiom, and
inflection.

This battle with language is also a battle over space. Brand chronicles
the violence to both body and landscape. As her forebears are forced into
an alien landscape, "spitting out the last spun syllables for cruelty, new
sound forming," creating sounds through their bleeding lips, they create, or recreate, a language in the context of violence, in the landscape

15. See the film dramatization of the Grace Nichols poetry collection, *I Is a Long
Memoried Woman,* directed by Frances-Anne Solomon (Toronto, Ontario: Leda
Serene Films, 1990).

16. Dionne Brand, *No Language Is Neutral.*

of Trinidad and Tobago, infused with blood sacrifice. Nation language then, birthed out of a history of violence, coercion, and a concerted effort to obliterate African identities, instead goes underground only to be reclaimed as a language precious to calypsonians and other descendants. Claimed and exhalted in public space, the Caribbean demotic/nation language/Creole/patois exists as a testimony to the syncretism of cultures that resulted from the survival of that which the colonial enterprise sought to obliterate. Sucking salt is characterized here, through language, as a transcendence of a legacy of violence (to both the body and the Caribbean landscape) and the creation of a new language expressing the complexities of Caribbean identities.[17]

Re-collected Language

Dionne Brand's *Bread Out of Stone: Recollections, Sex, Recognitions, Race, Dreaming, Politics* has helped me to tease out the symbolic connotations of salt, along with the conceptual meanings of "sucking salt," in order to transform the latter into an approach with which to critically analyze Caribbean women's literature. I have concluded that "sucking salt" becomes much more than the act of overcoming hardship; it is also a strategy for preparing oneself for impending hardship, as in an environment marked by constant upheaval, transition, and economic adversity. Here, Audre Lorde's discussion of her relationship with Grenada provides an important analogue:

> When I visited Grenada I saw the root of my mother's powers walking through the streets. I thought, this is the country of my foremothers, my forebearing mothers, those Black island women who defined themselves by what they did. "Island women make good wives; whatever happens, they've seen worse." There is a

17. Lovelace has an excellent discussion of this violence to landscape at the beginning of his novel *Salt*. He satirizes the difficulties that colonial officers experienced in their attempts at subduing Trinidad and Tobago. They had to conquer the Amerindians, the landscape, and the Africans forced into servitude. Writes Lovelace, "Watch the landscape of this island...and you know that they could never hold people here surrendered to unfreedom. The sky, the sea, every green leaf and tangle of vines sing freedom" (5).

softer edge of African sharpness upon these women, and they
swing through the rain-warm streets with an arrogant gentleness
that I remember in strength and vulnerability.[18]

Embedded in this statement is recognition of adversity and a commitment to transcendence. It communicates a sense of constant resistance
and challenge, undaunted by the inevitable hardships attached to everyday existence.

Brand's chapter entitled "Water More Than Flour" is a wonderful discussion of the ways that Caribbean women use language to resist hardship, even in the face of impossibility. She privileges women's space,
here located in the kitchen, as a space in which Caribbean women could
speak freely and with grace of the pain, economic adversity, and racial
and gender oppression that confronted them on a daily basis:

> More poetic, more expressive than any statement they could pro-
> duce to say "we are hungry and going to stay that way, and there
> are those out there who want us to be hungry, and we don't know
> when this is going to end, but it ain't right, and if we ever catch
> their ass it's going to be the big payback, but don't worry, god is
> going to take care of them."[19]

Even in the midst of great hardship, Caribbean women use language to
resist, to challenge, to mobilize for retaliation. For me then, "sucking
salt" carries with it the same challenge, the same preparedness to persevere and fight.

Inherent in the formulations of "water more than flour" and "sucking
salt" is a critique of dominant institutions and a commitment to survive. However, Brand's "water more than flour" seems to bring with it a
sense of impossibility that the metaphor of "sucking salt" does not have.
In my reading of her explanation, having "water more than flour" means
that one does not have the means to survive, not enough flour even to
make a bread, a "bake," or any other form of sustenance.[20] One therefore needs to solicit communal assistance, outside of the homespace.

18. Lorde, *Zami*, 9.
19. Brand, *Bread*, 124.
20. "Bakes" are made with flour, water, baking powder, sugar, cinnamon, and
sometimes eggs and vanilla extract and are fried in hot oil or shortening.

More specifically, when the metaphor "water more than flour" is read through the lens of contemporary Canadian racial politics, it describes a state of total hopelessness, the impossible situation in which Black women in the Americas are unable to escape racism and patriarchal domination. Brand reaches into her own personal history and reclaims the metaphor used by the women of the community in which she grew up to make connections between their lives and the contemporary lives of Black women in the Americas. She implies that despite the years of struggle of "so many Black women," and differences in historical context and geographical location, Black women today continue to exist in a state of crisis not unlike that of the women she knew as a child. "Water more than flour," they would say, "meaning nothing to eat, no sustenance; water more than flour, meaning that things were tough and would probably get tougher; water more than flour, to describe not only the physical but the spiritual state of want, meaning a thinness to life's possibilities, unerring hard times, an absence of joy, an absence of redemption or mercy or rescue."[21]

The impossibility of options described above implies Black women are unable and will never be able to create viable spaces of empowered resistance given the climate of economic, racial, and gender and heterosexist oppression existent in the late capitalist Americas. Black women have and do create such spaces, using language and the disruption of language as a powerful weapon. In my reading, the kitchens in which Brand and Marshall believe language is honed and disseminated is one such space. And where "bread out of stone" connotes hardness and impossibility, "sucking salt" is a demand for action. It could be argued that the former describes the point up to and just after migration (to metropolitan centers) at which Caribbean women realize that the lives constructed in new spaces have proven to be just as hopeless as the ones they left behind. What is clear is that, within the context of migration, both metaphors recall a culture of communal support that manifests in the determination of African Caribbean women to confront oppressions in the new spaces they enter, recreate communities, and, in their literature and creative writing, continue a tradition of social, political, economic, and cultural critique.

21. Brand, *Bread*, 124.

The spaces of which I am speaking are what Carole Boyce Davies refers to as a "safe space where Black women's speech can be heard." It is not as if Black women do not and are not speaking. Various institutional oppressions (sexism, racism, compulsory heterosexuality, phallocentrism) render the hearers of Black women's speech deaf. Boyce Davies argues that certain types of speech are erased by the dominant culture's insistence on overprivileging "rational discourse," or the parliamentary language of the elite. She, too, speaks of the importance of women-centered spaces in which Black women voice opposition and critique to others who share their perspectives and experiences. For instance, Boyce Davies reads the phrase used by the women in her own family in the Caribbean, "It's not everything you can talk, but..." as a formula for talk that, while reflecting all of the systems of oppression that seek to silence, carries in it a determination to challenge: "The placement of the conjunction *but* after the negation of... possibility... signaled a determination to articulate, to challenge, to reveal, to share. For the word *but* is more than a conjunction, it is also a subtle mark of opposition."[22]

Tales from the Garden and Beyond, by Hazelle Palmer, is a symphony of these oppositional voices. It is a collection of African Caribbean women's voices raised in adversity, protest, and triumph as they speak of their experiences in Barbados and Canada. The novel is built around Esmée, or Mrs. G., from Barbados, who now lives in Montreal. The story begins with Esmée's tale of how she escaped her abusive husband in Barbados and came to Canada; as her story continues, she describes her encounters with the poverty and hostility that have come to characterize her experience in Montreal. In "The Gardens," an inner-city community inhabited by Caribbean migrants, Esmée is able to cultivate warm friendships and nurturing relationships with other Caribbean women. Palmer's book is essentially a fictional oral history of the women in this working-class community, with each woman offering a different perspective on her life in "The Gardens" and beyond.

Marshall, Brand, Smith, Lorde, and several other writers discuss the functions of the kitchen space in very much the same ways. Kitchens become spaces in which women can gather together and give testimony to their encounters with racism and their loneliness, satisfying both

22. Boyce Davies, *Black Women, Writing,* 152.

their hunger for tastes of home and for understanding ears. Palmer writes:

> It was the loneliness that eventually brought Frances, Merry and Mrs. G. together. Each of them worked in other women's houses, cared for other women's children and husbands. On the weekends when they had time for themselves, they would meet in Frances' apartment, in the kitchen, to fix each other's hair, to play cards, and to talk.[23]

It is at these times that the three women can speak their stories without concern for unintelligibility. Although they are from different Caribbean islands, their "nation language" unites them in a circle of common history, struggle, and resistance. Here they speak with nostalgia of their homelands, but not without critique. Esmée, Frances, and Merry speak freely of the color, class, and economic stratification that existed in their homelands. As does Paule Marshall in *Brown Girl, Brownstones,* Hazelle Palmer paints a picture of "kitchen table talk" that highlights the telling of stories, characterization, and political critique in a language that in itself exists in opposition to centuries of exploitation and abuse. Here the transformative dimensions of "sucking salt" are evident in the ways that these women create community in which critique and strategies for resistance are cultivated.

The novel begins with an example of the transformative power of language. Esmée, with the assistance of her friend Tiny, plan the former's escape from her husband. Tiny, Esmée claims, never spoke "properly," "no matter how much schooling [she] had. Leaving out words, mispronouncing others." But it is the "bad talking" Tiny who gives her friend the moral support and courage necessary to leave her physically abusive husband. Uncompromising in her use of nation language and her attitudes towards men, she speaks forthrightly in her own tongue to criticize Esmée's husband's behavior. She states that she comes from a long line of women who resist patriarchal oppression:

> If it was me, I woulda poison he years ago. Go to the cemetery and get some old bones. Mash dem and spread the powder in his food a little bit at a time. It would take a little while, but the doctors

23. Hazelle Palmer, *Tales from the Garden and Beyond,* 84.

wouldn't know what take him when he take in sick and dead. . . .
My great grandmother kill she husband so, at least that's what my
mother tell me. I don't know if it's true but from the time I hear it,
I did like she. From long the women in me family don't take no
shit from no man.[24]

Her unwillingness to be confined within the master discourse of English
or to be abused by a man mark her as a resistant figure. She does not
suck the coarse salt of abuse like Esmée or of rejection like the woman
in Lillian Allen's poem.

Until reuniting with her childhood friend Tiny, Esmée suffers in
silence for fourteen years. Her husband, Henry, abuses her and her son,
Luke, almost daily. He reminds her constantly that her parents begged
him to marry her after she became pregnant with another man's child.
Her neighbors shun her while admiring Henry for his magnanimity despite the visible wounds and scars on Esmée's body. It is in Tiny's sitting
room, over sweet tea, that she is finally able to unburden herself of years
of silent suffering:

> [Tiny] went through the house to the kitchen and made some tea.
> She brought it back in two large enamel cups. The tea was sweet
> and the cream from the cow's milk floated on top as I drank it. We
> sat there that afternoon and talked for hours. My mouth was like a
> waterfall, words pouring out as free as water. I told her every-
> thing—about Luther, my marriage to Henry, about Luke, and the
> beatings Henry gave me.[25]

And in return, Tiny shares details of her life with her friend. The time
they spend together gives Esmée, for the first time in her life, the space
to vent and to receive support from another woman. And when Henry,
upon discovering their friendship, attempts to intimidate his wife into
ending her relationship with Tiny, the two women plot Esmée's escape.

Tiny's rebellious nature and forthright speech provide an example of
the type of character that Silvera describes who will not be silenced—
by a colonizing language or by anyone or anything else. She says exactly
what she wants, when she wants to, and to whomever she wants. Her

24. Ibid., 28, 36–37.
25. Ibid., 29–30.

rebellious spirit is matched equally by her wit. When told by Esmée's mother that learning to cook well will help her to find a husband, she replies, "I ent too interested in ketching one, nuh. I living well by meself." She continues that she and Edwin were "incompartable.... We didn't match ... Wrong last name. He name Edwin Small. Well you know how people would laugh after me when they hear me name. Tiny Small. I couldn't tek the pressure."[26] The above identifies a turning of language inside out to create a culturally specific, empowering mother tongue that African Caribbean Canadian women writers recreate in their texts.

After Esmée's departure for Canada, it is Tiny who verbally challenges Henry, "pispirating" him with insults.[27] Comically, "salt" here, through language, moves beyond transcendence into outright resistance. Using the imagery of showering Henry with urine, Palmer allows for Esmée's vindication. This can clearly be read as a critique of heterosexuality as well as of misogynistic violence. Esmée bestows Tiny with the authority to speak for her in very much the same way that Janie places her tongue in her friend Phoebe's mouth in Zora Neale Hurston's *Their Eyes Were Watching God*. In so doing, Esmée and Janie entrust their women friends to tell their stories, as well as to deprivilege the voices of the men that sought to silence them or speak for them. Tiny shatters this silence with a litany of insults. The most humiliating insult comes when she throws a "potty full of piss" onto Henry.[28] Here, Henry is literally forced to suck the coarse, stale salt of revenge from a woman who will not and does not fear him. Tiny has processed Esmée's anger, and her own residual anger, and having no further use for it, hurls it at Henry. This, coupled with Esmée's secret escape, is the sentence for his crimes. Whereas his first wife (whom he also abused) chose to "jump ship" and take her own life and that of her child to escape Henry's tyranny, Esmée sets sails to embark upon a new life in Canada.

26. Ibid., 37, 38.
27. *Pispirating* is a Barbadian term which means to verbally insult in the most skillfully vulgar and embarrassing way. Allsopp identifies *piss-pirade* as a verb, originating in Barbados, meaning "To delight in showing contempt for or causing the embarrassment of others; to vent anger (verbally)" (*Dictionary of Caribbean English*, 442).
28. Palmer, *Tales from the Garden*, 45.

Clearly, if "English is a foreign anguish," as Marlene Nourbese Philip asserts, the right speech of mother tongue must break the discursive silence enforced by a father tongue, colonized language, or patriarchal discourse. As Marshall points out earlier, the act of speaking for women is a powerful one, especially when speaking against exploitation or abuse. The language that Tiny uses, and that Silvera uses in "Remembering G," emerged from the effort to maintain an identity, through language, that had been maligned. The subversive use of nation language, here, responds not only to the legacies of colonization, but also to gender inequity and more specifically to domestic abuse. Tiny and Silvera's characters must speak in nation language in order to challenge mistreatment, because in nation language, "the noise that it makes is part of the meaning, and if you ignore the noise (or what you would think of as noise . . .), then you lose part of the meaning."[29]

Palmer skillfully writes the lives of working-class Caribbean women in Montreal, expertly fusing language, personal history, and resistance. More importantly, language is here located within the context of gender, class, and race. Esmée's economic dependence, shame, and fear render her silent in the midst of brutality. Tiny's contrasting independence and refusal to be cowed by men or dominant discursive formations exemplify the articulation of a subjectivity that knows no boundaries.

Beyond the boundaries of linguistic censorship, African Caribbean Canadian migrants wage a war with words that transcends confrontation with father tongue. Their works create and portray spaces carved out by themselves and others in which language acts as a lifeline to communities of other Caribbean women in Canada, their islands of birth, and women of African descent around the world. Here nation language becomes much more than artifice; its location between material socio-historical, political, and economic realities identify it as a necessity.

Despite this necessity, African Caribbean Canadian writers continue to struggle with the problematic of language. For in spite of the challenge that nation language offers to Standard English, for many, including Marlene Nourbese Philip, Standard Endlish is the only language most of the writers discussed in this chapter have at their disposal:

29. Brathwaite, *History*, 271.

In the absence of any other language by which the past may be repossessed, reclaimed and its most painful aspects transcended, English in its broadest spectrum must be made to do the job. To say that the experience can only be expressed in standard English (if there is such a thing) or only in the Caribbean demotic (there is such a thing) is, in fact, to limit the experience for the African artist working in the Caribbean demotic. It is in the continuum of expression from standard to Caribbean English that the veracity of the experience lies.[30]

She continues that African Caribbean artists and writers must face the challenge presented by the language called Standard English. It must constantly be acted upon, destroyed, and reconstructed in order to create a language that neither destroys nor obliterates history, identity, or self-constructed image and imagination of subjectivity. Philip, Brand, and Silvera accept this challenge, using language to disrupt, transform, and transcend. Nelly Furman asserts, "not only are we born into language which molds us, but any knowledge of the world which we experience is itself also articulated in language."[31] Therefore, Caribbean women writers must struggle to dismantle demoralizing images of Caribbean womanhood and instead construct self-created and empowering i-mages in a language of resistance.

Issues of language and resistance are foregrounded in the writings of African Caribbean Canadian women. In their works, "sucking salt" takes the shape of linguistic resistance—via "nation language" or the "Caribbean demotic"—to historical erasure and to silencing. Caribbean women writers in Canada such as Dionne Brand, Marlene Nourbese Philip, and Makeda Silvera address the conflict between writing in Standard English and Caribbean English. These writers speak and write against racism and gender oppression with "mother tongue," a language of resistance. Mother tongue, though similar to "nation language," is specific to the experience of African Caribbean women.

30. Philip, *She Tries*, 18.
31. Cited in Boyce Davies, "Other Tongues," 161.

Six Refugees of a World on Fire

Kitchen Place and Refugee Space in the Poetics of Paule Marshall and Edwidge Danticat

T wo passages in Paule Marshall's essay "The Making of a Writer: From the Poets in the Kitchen" especially resonate with the conceptual meanings of sucking salt, especially in relationship to the transcendence of adversity:

> In this man world yuh got to take yuh mouth and make a gun!

> Some people, they declared, didn't know how to deal with adversity. They didn't know that you had to "tie up your belly" (hold pain, that is) when things got rough and go on with life.[1]

The idea of taking one's mouth and making it a gun describes how one uses voice and language as a weapon: "In this man world yuh got to take yuh mouth and make a gun!" Paule Marshall portrays the ways in which Caribbean women, in the context of the kitchen, created poetry of resistance against exploitation in their everyday lives. *Merle and Other Stories* is a collection that chronicles Marshall's development as a writer, beginning with the instructive space of the kitchen.

Marshall's work has been instrumental in my own development as a scholar and literary theorist. It was *Brown Girl, Brownstones* that first

---

1. Marshall, "Making of a Writer," 7, 5.

piqued my interest in Caribbean women's literature and issues of migration. In Selena Boyce, the protagonist of the text, I saw a reflection of myself as a second-generation Caribbean migrant in New York City. Most dramatic was Marshall's representation of the everyday speech of Barbadian women. I had never before seen this language, which I had grown up with, represented with such skill on the page. Marshall had captured the lyrical nature of this language without sacrificing its political content. She had privileged the everyday speech of Black women in a space that mainstream feminist discourse had labeled a prison—the kitchen. At the beginning of "From the Poets in the Kitchen," Marshall describes a conversation with a colleague, who pointed out to her what an empowering space the kitchen could be, especially for young girls:

> In discussing his formative years, he didn't realize it but he seriously endangered his life by remarking that women writers are luckier than those of his sex because they usually spend so much time as children around their mothers and their mothers' friends in the kitchen.
>
> . . . But my guest wasn't really being sexist or trying to be provocative or even spoiling for a fight. What he meant—when he got around to explaining himself more fully—was that, given the way children are (or were) raised in our society, with little girls kept closer to home and their mothers, the woman writer stands a better chance of being exposed, while growing up, to the kind of talk that goes on among women, more often than not in the kitchen; and that this experience gives her an edge over her male counterpart by instilling in her an appreciation for ordinary speech.[2]

As a young girl, I never thought that being in the kitchen with the women in my family gave me an edge. In fact, it was the place that I was often banished to by my uncles and great-uncles when they caught me trying to listen in on their conversations. But it was between my mother and her sisters that I learned our family history and lessons on living life as a woman. The ordinary speech of the kitchen space was instructional. It was amazing to read Marshall describe what I recognized as a truth in my own life:

2. Ibid., 3.

> [My colleague] didn't know it, but he was essentially describing my experience as a little girl. I grew up among poets. Now they didn't look like poets—whatever that breed is supposed to look like. Nothing about them suggested that poetry was their calling. They were just a group of ordinary housewives and mothers, my mother included, who dressed in a way (shapeless house dresses, dowdy felt hats and long, dark, solemn coats) that made it impossible for me to imagine they had ever been young.

This resonated deeply with me—although the Gadsby women belonged to a later generation of migrants (my eldest aunt arrived in New York City in 1945) and are all professional women, the language in which they expressed themselves in the kitchen space was the ordinary language—yet sheer poetry—of which Marshall speaks. The women who sat around the kitchen in Marshall's childhood used their time there to talk politics, swap advice and gossip, and share hopes and dreams for the future. They were Garveyites, FDR supporters, mothers, cleaning women, and political theorists. Although they had little or no true political power, "they fought back, using the only weapon at their command: the spoken word."[3]

The notions of ordinary language, women's speech, alternative sites of theory, and constructions of migratory subjectivity in these alternative sites provide a useful framework for examining the power of "kitchen table talk." Marshall's excellent essay is a fine place to begin as we extend our ongoing discussion of language to an examination of the "word-shop of the kitchen" and its representation in Breath, Eyes, Memory by Edwidge Danticat. The link between Marshall and Danticat is natural, for the latter, in her dedication to Breath, Eyes, Memory, conveys her gratitude to the former as teacher and literary foremother. Although she does not write her novels in Creole or French, Danticat has been inspired by Marshall's ability to capture the everyday speech of working-class Caribbean people on the page. Using the legacy of the women from her childhood as her guide, Marshall creates a narrative world with women at its center. The language generated in this space becomes a political tool, one that must be policed or controlled.

3. Ibid., 7.

Everyday Language and Creative Resistance

Marshall represents language that was never meant for the page. Witnessing these exchanges taught her how to re-present everyday speech in a written form. In *Merle and Other Stories,* the introduction to each chapter provides a personal context to the stories, charting her own historical journey through language and writing. In the essay "The Making of a Writer: From the Poets in the Kitchen," Marshall talks about the ways in which the women in her childhood fought for control of their lives. This fight manifested itself in the kitchen, where these women, unencumbered by their White employers, husbands, or the probing eyes of strangers, could speak freely of their battles with racism, economic degradation, and patriarchy. Identifying the world as being the possession of men or "this man," they acknowledged the existence of racism, patriarchy, classism, and gender-based oppression, while making it clear that they would fight with their voices. "This man" (or "the man") takes metaphorical shape in White men and Black men, but also in imperialism and capitalism. Although they believed that, in America, "you could at least see your way to make a dollar," buy homes, and educate children, they understood that they would have to constantly battle American racism and prejudice. "This man" country did not welcome them, except in their role as laborers. Talk and language provided their outlet and refuge. They cut holes in the invisible space they had been forced into, which Marshall likens to that inhabited by Ralph Ellison's invisible man:

> Indeed you might say they suffered a triple invisibility, being black, female and foreigners. They really didn't count in American society except as a source of cheap labor. But given the kind of women they were, they couldn't tolerate the fact of their invisibility, their powerlessness. And they fought back, using the only weapon at their command: the spoken word.[4]

It could be argued that these women, although rendered "invisible" by the American mainstream, were never truly hidden. They were highly visible, as Marshall writes, working as day domestics in the homes of White people on the upper west side of Manhattan while at the same

4. Ibid.

time densely populating Brooklyn and Harlem, buying homes, pushing their children into the public school system, and contributing money to political movements:

> If F.D.R. was their hero, Marcus Garvey was their God. The name of the fiery, Jamaica-born black nationalist of the 20's was constantly invoked around the table. For he had been their leader when they first came to the United States from the West Indies shortly after World War I. They had contributed to his organization, the United Negro Improvement Association (UNIA), out of their meager salaries, bought shares in his ill-fated Black Star Shipping Line, and at the height of the movement they had marched as members of his "nurses' brigade" in their white uniforms up Seventh Avenue in Harlem during the great Garvey Day Parades. Garvey: He lived on through the power of their memories.[5]

Therefore, while seemingly silent as individuals in relationship to mainstream America, these women lent their collective voices to anticolonial, anti-imperialist struggle.

Marshall also credits Paul Laurence Dunbar and John Updike for providing useful examples of the power of language and its many uses. She respects Dunbar's dialect poetry for showing her the extent to which Black peoples have transformed a language imposed on them. Language is an integral element of reconstructing "our personality on our own terms":

> I see writers as image-makers, and one of the ways that we can begin offering images of oursel[ves] which truly reflect us, which begin to throw off the negative images the West has imposed on us, is to begin having our literature offer to the black reader the image of himself that is positive and creative. I don't think a people really progress[es] until they think positively of themselves. Cultural revolution is about how you see yourself. What you think of yourself is part and parcel of other aspects of the revolution, the political revolution. You can't have the one without the other.[6]

5. Ibid., 5.
6. In Ogundipe-Leslie, "Re-creating Ourselves," 22.

This belief in the centrality of language to positive self-image mirrors that of Canadian-based writer Marlene Nourbese Philip, in her essay, "The Absence of Writing, or How I Became a Spy," written twenty years after "From the Poets."[7] Philip discusses the importance of image, or i-mage, and she concludes that the Caribbean writer must use the "Caribbean demotic," as it is a language born of struggle and therefore the only one through which she can adequately communicate the legacies of the Middle Passage. For this same reason, Marshall feels that the role of the writer is extremely important, for "it is the writer's great contribution to create new images that will overcome the negative psychological images we have because of our history."[8]

"The poets in the kitchen" of Marshall's youth utilize this "Caribbean demotic" at the level of community. Marshall represents their language on the page in order to present with authenticity the ways in which they understood themselves and their lives in migration. Language in this context is as much a weapon as it is a refuge. The kitchen spaces that Marshall describes provide an outlet for creative linguistic responses to past and present oppressions—in Barbados, "poor but sweet"; in the United States, "this man country." In this context, *refuge* and *refugee* take on new meanings. If we can borrow from the present-day example set by the hip-hop group the Fugees, the image of "refugee" connotes more than mere escape from persecution. It is also a creative, linguistic, and lyrical challenge to subjugation with the use of voice.

Marshall develops this narrative of political resistance through language in her novels. In *Brown Girl, Brownstones,* Florrie Trotman reminds the reader that "in this white-man world you got to take yuh moth and make a gun." In this case, she explicitly identifies "the man" as White, a clear affirmation of a history of racism and colonial oppression that could not be escaped by leaving Barbados. To be Black in the world, then, demands recognition of racism and gender inequalities, but it does not demand acceptance of abuse. Also invoking the sea imagery that, as Gavin Jones has pointed out, pervades the novel, "This spoken language, like the images of the sea and of prisms in the novel, is another element in Marshall's exploration of how her characters are defined by

---

7. This essay is the first introduction to Philip, *She Tries.*
8. In Ogundipe-Leslie, "Re-creating Ourselves," 24.

the concatenation of cultural difference." Marshall's use of "the adjectival opposites" often used in Barbadian speech, such as "nice nasty" and "beautiful ugly," allows her to clarify the issues of difference and cultural identity experienced each day by the poets in the kitchen. The contradictions of these experiences are mirrored in the contradictory connotations and imagery of the sea. "By combining an examination of diasporic sea imagery and the racial dynamics of vision in *Brown Girl*, we can appreciate how Marshall exposes not so much the possibilities as the problems of establishing a unified black consciousness in a world driven by competing definitions of the self."[9]

In her foreword to the second edition of *This Bridge Called My Back: Writings by Radical Women of Color*, Cherríe Moraga suggests that the need for links between women of color throughout the United States "grows more and more urgent as the number of recently-immigrated people of color in the U.S. grows in enormous proportions, as we begin to see ourselves all as refugees of a world on fire." Moraga's words, written in 1983, have proven prophetic, for they especially ring true today. She chronicles the devastation caused by this global fire and poses the question, What place does Third World feminism have in all of this? What are the particular oppressions suffered by women of color all across the earth? And, faced with these various oppressions, what purpose do words have? She rhetorically asks, using the power of her own mother tongue: ¿"Cara a cara con el enemigo de qué valen mis palabras? (Face to face with the enemy, what good are my words?)"[10]

The determination of the women around Paule Marshall's kitchen table to "take yuh mouth and make a gun" is the answer to this question. Despite Moraga's disappointment with the realization that much of what she writes may not be read by all of the people she attempts to reach, she continues to write. "The political writer... is the ultimate optimist, believing people are capable of change and using words as one way to try and penetrate the privatism of our lives." I would argue then, that Paule Marshall and Edwidge Danticat are both creative political writers, challenging the various oppressions confronted by Black

9. Gavin Jones, "'The Sea Ain't Got No Back Door': The Problems of Black Consciousness in Paule Marshall's *Brown Girl, Brownstones*," 603, 597.
10. In Moraga and Anzaldúa, *This Bridge*, 3.

women daily, using words as their weapons. In their fiction they represent everyday guerrillas who wage war on the violence of exclusion and erasure. Like Moraga, they write and speak "to anyone who will listen with their ears open (even if only a crack) to the currents of change around them."[11]

The currents of change fan the fires of rebellion in the midst of a world on fire. Marshall and Danticat represent two generations of second-generation migrants to the United States, in their case New York City, whose work challenges racist, imperialistic, and sexist representations of Caribbean women. For them, refugee identity does not necessitate degradation. It exists and evolves in a space that harbors creativity, specifically creative resistance through language. With their writing they shoot speech directly at a master narrative of exclusion. Marshall and Danticat recall women forced to flee nations ravaged by the fires of economic scarcity, poverty, and corruption, who challenge obstacles through voice and writing. Marshall quotes the Polish émigré Czeslaw Milosz, writer and Nobel Laureate: "Language is the only homeland." For the poets in the kitchen, language was both homeland and refuge. But as bell hooks has pointed out, and as the Fugees represent, this space of refuge, or refugee camp, is a site of creative resistance.[12] Theory is produced at all levels of African diasporic cultural production, where the margin becomes the center. In my conception, "refugee space" is not merely a space characterized by weakness and degradation—it is a site of constant production of creative resistance to oppression.

"The Sea Ain' Got No Back Door"

The sea signifies in multiple ways in *Brown Girl*. First, it physically separates Selena Boyce's Barbadian family in New York from the island.

11. Ibid.

12. In *Feminist Theory: From Margin to Center*, bell hooks writes that existence in the margins allowed members of the Kentucky community where she grew up to develop an understanding of both the margins and the "main body" of the culture: "This sense of wholeness, impressed upon our consciousness by the structure of our daily lives, provided us an oppositional world view—a mode of seeing unknown to most of our oppressors, that sustained us, aided us in our struggle to transcend poverty and despair, strengthened our sense of self and our solidarity" (preface to the first edition).

When viewed against the backdrop of the Middle Passage, the sea takes
on the added dimension of death and dislocation. In addition, as Gavin
Jones points out, the sea symbolizes constant change and movement:
"While several critics have pointed to architectural imagery as the bind-
ing force of *Brown Girl,* the image of the sea seems more fundamental
to the novel, mainly because it resonates in so many different areas: most
importantly, those of the diaspora, ethnicity, and sexuality. The sea has
a thematic inclusiveness, flexibility and fluidity; upon it float diverse
ideas of difference." Jones contends that Marshall's sea imagery communicates a Black Atlantic consciousness, giving rise to unique intellectual
traditions and ideas and resulting in the emergence of cultural transnational identities.[13]

A clear example of this is seen in the failure of Deighton Boyce, Selina's
father, to resolve these new identities without losing himself in a preoccupation with material success. He chooses to "jump ship," to drown in
the sea, upon returning to Barbados after deportation from the United
States for illegal immigration. He does this not to escape enslavement as
many of his African ancestors might have, but to escape the shame of
returning home empty-handed. His memories of Barbados are refracted
through his impoverished childhood and racism. In a reversal of the
Middle Passage, Deighton Boyce chooses to suck salt. For him, the sea
truly has no back door; he can either drown or swim. He feels trapped,
unable to create fortune at home or abroad. The disillusionment of his
migration experience is not lost: "Time fled as the mist fled and he was
a boy again, diving for the coins the tourists tossed into the sea, and he
saw the one he wanted most in the bright disk of the sun."[14] The shining
coins represent his unrealized potential abroad. The land that he had
possessed in Barbados had been sold behind his back by Silla, his wife.
Deighton jumps into the sea, choosing to suck salt and die rather than
live without his pride. Unable to stay in Brooklyn, and returning without riches, he ends his life.

Suggie Skeete, the sexually uninhibited lodger in the Boyce household, confirms the inevitability of Deighton's fate by refusing it for herself. She chooses to stay in the United States and struggle rather then

13. Jones, "Sea," 598.
14. Marshall, *Brown Girl,* 190.

return home to the poverty she left behind. For her, Brooklyn provides opportunities unavailable to poor Black women in Barbados: "Go back? Where? Home, you mean? . . . Me go back there? You think I looking to dead before my time? Do you know how bad those malicious brutes would lick their mouth on me if I went back the same way I left? Tell muh, why you think your father is at the bottom of the sea tonight?" The Middle Passage reference is clear, yet reversed: Suggie has embraced a new identity in migration, that of the woman who has gone "overseas," and she expects to return home only after having taken full advantage of whatever opportunities she finds in New York. Return is no longer a simple matter of traveling "home" across the Atlantic Ocean. Interestingly, Jones suggests that Marshall genders the sea as female via Suggie's sexuality. "It is the sea that carries away Suggie Skeete's pink panties, marking her first sexual experience at the age of twelve, and it is the image of drowning—this time in her partner Clive Springer's 'sea' of masculinity—that describes Selina's first sexual experience."[15] Again we see the metaphor of salt—this time, as it relates to gender, race and sexuality.

Selena Boyce learns the lessons from her father's suicide, Suggie's practicality, and her mother's tenacious commitment to survival at all costs. Her "sea change" is the result of an emerging identity in migration, one shaped by values of her community and a streak of individualism that frees her from obligation to her family and community. One wonders if this disconnection from community will lead to Selena's downfall; I contend that this outcome is not inevitable. It could be argued that she must extricate herself from the insularity of her mother's house and her small Barbadian community in order to grow emotionally. Gavin Jones sees this departure as logical, for Selena must distinguish herself from her parents and their wave of migration: "Like a dark sea nudging its way onto a white beach and staining the sand, they came." When she rejects the college scholarship offered to her by the members of the Association of Barbados Homeowners and Businessmen, she remarks that the faces of her elders appear as "a dark sea—alive under the sun with endless mutations of the one color."[16]

15. Ibid., 208; Jones, "Sea," 599.
16. Marshall, *Brown Girl,* 4, 302–3.

Jones submits that the former reference to the sea symbolizes a narrative of diaspora, another level of dispersal. I would caution against a conflation of diaspora and migration, while acknowledging that the sea carries multiple articulations of diaspora. However, Marshall is clear in *Brown Girl* that these identities created in New York, although diasporic, are migratory identities shaped by a multiplicity of identities in the shadow of capitalism and twentieth-century racial politics. For although the sea "contains contradictory multitudes—it is the sea of female creativity, Diasporic consciousness, and African history, yet also the sea of colonial exploitation, industrial decay, and obliteration of the black past—Marshall's novel as a whole proposes a sense of selfhood which, like a prism, contains many faces, each one refracting at an acute angle of difference."[17]

As I already noted, Caribbean women's creative expression must be understood as labor, as cultural production. In her comparative study of the emergence of Caribbean Women's Writing, Belinda Edmondson notes, "My impression of the works of Marshall . . . was similar to that of my impression of Lamming et al.: like the prior generation, the women's central concern was the reconfiguration of the Caribbean space, on which colonial experience has left an indelible print." Marshall and Danticat, both descendants of economic migrants to New York City, are "'making' the West Indian nation from another direction. . . . Immigrant women, though immigrant, help to produce the capital of the West Indies, in the form of the obvious—by sending goods to their families 'back home'—and not-so-obvious, the production of narratives as a different kind of 'cultural capital.'"[18]

One of the characters in Marshall's fiction for whom the "making" of a Caribbean nation is important is Merle Kinbona. In the preface to the short story "Merle" in *Merle and Other Stories*, Marshall calls her "A Third World revolutionary spirit."[19] Although not based in New York, Merle is a great example of a subjectivity that emerges out of the experience of migration. Born in the Caribbean, Merle Kinbona commits her life

17. Jones, "Sea," 605.
18. Belinda Edmondson, *Making Men: Gender, Literary Authority, and Women's Writing in Caribbean Narrative*, 3, 10–11.
19. Marshall, *Merle*, 109.

to defending "the little fella," those plagued by poverty and injustice. Marshall explains,

> Merle remains the most alive of my characters. Indeed, it seems to me she has escaped the pages...altogether and is abroad in the world. I envision her striding restlessly up and down the hemisphere from Argentina to Canada, and back and forth across the Atlantic between here and Africa, all the while speaking her mind in the same forthright way as in the book. She can be heard condemning all forms of exploitation, injustice, and greed. In El Salvador, Harlem, Haiti, at the Plaza de Mayo in Buenos Aires and amid the favelas of Rio de Janeiro, wherever she goes, she continues to exhort "the little fella" as she calls the poor and oppressed to resist, to organize, to rise up against the condition of their lives. Like Gandhi, she considers poverty the greatest violence that can be done a people. I hear her inveighing constantly against the arms race, the Bomb, against technology run amok.[20]

Merle is the quintessential migrating revolutionary subject, her political allegiances erasing national boundaries. Merle sees herself as a citizen of the Black world, with the responsibility to fight for the freedom of Black peoples globally. Merle's Pan-African consciousness is most clearly developed in *The Chosen Place, the Timeless People*. In many ways, she is a fictional mirror image of Claudia Jones, espousing a leftist critique of capitalism and its aftermath internationally: "The most passionate and political of all [Marshall's] heroines," Merle struggles to discover what her role will be in effecting positive political and social change. While many of the characters around her mistake her passion for madness, Merle fights constantly with the desire to give up, all the while knowing that submission for her will signal spiritual death: "Some people act, some think, some feel, but I talk, and if I was to ever stop that'd be the end of me."[21]

Her commitment to change, insistence on challenging neocolonialism, and alleged madness can be read within the context of "sucking salt." Here the metaphor is expressed in the process by which oppres-

20. Ibid.
21. Ibid., 116, 118.

sion and resistance can both weaken and strengthen Black women in particular. Merle's exhaustion—caused by constant struggle with the colonial government in Bournehills and by her own unresolved history with Black Nationalism—actually strengthens her resolve to continue to advocate for the poor. Merle tells Lyle Hutson, a lawyer in Bournehills who has turned away from activism long ago: "I've had to pay with my sanity for the right to speak my mind so you know I must talk!" Merle's political awareness and savvy is evident throughout the text as she blasts development schemes from the west; "Foreign advisors and experts! They're a plague on us in the West Indies." A daughter of the sixties, her feminist and womanist affiliations are evident as she implores Lyle to "see to it that the men don't go off by themselves as usual and leave the women sitting alone in a corner someplace like they're in purdah."[22]

Merle provides a perfect example of the function of "a daughter" of the West Indies, in keeping with Danticat's vision of the role the "daughters of Haiti" must play in relationship to their homeland and "homes" constructed elsewhere. Committed to remaining in the Caribbean, she struggles to beat back imperialism in the region and the erasure of history at a variety of levels. Fired from her job at the local high school for teaching Caribbean history, she works at the island almshouse, all the while maintaining close contact with the political and economic life of the country. She charges, "Those English were the biggest obeah men out when you considered what they did to our minds."[23] Born into a relatively prestigious family, sent to the finest school on the island, and educated in England, Merle had rejected the trappings of a comfortable neocolonial lifestyle, choosing class suicide instead, a tireless advocate for the "little fella."

In *The Chosen Place, the Timeless People,* Merle's role as revolutionary is fully developed. She struggles in defense of the people of Bournehills, fighting what she sees as the threat of Western imperialism. Having traveled to England as a student, where she developed her socialist sensibilities, she returns home after a failed marriage to promote socialism as a solution to neocolonial corruption. She exists as a person who has suffered under the worst that colonialism has had to offer—alienated

22. Ibid., 118.
23. Ibid., 122.

identities, compulsory heterosexuality (her relationship with a woman in England so angers her Ugandan husband that he leaves her, taking their child), and narrow nationalism. Marshall further explains Merle's character:

> Merle Kinbona, meaning "good kin," for me is not only a black woman who is struggling for her identity, struggling to assert herself, to give meaning to her life, she is also reflective of the horrendous colonial experiences we have all undergone, and her struggle to bring together all those influences that have gone into making her so that she could fashion out of it a whole person. So she in a sense reflects the struggle of black people to come into her own.[24]

Merle's allegiance to the "little fella" and her commitment to fighting for the rights of the dispossessed nearly result in her psychological breakdown. Her return to Africa is made symbolically via South America and the Caribbean, completely avoiding the West. By the end of the novel, Merle travels to Uganda to see her daughter in a first step toward finding wholeness. At this point, the imagery of the Middle Passage is evoked again, as Merle traces a reverse passage to Africa, bridging a gap between the Caribbean and Africa.

The possibilities for sucking salt via traversing the sea and physical return to the Caribbean and Africa are explored in great detail in *The Chosen Place, the Timeless People*. Bourne Island, the island that pushes farthest to the east (like Barbados) appears to be isolated—lost at sea, if you will—and mired in a neocolonial model of social and political organization. Its proximity to Africa is explicit; it is located in the heart of the Black Atlantic world, "amid an immensity of sea and sky, becalmed now that its turbulent history was past, facing east, the open sea, and across the sea, hidden beyond the horizon, the colossus of Africa."[25] In Merle's body, the convergence of this history and the possibilities for the future of Bourne Island (and, by extension, all peoples of Africa and the African Diaspora) create a tempest, which is mirrored in the turbulence of the sea. Much is made of flooding and "spilling over" in the novel, as Bournehills is constantly in danger of being washed away by

---

24. In Ogundipe-Leslie, "Re-creating Ourselves," 20.
25. Marshall, *Chosen Place*, 13.

rain and sea. Merle, too, is always on the verge of spilling over, slipping into depression whenever she remembers the daughter stolen away by her African husband, or when the demands of life as a full-time activist and political agitator become too much for her. Here, sucking salt takes its toll on Merle, who is unable to balance her desire to be of use to her fellow citizens with her need to heal from a series of emotional wounds.

A truly diasporic subject, Merle is directly connected to Africa and to the New World, devoting her full energy to create a hopeful political landscape on Bourne Island. She battles local corruption, neocolonial elites, and foreign "aid," personified in the characters Saul and Harriet. Much like Velma in Toni Cade Bambara's *The Salt Eaters*, Merle must learn "the difference between eating salt as an antidote to snakebite and turning into salt, succumbing to the serpent."[26] Both Velma and Merle exemplify the specific experience of Black female diasporic identity engaged in political struggle. The difficulties of understanding the meaning of sucking salt, and surviving whole in order to continue the important activist work necessary for the continued survival of diasporic peoples, demand a sense of common interest among Africans and peoples of African descent, forever linked by the experience of Atlantic slavery:

> [Velma] thought she knew that. At some point in her life she was sure Douglass, Tubman, the slave narratives, the songs, the table, Delaney, Ida Wells, Blyden, Du Bois, Garvey, the singers, her parents, Malcolm, Coltrane, the poets, her comrades, her godmother, her neighbors, had taught her that. Thought she knew how to build immunity to the sting of the serpent that turned would-be cells, could-be cadres into cargo cults. Thought she knew how to build resistance, make the journey to the center of the circle, stay poised and centered in the work and not fly off, stay centered in the best of her people's traditions and not be available to madness, not become intoxicated by the heady brew of degrees and career and congratulations for nothing done.... Thought the workers of the sixties had pulled the Family safely out of range of the serpent's fangs so the workers of the seventies could drain the poisons, repair damaged tissues, retrain the heartworks, realign the spine...[27]

26. Toni Cade Bambara, *The Salt Eaters*, 8.
27. Ibid., 258.

Reconnection to this legacy demands baptism in the tears of the ancestors, to reintroduce the taste of salt via the Middle Passage and remind the current generation what their investments should be. When Minnie, a healer in Bambara's fictional community of Claybourne, Georgia, begins to question why she should help Velma find the path to healing, her ancestral mother, Old Wife, reminds her that she must:

> [R]ip them fancy clothes off... and thrash out into them waters, churn up all them bones we dropped from the old ships, churn up all that brine from the salty deep where our tears sank, and you grab them chirren by the neck and bop'm a good one and drag'm on back to shore and fling'm down and jump to it, pumping and cussing, fussing and cracking they ribs if ya have to to let'm live, Min. Cause love won't let you let'm go.[28]

This commitment directly mirrors Marshall's own commitments as a writer, which she communicates through Merle. She explains that, in *The Chosen Place,*

> there is a conscious attempt to project the view of the future to which I am personally committed. Stated simply it is a view, a vision if you will, which sees the rise through revolutionary struggle of the darker peoples of the world and as a necessary corollary, the decline and eclipse of America and the West.[29]

The process of "churning up the bones" of revolutionary struggle permeates the novel. According to Jane Olmstead, the sea challenges "both visitors and island dwellers to confront the past, their histories, or be destroyed in the process."[30] There is no "back door" through which to escape; confrontation must occur in order for to progress occur.

In *Praisesong for the Widow,* Marshall provides another example of a woman who must achieve wholeness via return. Returning to New York City and then to the Caribbean, the Middle Passage is represented again, this time to make links between African, African American, and

28. Ibid., 61.
29. Marshall, "Shaping," 108.
30. Jane Olmstead, "The Pull to Memory and the Language of Place in Paule Marshall's *The Chosen Place, the Timeless People* and *Praisesong for the Widow,*" 249.

Caribbean history and culture. At the beginning of *Praisesong for the Widow*, Avey Johnson has lost all allegiance to "the little fella," in this case the Black working class. Although complacent in her middle-class life, she has become bored and dissatisfied. While traveling on a cruise, she is plagued by Middle Passage nightmares in which she is engaged in a struggle with her Great Aunt Cuney. The cruise represents a reverse Middle Passage of sorts for Avey. While aboard the cruise ship she is plagued by dreams, disorientation, and frequent nausea. The cruise also represents Avey's complete disconnection from her southern rural roots on Tatem Island, South Carolina (modeled after the Sea Islands off the coast of Georgia and South Carolina). The cruise also represents a reverse Middle Passage in showing Avey's ability to embrace the trappings of middle-class life, signified by her voyage to the colonies as a privileged passenger on board the cruise ship, followed by her personal transformation. As Edmondson points out, "The travelers are First World consumers, who consume the product of the Caribbean and then leave. Avey is a participant in this act perpetrated on black and non-white Caribbean peoples and as such has consolidated her 'success' by 'evolving'... from being one of the black peoples acted upon in such ways... to being one of the actors."[31]

National identity in relationship to the Caribbean becomes blurred in *Praisesong*, as Avey embarks on a quest for self-identity. Refusing to reboard the ship after a stop in Grenada, she decides to take a plane back to New York. But she changes this plan when, after meeting Lebert Joseph, an elderly man from Carriacou, she accepts his invitation to travel with him to the small island for a performance of the Big Drum Ritual. Lebert Joseph asks Avey, "What's your nation?" demanding that she identify what African nation she belongs to. Avey of course does not know. At this point, *nation* does not refer to geographical spaces with distinct laws, governments, economies, and cultures. First, it is defined by a people linked by culture and experience that is not limited to geography. Edmondson, paraphrasing Luce Irigaray, argues that "woman" is always in exile from "nation." Avey sails from the nation of the United States to the island nation of Grenada and then to Carriacou to discover in fact what her nation is. Lacking a sense of belonging in

31. Edmondson, *Making Men*, 161–62.

New York in the comfortable, middle-class life created for her by her husband, and disgusted by her cruise, she finds her "mother/land" in the Caribbean.[32] The "mothers" in this case are her Great Aunt Cuney and her grandmother (both of whom are ancestral figures, along with Lebert Joseph). Here grandmother and great aunt impressed upon the young Avey the importance of remembering the history of her ancestors on Tatem Island. This history is passed down to her through the Ibo Landing story—the tale of the Ibos, who, upon seeing what lay in store for them on the shores of America, turned on their heels and walked back to Iboland. By going to the Caribbean, Avey reconnects with this history. In the Big Drum performance, "nation" is made at the level of identification with origins, and with a history in constant danger of erasure.

No longer able to recognize herself, not even in the mirror, she must return to her past. This return takes the form of travel to the Caribbean on a cruise, where she loses her way and finds it again on Carriacou. When asked to name her national identity, her inability to respond is met with people's insistence on figuring it out for her. It is significant that Avey travels to the Caribbean to recall her nation, for without a nation to call her own, Avey is a refugee of sorts, displaced and confused. The pain in her stomach that forces her to abruptly leave the cruise ship, her dreams about her Great Aunt Cuney, and her overall discomfort force her to wander in a limbo that is not the United States, not the Caribbean, not Africa, not anywhere. It is in her participation in the Big Drum Ritual and in her exile, so to speak, on Carriacou, that she finds her nation:

> [T]he quest to salvage blackness also becomes a journey to reconnect to a feminine identity that has been distorted by First World, masculine-associated modernity. The journey to the Caribbean is effectively a "return" to the womb; the islands, surrounded by water, inhabiting nowhere in particular, imitate the conditions of the child's (pre)historic memory of the formative possibilities of identity.[33]

32. Marshall, *Praisesong*, 167; Edmondson, *Making Men*, 164.
33. Edmondson, *Making Men*, 164.

Avey was free of this distortion during her childhood visits to Tatem Island and when she recollects being part of an international community in New York City, a space in which Black southerners and Caribbeans met in fellowship for annual excursions and cultural events. The First World of which Edmondson speaks then, does not consist merely of "masculine-associated modernity." Within it exist multiple narratives of identity, which Avey had unfortunately chosen to forget. Although I agree with Edmondson that it is quite interesting that Avey, an American woman, must travel to the Caribbean to reclaim her identity, it makes perfect sense that she would need to do so. For in the New York of her childhood, as described in *Praisesong*, and in her memories of Tatem, it is perfectly logical that she would travel to one of the most diverse regions for peoples of the African diaspora to redefine her self. Her memories of Tatem are inextricably tied to an African identity in America, as much as the experience of the Caribbean is linked to an experience of being of African descent in the Americas.

Edmondson argues that the Caribbean is a vehicle for Avey's construction of an African American identity: "The Caribbean in this arrangement, Not-Africa and Not-Black America, but both entities are present in its construction. It must be emphasized that Avey returns to America, after all. She has utilized the Caribbean experience to effect her completion as an *African American*. Her concerns are finally, local ones."[34] This claim ignores the fact that Marshall purposefully uses Avey to make connections between the experiences of Black peoples in diaspora. And more important than Avey's concerns, as a fictional character in a novel, are Marshall's concerns. In her interview with 'Molara Ogundipe-Leslie (six years before the publication of *Praisesong*), Marshall had culminated her idea of diasporic identity that she began to pursue with Selina Boyce in *Brown Girl*. As a character, Avey must deal with the damaging effects of decadence on her spirit and psyche. In her discussion of *The Chosen Place*, Marshall tells Ogundipe-Leslie,

---

34. Ibid. This reading suggests that Avey manipulated the Caribbean and the people of Carriacou, exploiting its cultural capital for her own spiritual needs. This is a reading with which I must disagree. Avey never planned to go to Carriacou; her arrival there is without guile or expectation. It is her desire not to lounge in decadence that initiates her journey to the island.

I see decadence as one of the insidious exports of the western
world to the Third World: a whole emphasis on a kind of cush-
ioned and comfortable but essentially meaningless bourgeois life.
And to make that so attractive that people become centered on self,
which makes it almost impossible to think in terms of nation, to
think in terms of the good of society. The emphasis resides mainly
on the how-am-I-going-to-make-it-for-myself? ... I see that hap-
pening time and time again, not only in West Indian societies, but
in African societies and in black American society.[35]

Is this not also the case with Avey? Marshall makes diaspora through
Avey on several levels. For example, the patois that Avey hears in Grenada
and Martinique reminds her of the linguistic rhythms in Tatem. Again,
connections are made constantly between Black cultures in Africa, the
United States, and the Caribbean.

Sucking salt, for Avey, takes the form of rootlessness and total disconnection from community. Community becomes replaced with material
possessions and status symbols, such as the ability to go on a cruise, that
leave Avey feeling empty. It could also be argued that Avey's experience
in Carriacou underscores the complexity of African American culture,
particularly in urban centers such in New York, in which Blackness is
interpolated in several ways. Again, if we understand the term *African
American* as referring to "Africans in the Americas," conceptually, the
space that Avey navigates between the Caribbean and New York is not
demarcated by national borders as we understand them. Therefore,
although she does travel to the Caribbean as "First World" tourist traveling to the "Third World," she is also a diasporic, migrating subject,
traveling through her own history and back to the present.

In addition, the existence of the church sermon from Avey's childhood (just before the section entitled "The Beg Pardon") is what initiates the purging, or bodily cleansing, that she experiences aboard the
schooner to Carriacou. It could be argued that since she is about to
enter a sacred space, in which she must ask the ancestors forgiveness for
having forgotten to honor them, both her body and spirit must be
cleansed. So, the church sermon functions as the means by which her
soul is cleansed. Joyce Pettis's interpretation of the episode is insightful:

35. In Ogundipe-Leslie, "Re-creating Ourselves," 20.

As Avey recalls the preacher's demand that the congregation rid themselves of the "stones of sin," Avey rids herself of the spiritually strangling materialistic force symbolized through food images, the bloated mass that has marked her extravagance. The sermon, the women on board the schooner (who remind her of churchwomen from her childhood), and the murmured "bon" chorus from the schooner passengers (resonating with the response of the congregation) conflate Christianity, the Middle Passage, West African cultural behaviors, and the transit of African peoples. Avey's loss of control over bodily functions signifies continuation of her return to a childlike state, a process that began during her recollection of life on Halsey Street and an essential state that precedes completion of the journey.[36]

Upon her return to New York, Avey is no longer merely a child of this space. She is a child of the diaspora—whole, and rooted in spirit. Her experience as a "refugee of a world on fire" takes her on a journey toward wholeness that ends with a reintegration of the various pieces of herself she had lost in her quest for bourgeois privilege. Thus Avey, like Merle, becomes a bridge across the sea of African diasporic history, culture, and politics. Here, refugee status entails reconnection, rebirth, and wholeness. Upon her return to New York City, Avey is once again a child of the diaspora, rooted in spirit.

Edwidge Danticat's work utilizes the fact of refugee consciousness, which is omnipresent in the lives of many Haitians, who have risked everything to escape abject poverty and military violence in Haiti. "Children of the Sea," the first short story in her collection *Krik? Krak!* is her representation of this experience as it is written into the lives of two young people who preserve their love for each other in letters. The sea separates the lovers, as the young man escapes political persecution for antigovernment protest by boarding a small boat bound for Miami. He leaves his true love behind with her parents, who struggle to protect her from the Tonton Macoutes, the militia force under the control of the corrupt dictator François "Papa Doc" Duvalier.

Danticat uses the epistolary form to explore the emotional worlds of these two young people, providing the reader with insight into the

36. Joyce Pettis, *Toward Wholeness in Paule Marshall's Fiction*, 127.

circumstances that would force Haitians to flee their homeland in small, rickety boats in hope of arriving in Miami or even of being apprehended by the U.S. Coast Guard. The young couple seek solace in their letters, even though they know that their words will never physically reach their desired destinations. They obtain comfort in writing their letters, finding a refuge in language. Even as the young man realizes that he will soon die, he writes, "I know you will probably never see this, but it was nice imagining that I had you here to talk to."[37]

He calls himself one of the "children of the sea," "those who have escaped the chains of slavery to form a world beneath the heavens and the blood-drenched earth where you live." Refusing to view his impending death as defeat, the young man reconstructs himself as entering into another consciousness in which Africans and peoples of African descent continue to challenge efforts to destroy or enslave them. They live free beneath the heavens in the depths of the sea, with Agwé, the spirit of the water.[38] The sea, then, provides refuge, retaining the histories and memories of those who pass through her waters. She is merciful, yet merciless, as she consumes the bodies of yet more Haitian refugees, closing the door on this life and opening into the next.

Obvious parallels can be made with the Middle Passage texts of D'Aguiar, Lovelace, and Glissant, discussed earlier. The salt and sea trope is pervasive in African Caribbean literature; the phrase "the sea ain't got not back door" is taken from both *Breath, Eyes, Memory* by Danticat and "The Making of a Writer" by Marshall. The latter writes of the women who sat in fellowship around her mother's kitchen table: "'The sea ain' got no back door,' they would say, meaning that it wasn't like a house where if there was a fire you could run out the back. Meaning that it was not to be trifled with. And meaning perhaps in a larger sense that man should treat all of nature with caution and respect." In *Breath, Eyes, Memory*, Grandmè Ifé reminds Sophie that "the sea, she has no back door."[39] As the characters in each work maintain that the sea has no back door, no mercy, they constantly navigate their way back and forth across this same sea, via memory, language, and writing, as do the

37. Danticat, *Krik? Krak!* 27.
38. Ibid., 27, 20.
39. Marshall, "Making of a Writer," 8; Danticat, *Breath, Eyes, Memory,* 99.

authors of these texts. The metaphorical dimensions of the sea exist as part of the consciousness of Caribbeans, who usually engage the sea, at some level, every day.

This conception of the sea is also a nice response to Paul Gilroy's articulation of the Black Atlantic and the circulation of ideas, history, and culture trafficked among communities of women. Not only do these ideas circulate across the Atlantic, but also they are buried in them, just as consciousness of the cultural and historical significance of the sea is a part of African diasporic identity. The memory of the Middle Passage is reproduced in the numerous implicit and explicit references discussed earlier, in literature, music, orature, and folklore. An example is Bob Marley's "Redemption Song," in which he chronicles the experience of the Middle Passage ("Old Pirates Yes They Rob I") and calls for a song of freedom to rescue Africans in the diaspora and on the continent from the legacy of slavery ("We Forward In This Generation Triumphantly"). In the song, he speaks of a "Bottomless Pit," a clear reference to the hold of the slave ship, which is the limbic space between Africa and the New World. The spiritual memory of this experience finds its way into every manifestation of African liberation politics.[40]

Breath, Eyes, Memory highlights the importance of memory (or re-memory, as we have learned from Toni Morrison's *Beloved*) in the African diasporic imagination. Characters in the text make frequent mention of Guinea as the ancestral resting place of those who have passed on. For example, Danticat's Louise tells Sophie that her mother, Man Grace, is "gone, my mother is dead now. She is in Guinea ahead of me." Louise then recalls remembrances of Africa when she tells Sophie of her plans to travel to America by boat:

> It has been a long time since our people walked to Africa, they say. The sea, it has no doors. They say the sharks from here to there, they can only eat Haitian flesh. That is all they know how to eat.
>
> Why would you want to make the trip if you've heard all of that?
>
> Spilled water is better than a broken jar. All I need is five hundred gourdes.
>
> I know the other side. Thousands of people wash up on the shores. They put it on television, in newspapers.

40. Bob Marley, "Redemption Song."

People here too. We pray for them and bury them. Stop. Let us
stop talking so bad.[41]

The persistence of diaspora is evident here, as the Middle Passage maintains prominence in the experience of diaspora Africans. In this case,
the journey is made out of economic necessity.

In an essay entitled "We Are Ugly, but We Are Here," Danticat references Guinea, or Guinin, again: "When they were enslaved, our foremothers believed that when they died their spirits would return to Africa,
most specifically to a peaceful land we call Guinin, where gods and god-
desses live." Her grandmother taught her,

> the past is full of examples when our foremothers and forefathers
> showed such deep trust in the sea that they would jump off slave
> ships and let the waves embrace them. They too believed that the
> sea was the beginning and the end of all things, the road to free-
> dom and their entrance to Guinin. These women have been part
> of the very construction of my being ever since I was a little girl.
> Women like my grandmother who had taught me the story of
> Anacaona, the queen.[42]

The grandmother functions as a crossroads figure who provides the
link between the ancestors and subsequent generations of women. It is
through her line that diasporic information is passed on.

Danticat presents examples of the mythology of diaspora in the lore
embedded in Haitian orature. Grandmè Ifé tells a story of a little girl
who outwits a beautiful lark that attempts to steal her away to a faraway
land across the sea:

> As soon as the little girl got on the bird's back, the bird said to the
> girl, I didn't tell you this because it was a small thing, but in the
> land I am taking you to, there is a king there who will die if he does
> not have a little girl's heart. The girl she said, I didn't tell you this
> because it was a small thing, but little girls, they leave their hearts
> at home when they walk outside. Hearts are so precious. They don't
> want to lose them. The bird, clever as it was, it said to the girl, You
> might want to return to your home and pick up your heart. It is a

41. Danticat, *Breath, Eyes, Memory*, 98, 99.
42. Edwidge Danticat, "We Are Ugly, but We Are Here," 6.

small matter, but you may need it. So the girl, she said, Okay, let us go back and get my heart. The bird took her home and put her down on the ground. He told her he would wait for her to come back with her heart. The girl ran and ran all the way to her family village and never did she come back to the bird. If you see a handsome lark in a tree, you had better know that he is waiting for a very very pretty little girl who will never come back to him.[43]

The little girl, frightened of what awaits her in the faraway land, outwits the bird, tricking him into returning her home. It could be argued that this tale was created in response to the experience of the Middle Passage, as a cautionary tale to warn the descendants of enslaved Africans against the dangers of beguiling strangers. Through the oral wizardry of Grandmè Ifé, Danticat has woven a mythology of diaspora, a rationalization of the experience of Atlantic slavery, underscoring the potential perils of the sea.

Danticat extends this tradition of ancestral intervention through the body of her work, as does Marshall. Joyce Pettis's thorough study of Paule Marshall's works, *Toward Wholeness in Paule Marshall's Fiction* provides an extensive discussion of the ways in which key ancestral figures help women find spiritual wholeness. Da-duh, Marshall's own grandmother, appears in *Praisesong* as Great Aunt Cuney, in *Brown Girl, Brownstones,* and in the short stories "To Da-Duh in Memoriam," "Reena," and "British Guiana" in *Merle: A Novella and Other Stories.* In her introduction to "To Da-Duh," Marshall remarks, "She's an ancestor figure, symbolic for me of the long line of black women and men— African and New World—who made my being possible, and whose spirit I believe continues to animate my life and work. I wish to acknowledge and celebrate them. I am, in a word, an unabashed ancestor worshipper."[44] Pettis's study relies heavily on Afrocentric scholarship on psychology, and she argues that Marshall's work is preoccupied with making connections among the experiences of Africans in diaspora. Unlike other African American women writers, Marshall's project is to highlight the multiplicity and simultaneity of African and African diasporic experiences. Her location as both African American and African Caribbean

43. Danticat, *Breath, Eyes, Memory,* 125.
44. Marshall, *Merle,* 95.

has given her the perspective necessary to understand both experiences and identify the similarities inherent in them:

> I think that I am in a unique position. I know that people have trouble defining me as a black American or Caribbean writer. I fall between two stools, I'm neither West Indian nor black American. My parents were from the West Indies and they gave me a very strong sense of the culture out of which they came. That was one of the things that molded me as a person and a writer. Yet on the other hand I was born in Brooklyn, went to public schools and I'm very much a black American. I have got my feet in both camps, so that I am able to understand and respond to black American culture as well as West Indian writers who feel their situation is unique and apart from the black American experience. Similarly, I have no patience with black American writers who feel that the Caribbean is exotic and curious and different. To me it's all part of the same thing. There may be differences of expression, but at the base it's the same cultural expression.[45]

Pettis contends, "Marshall's personal synthesis of Afro-Caribbean and African American heritages is thus crucial to her vantage point of inter-connecting yet disparate cultures." She continues to describe Marshall's use of fiction to unite the various aspects of diasporic culture:

> Marshall's major fiction . . . constitutes a successive working out of falsely divisive cultural signs; each of Marshall's first three novels, which she rightly conceives as a trilogy, concludes with the pro-tagonist undertaking both a physical and spiritual journey that moves her closer to the destination that will dissolve petty cultural differences because it will affirm acceptance of the spiritual origin of the African diaspora. Marshall's vision, with liberty to transcend black culture within the United States, thus enriches and distin-guishes her fiction. Her intimacy with three cultures and her imagi-native visioning invites her criticism and questioning of them all.[46]

As Grandmè Ifé provides a link for Sophie between Haiti and the United States, Da-Duh, Great Aunt Cuney, and Lebert Joseph are ancestral

---

45. In Ogundipe-Leslie, "Re-creating Ourselves," 23–24.
46. Pettis, *Toward Wholeness,* 33, 34.

figures who facilitate Avey Johnson's path to spiritual wholeness. The sea, though it mercilessly lacks a "back door" and thus provides mortal danger, nevertheless provides a passage for interconnection with ancestors, history, identity, and spiritual rebirth.

"You Can't Beat These Children as You Would Like . . . After All, These Is New York Children!"

Marshall describes the ways in which the Barbadian migrants of her childhood adapted their parenting to conform to the laws they were now confronted with in New York City: "You can't beat these children as you would like, you know, because the authorities in this place will dash you in jail for them. After all, these is New York children." Immigrant mothers and fathers learned they could not discipline their children with complete impunity, because, in essence, the surrounding American culture preempted their parental authority. Marshall explains what it was like to be the child of such parents: "Not only were we different, American, we had, as they saw it, escaped their ultimate authority." So the adults were "confronted . . . by a world they could not encompass, which even limited their rights as parents, and at the same time finding themselves permanently separated from the world they had known, they took refuge in language."[47] Language became homeland.

For Marshall and Danticat, returning to a geographical homeland is not difficult. As "New York children," both authors, by virtue of their economic status, have access to the Caribbean in ways that their parents may have lacked. They return both physically and literarily. As a second-generation migrant, Marshall's relationship to the Caribbean exists at the level of culture and the remembrances of the first generation. Thus Marshall constructs Selena Boyce and Avey Johnson, women for whom "back home" is a place of legend, reconstructed by elders. Marshall has herself "returned" or visited Barbados several times in childhood and adulthood.[48] And as an author, she returns to the Caribbean through her characters.

47. Marshall, "Making of a Writer," 7.
48. Marshall writes in the preface to the novella "Barbados" (in both *Soul Clap Hands* and *Merle*) that she wrote *Brown Girl, Brownstones* on Barbados in 1958. The

I have chosen to focus on the works of Marshall and Danticat for several reasons. First, each represents complex subjectivities in migration. Second, migration to New York brings with it a very particular experience of migration. Marshall and Danticat convey the stories of women who migrated to the United States, New York City specifically, at very particular points in history. Marshall's parents migrated to the United States just after World War I, at a time when the nation was anxious to supplement the labor force. They left preindependence Barbados behind to escape economic scarcity. Danticat, born in Haiti, migrated to the United States with her family under similar yet different circumstances:

> I was born under Haiti's dictatorial Duvalier regime. When I was four, my parents left Haiti to seek a better life in the United States. I must admit that their motives were more economic than political. But as anyone who knows Haiti will tell you, economics and politics are very intrinsically related in Haiti. Who is in power determines to a great extent whether or not people will eat.[49]

For Danticat, Haiti is a part of her immediate memory. A first-generation Haitian American, her connection to the island is much stronger. She has a vivid memory of the necessity of moving to America. In "We Are Ugly, but We Are Here," Danticat speaks of her personal memories of the violence of the Duvalier regime and of the collective memories and legacy of colonial violence against the indigenous peoples of Haiti and the Africans enslaved there. In the title of the essay, Danticat gives testimony to the survival of all Haitian women, despite what they have endured:

> Nou led, Nou la . . . We are ugly, but we are here. Like the modesty that is somewhat common in Haitian culture, this saying makes a deeper claim for poor Haitian women than maintaining beauty, be it skin deep or otherwise. For most of us, what is worth celebrating is the fact that we are here, that we against all the odds exist. To

---

novella "Barbados" "came to" her as she wrote it on the island while she was staying in a rooming house owned by the man upon who the story is based" (*Merle*, 51). "To Da-Duh, in Memoriam" is her most autobiographical story, written about a visit she paid to her grandmother when Marshall was nine (95).

    49. Danticat, "We Are Ugly," 2.

the women who might greet each other with this saying when they meet along the countryside, the very essence of life lies in survival. It is always worth reminding our sisters that we have lived yet another day to answer the roll call of an often painful and very difficult life.[50]

In her essay, she remembers Anacaona, an Arawak woman who fought the Spanish until she was raped and murdered; as Danticat tells the tale, she explains that Anacaona was a queen:

> She was an Arawak Indian. She was a poet, dancer, and even a painter. She ruled over the western part of an island so lush and green that the Arawaks called it Ayiti, land of high. When the Spaniards came from across the sea to look for gold, Anacaona was one of their first victims. She was raped and killed and her village pillaged in a tradition of ongoing cruelty and atrocity. Anacaona's land is now the poorest country in the Western hemisphere, a place of continuous political unrest.[51]

Danticat struggles to discern where she—as a Haitian, American, woman writer, a Haitian who has lived more than half of her life in America—fits into "all of this": Haiti's history of rebellion, anticolonial struggle, violence, and poverty. "All of this now brings many questions buzzing to my head. Where was really my place in all of this? What was my grandmother's place? What is the legacy of the daughters of Anacaona? What do we all have left to remember, the daughters of Haiti?" Anacaona, rebel woman, poet, dancer, painter, is the consummate revolutionary, her commitment to her people fused with her creative vision. If we follow Sylvia Wynter's suggestion to give voice to Sycorax, the erased mother of Caliban in Shakespeare's The Tempest, Anacaona is the voice of this dispossessed Caribbean woman. Danticat chooses to write of Anacaona and her daughters, to allow them to speak "through the blunt tip of [her] pencil."[52] These "Kitchen poets," as she calls them, are women who urge

---

50. Ibid., 5.
51. Ibid., 2.
52. Ibid., 4; Sylvia Wynter, "Afterword: Beyond Miranda's Meanings: Un/silencing the 'Demonic Ground' of Caliban's 'Woman,'" in Boyce Davies and Savory Fido, Out of the Kumbla, 355–72; Danticat, Krik? Krack! 222.

her to write for all those who have had no one to speak for them. The act of writing is a way to immortalize these women and their stories:

> When [your mother] was done [braiding your hair] she would ask you to name each braid after those nine hundred and ninety-nine women who were boiling in your blood, and since you had written them down and memorized them, the names would come rolling off your tongue. And this was your testament to the say that these women lived and died and lived again.[53]

These kitchen poets, who spoke at the level of food, "slip phrases into their stew and wrap meaning around their pork before frying it. They make narrative dumplings and stuff their daughter's mouths so they say nothing more."[54]

Audre Lorde's discussion of the erotic is useful here. If the erotic can be described as "an assertion of the life force of women; of that creative energy empowered, the knowledge and use of which we are now reclaiming in our language, or history, or dancing, or loving, or work, or lives,"[55] then Anacaona personifies the uses of the erotic in the life of an artist and activist who uses her creative energies in her work. In beginning her essay with the history of Anacaona, Danticat provides an example of the role of the Haitian woman writer/artist/cultural worker in Haiti and abroad.

In the process of writing about the "daughters of Haiti," Danticat draws from the erotic, to quote Lorde again, as "a resource within each of us that lies in a deeply female and spiritual plane, firmly rooted in the power of our unexpressed or unrecognized feelings." In honor of the spirit of survival, Danticat argues "that to this day a woman remembers to name her child Anacaona, a name which resonates both the splendor and agony of a past that haunts so many women." Danticat makes a commitment to documenting these "unrecognized feelings," dedicating *Breath, Eyes, Memory* to "[t]he brave women of Haiti, grandmothers, mothers, aunts, sisters, cousins, daughters, and friends, on this shore and

---

53. Danticat, *Krik? Krack!* 224.
54. Ibid., 219–20.
55. Lorde, "Uses of the Erotic: The Erotic as Power," in *Sister Outsider,* 55.

other shores." In her fiction, Danticat remembers these women, recall-
ing them from the experiences of her childhood in Haiti and New York:
"The women's stories never manage to make the front page. However
they do exist."[56]

Danticat addresses issues of language as crucial to the representation
of these stories. As a Haitian who writes in English, she attempts to capture the beauty and lyricism of Creole without betrayal. Her ancestors
created a language that was "half of one language and half another.
They spoke the French and Spanish of their captors mixed in with their
own African language," to create a Creole "with which to describe their
new surroundings, a language from which colorful phrases blossomed
to fit the desperate circumstances." In this language, they spoke in codes,
such as "How are we today, my sister?" "I am ugly, but I am here." When
her ancestors communicated with their gods, it seemed as if they were
"speaking in tongues." Writing in English, then, Danticat speaks in yet
another tongue, developed as a result of the experience of migration and
survival. She writes in a language that is a culturally specific representation of English that speaks of the particular experiences of Haitians
women in America.

Belinda Edmondson contends that Caribbean women writers transform Caribbean space in their literature. Edmondson uses Marshall's
claim in the preface to the collection *Soul Clap Hands and Sing* that the
settings for all the novellas begin with the letter *B:* "from Brooklyn to
Brazil," for example, and that "the parameters of the nation space are
expanded both figuratively and literally to include Brooklyn as well as
Barbados."[57] In so doing, the Caribbean becomes more than just the
Barbados that figured prominently in Marshall's household and in the
memories of her parents; it is located all over the world.

The creative theorizations on migration emerging out of Marshall
and Danticat's oeuvre are particularly striking, as they appear literally
and in a different version in Danticat's *Breath, Eyes, Memory.* The phrase
"The sea ain' got no back door," used by both Danticat and Marshall,

---

56. Ibid., 53; Danticat, "We Are Ugly," 4; Danticat, *Breath, Eyes, Memory,* v;
Danticat, "We Are Ugly," 4.
57. Edmondson, *Making Men,* 14.

reminds human beings—particularly Africans who crossed the Middle Passage—that the sea is a powerful force of nature, that it is as dangerous as it is beautiful. The imagery of the sea, the passageway into the United States, here with the point of disembarkation often being New York City, provides a link between "back home" and "this man's country."[58] I choose here to focus on selected writings by Marshall and Danticat because in the works highlighted they speak of the experience of migration from the Caribbean to New York City, specifically Brooklyn. They tell stories of first- and second-generation women migrants and the emergence of new identities in migration. They are both Caribbean and American at the same time, attempting to decipher the complex matrix of American Blackness. Clearly, there are many other Caribbean women who write of migration to New York. However, the intersections between the works of Marshall and Danticat, along with the personal relationship between the two, exemplify a generational discourse between writers that begs examination. Although the sea has no "back door," it continues to inspire dialogue about identity, gender, race, and the history of enslavement.

The imagery of the sea connotes this movement through identities, marking a dividing line between old and new, slavery and freedom, forgotten histories and ancestries regained. Peoples of African descent are no strangers to the dangers of the sea, whether represented historically by the Middle Passage or contemporarily by the often fatal journey made by Haitian refugees to the United States. Nor have we forgotten the mercy shown to our ancestors by the sea when they chose to plunge into her waters rather than endure another day in bondage. The sea then, with no back doors, propels us forward, while constantly reminding us of a not-so-distant past. For as the tide splashes against the shore, the waves simultaneously carry onto the shoreline as much as they carry away, back into the sea. Thus, as generations of Caribbeans migrate to North America, South America, Europe, and throughout the Caribbean, they carry an identity that, as it is changed by the experience of migration, is passed on to subsequent generations. The experiences of the second generation, as exemplified in the works of Marshall and Danticat, give rise to complex subjectivities.

58. Danticat, *Breath, Eyes, Memory*, 6.

Postscript

Rose, dressed in a pair of men's baggy work pants and a big shirt with a belt drawn tightly around her waist, marches down to the rum shop on payday. Garfield would be there with his friends, telling lies and buying drinks to wash away the raw taste of the workweek, the sweet heat of the rum caressing the tongue, biting it ever so slightly, slowly easing down the throat into the stomach. Although her husband always provided for his family, Rose knew that the days spent in the sugar refinery, seduced by the hot syrupy aroma of boiling cane juice, would whet the men's appetite for rum, an appetite whose hunger could easily exceed Garfield's wages. The promise of this liquid reward made the burden of hot, backbreaking work almost bearable. However, Rose had a household to run. So, under the camouflage of night she went in search of her husband.

I begin this postscript with the image of my grandmother, a solitary figure marching into the night in search of the means to support her family. Masquerading as a man in order to enter into a masculine space, she mobilized against the possibility of poverty, stomping through the night air to obtain the necessary resources to maintain her household. The image of Delia Rose Gadsby traveling "under the camouflage of night" has remained with me throughout this study. It reminds me of the sacrifices that she must have made to raise her children in the 1940s through the 1960s, and how difficult this task must have been at times.

173

Had she not been as hard as she was, the lives of her children might have been radically different. She instilled in them the importance of self-preservation and survival against all odds, even if this survival demanded assuming another identity.

As the granddaughter of Delia Rose, I honor her for creating women who know the importance of survival, despite difficulty, and who passed this skill on to their children. The imagery of travel into unfamiliar territory recalls another image, that of my mother, conspicuously inconspicuous in old women's clothing, attempting to appear so insignificant that customs officers at the U.S.-Canadian border would have no cause to ask for her citizenship papers. All of the migrations, movements, and journeys made by my grandmother, mother, and aunts have shaped my own experience in the United States. As a Black woman in the academy, a daughter of a working- and middle-class mother, I see myself walking into this study with the desire to create something new, to use the space created for me by my mother for the opportunity to theorize new worlds in migration.

The image of my grandmother walking into the darkness, on a mission so to speak, serves as a metaphor for the orientation of this study. My work exists in that open space after postmodernist, postcolonial interventions, acknowledging the sentiment by several theorists of the inadequacy of some of the current theoretical formulations of identity. This study offers alternative research on Caribbean literature that looks directly to Caribbean culture for new theories of analysis. Finding parallels among texts, literature, and culture, I foreground the discussion of salt and "sucking salt" as a new conceptual environment for the evaluation of Caribbean women's writing. "Sucking salt" is a metaphor for hardship that implies mobilization against further suffering. To "suck salt" is to be in a situation of scarcity, when one has almost nothing to ensure survival. Literally, when one has no food, "sucking salt" encourages thirst, causing one to drink water, which makes the stomach full. "Sucking salt" allows one to survive and live to survive again. At the level of diaspora, the term connotes transcendence of adversity and creative resistance. "Sucking salt," indeed, is a metaphor for diaspora, particularly in relationship to the Middle Passage that links the history and culture of Africans in diaspora and the continent as well.

The preparation of salted codfish provides a practical example of the taking on of salt at the level of hardship and negotiation beyond it. One of the foods rationed to slaves, along with the scraps of meat, grain, and other provisions they were forced to eat out of necessity, saltfish carries with it the symbolic meanings of "sucking salt" discussed here. Salted codfish was imported to the Caribbean from England (and later Newfoundland) precisely because it was inexpensive and would not decompose during transportation. It is inedible until most of the salt is extracted from it via boiling or soaking. This is a delicate procedure, for if too much salt is removed, it will be bland. Once the excess salt has been removed, it becomes the main ingredient in a dish that can easily be stretched, if necessary. The horror of being given this type of food to eat in its uncooked form, which was often beginning to spoil even before it was salt-cured, can only be mediated by the skill with which enslaved African Caribbeans transformed it into a delicacy. This level of creativity takes the form of what Barbadian novelist Austin Clarke refers to as a "philosophy of cultural improvisation." His *Pig Tails 'n Breadfruit* is an excellent memoir and recipe book that places recipes for traditional Barbadian dishes within the context of working-class life on the island in the 1940s and 1950s. Clarke foregrounds the importance of class and food preparation as it relates to a philosophy of survival emerging out of the experience of slavery. In a situation of scarcity or desperation, one must piece together anything to make the impossible possible. Clarke's mother's eloquent articulation of this philosophy is instructive here: "If you don't have a horse, ride a cow. Or jackass. Or a mule."[1] In a similar way, "sucking salt" for survival is located within Caribbean culture and identity.

A study of the metaphorical and literal significance of salt in Caribbean culture and consciousness has not been explored in the scholarship on literature of the region. My work seeks to begin filling this void. It has been examined in fiction by Caribbean authors such as Fred D'Aguiar, Earl Lovelace, and Edouard Glissant, Mary Prince, and other authors discussed in this study. The present study seeks to take its place beside similar studies of the notions of "sweetness," however, such as Sydney Mintz's *Sweetness and Power*, which deals with the history of

---

1. Austin Clarke, *Pig Tails 'n Breadfruit: Rituals of Slave Food,* 90.

sugar in relationship to colonialism and power in the Caribbean and Europe. The notion of "sweetness," though similar in its connection to power and struggle, differs from the conception of "sucking salt" in that *sweetness* connotes abundance, whereas *sucking salt* connotes scarcity. "Sweetness" has been employed in Caribbean popular culture extensively, in relationship to food, sexuality, and aesthetics. The double entendre in many calypsos shows a strong connection between the three, as we have seen in Sparrow's use of "sweetness" in relationship to saltfish and woman's sexuality ("All saltfish sweet!").

In music, salt and sexuality are represented in various forms. The Mighty Sparrow's song "Saltfish," for example, represents both salt and "sucking salt" in relation to Caribbean women's sexuality; it communicates criticism of women as well as a celebration of female sensuality and eroticism. Saltfish, when taken orally as food, is literally an entrée that, if prepared well, is a work of art. Caribbeans use *sweetness* to describe a person or thing of great beauty, as well as a work of culinary art. Austin Clarke has a clear definition and illustration of the connotations of *sweetness* in his memoir:

> Barbadians use the term "sweet" to express our love and appreciation for all food that is cooked appetizingly.
>
> "My mother does-cook sweet-sweet-sweet," I used to tell my friends. The older boys, with more learned references and wider experiences, talked about a different kind of "sweetness," which had nothing to do with food. Their appreciation of "sweetness" referred to girls whose attention they hoped to attract. And they would claim, "Boy, I know she sweet! She *look* sweet!"[2]

Sweetness is thus expanded to connote and connect the politics of the kitchen and the bedroom. My discussion of "sucking salt" marks a similar notion in the converse to Clarke's representation in that the theoretical models for the exploration of Caribbean life and culture are taken from Caribbean culture itself and utilized at the level of literature.

My conception of "sucking salt" was developed through an examination of Caribbean culture and history articulated through orature and

2. Ibid., 4–5.

literature by women, on women. "Sucking salt," indeed, is part of a new lexicon, an extension of the "New World Language" developed by Gayl Jones in Corregidora through jazz discourse. Calypso, soca, zouk, rasin, kompa, reggae, and so on are yet more articulations of this New World Language, exemplifying the contradictions, complexities, and international dimensions of Caribbean culture.

This study offers new frameworks for the examination of Caribbean women's writing, and, by extension, literature by women of various diasporas, specifically the African diaspora. Feminist theories of subjectivity and the importance of writing and language are central. As Alice Walker, Marlene Nourbese Philip, and Audre Lorde have argued, writing is often a matter of survival. In my study, I give testimony of this survival, chronicling the ways in which Black women writers write of both the struggles to survive despite adversity and the joyfulness of life itself. Within my own family history and within the many descriptions in Caribbean women's literature of migration from the Caribbean to Canada, England, and the United States, Caribbean women have given voice to their lived experiences of migration and diaspora into their works. These stories—oral and written—explore the complexities of African diasporic cultures, including issues such as migration, sexuality, gender politics, identity, and popular culture.

My linking of literary representations of Caribbean women's migration with information of the lived experience of migration chronicled in interviews and oral narratives has taught me valuable lessons. First, migration is shaped by much more than economic imperatives. Of course, it cannot be argued that poverty and lack of educational opportunities have not affected patterns or rationales for movement from one space to another. However, there is a whole spectrum of justifications for these movements that cannot be explained by economic analyses and traditional historical studies. Mary Chamberlain, Patricia Pessar, and Carole Boyce Davies have provided excellent models for analyzing migration in history, anthropology, and literature, and their models return to the subjects of migrations themselves. Locating myself as the result of a series of movements beginning with the Middle Passage and culminating in my birth in the United States, I have been able to understand migration with greater complexity. Constant movement, travel, and flights to and from the Caribbean, England, and Canada have shaped my understanding of Caribbean identity in a way that merely conducting research on the area could not. The Caribbean and the northern regions of South America have extended from the narrow chain of islands into Europe, North America, and even Africa.

In my examination of Caribbean women's writing, I seek to challenge the notion of literature as artifice, as extraordinary reproductions of everyday lived experiences. Instead, I contend that Caribbean women who write of migration generally reproduce the experience of migration as a creative way of examining new theoretical and geographical spaces created as a result. If we understand migration as occurring along circuits, as Pessar argues, we can understand how Boyce Davies's mother's migrations can redefine space, as she tells us at the beginning of *Black Women, Writing, and Identity.* The women of which I write exist in a variety of spaces simultaneously, each of which functions as home in different ways. Caribbean identities are therefore always works in progress, affecting and being affected by the spaces passed into and through. Conceptualizing migration in this way has helped me to understand my mother's migrations more clearly, providing a context for that of her sisters, and as a result, for my own as well.

This book ends where the next one must necessarily begin: An extensive discussion of Caribbean women's construction of our own sexualities in literature and culture must be developed. In addition, we must further explore how these women create new worlds in migration, and how the spaces to which they migrate are affected by their presence. The issue of identity in this context is crucial here. For where does Caribbean identity end and total assimilation into American, or Canadian, or British identity begin?

As I carry with me an identity that is very specific to place and spaces in which I was raised, I am beginning to realize that my own migrations "redefine space." In my examination of Caribbean cultures in migration, specifically those resulting from the experiences of those born to Caribbean parents outside the region, I have organized my thoughts around the consciousness of someone born under these circumstances as a Black woman in New York who identifies as Caribbean, extending outward into a discussion of first- and second-generation migration experiences. Such extension is significant for many, particularly in cities such as New York and Miami, where Caribbean communities fiercely maintain a vibrant Caribbean culture mediated by the proliferation of American culture, with constant interaction with the Caribbean region. Frequent and fairly reasonable travel between the United States and various islands allows many to move between "homes." Whether one travels by airplane, boat, or bus, economic and cultural transmission is facilitated.

For those of us born in these communities, the Caribbean was as much a part of our everyday experiences as *Soul Train* or block parties. Excursion trips to recreational parks in upstate New York (such as Peg Leg Bates and Bear Mountain) coincided with Budweiser Superfests and Freshfest concerts. We were as "at home" in these spaces as we were in Brooklyn at the Caribbean Carnival on Eastern Parkway in full costume. We traveled "home" to the Caribbean for Christmas, Easter, Carnival, Crop Over, and summer vacations, staying with relatives who would in turn visit us the following year. In the Caribbean, we are "American born," "Jamerican," and "Bajan Yankees." In the United States, we are "Caribbean Americans." The Caribbean, the United States, and Europe have been forever changed by generations who left, leave, and return again and again in circuits, circulating goods, capital, and people. So the Caribbean exists internationally, constantly repeating, recreating, reproducing.

Future research in this area must acknowledge the international dimensions of Caribbean literature and identity. It must move beyond a philosophy of fragmentation into one that examines the wholeness of a cultural identity bred in diaspora and shaped by migrations. To create innovative and relevant approaches to Caribbean and other literatures of the African diaspora, scholars must look to the cultural production of these cultures at all levels for continuities and discontinuities. If we look carefully, we will see that the raw material for new and interesting discussions emerge with abundance from the subjects of the literature ourselves. For, as Audre Lorde taught us,

> We carry our traditions with us. Buying boxes of Red Cross Salt and a fresh corn straw broom for my new apartment in Westchester: New job, new house, new living the old in a new way. Recreating in words the women who helped give [us] substance.... Their names, selves, faces feed me like corn before labor. I live

each of them as a piece of me, and I choose these words with the same grave concern with which I choose to push speech into poetry, the mattering core, the forward visions of all our lives.[3]

Delia Rose was a hard woman, "falling out" with friends often. But she was hard because she had to be. Holding together a family of eight children and a husband demanded hardness. But she loved them, and she gave her girls the skills necessary to survive beyond the shores of Barbados. And in turn they try to impart these skills to their own children, pushing us out into the world with a bit of salt tucked behind each ear.

3. Lorde, *Zami*, 255–56.

Literature Review

The works of numerous scholars and literary and cultural theorists have contributed to my understanding of the subjects of this book. Many of these are mentioned in Chapter 1, but below I present additional discussion of these influential texts.

Carole Boyce Davies's work on literary representations of Black women's migrations, critiques of institutional dominance, and discussions of race and Black women's migrations have been particularly useful to my analysis.[1] Boyce Davies offers concepts such as "uprising textualities" created by Black women writers that exist independently of totalizing Western academic theory. These writers move us beyond the boundaries of colonialism and academic categorization (including the omnipresent "posts" of postmodernism, postcoloniality, postfeminism, poststructuralism, and so on) to construct creatively resistant spaces. My own work moves beyond the "post" formulations as well. Although I recognize the attempt of each theoretical intervention to decenter the West and Western constructions of Otherness and destabilize master narratives, I believe that in the insistence on decentralization, each formulation falls into the trap of revolving around the West once again.

---

1. See Boyce Davies, *Black Women, Writing;* and Carole Boyce Davies and 'Molara Ogundipe-Leslie, eds., *Moving beyond Boundaries,* vol. 1, *International Dimensions of Black Women's Writing,* and vol. 2, *Black Women's Diasporas.*

Basically, the constant attempt to prove the inherent value of the "Other" as equal to that designated by the West undermines any theorization on identity that does not factor in the existence of the West and its already acknowledged flawed notions of subordinated identities. I find it much more useful to begin thinking about identity without depending on a dichotomous relationship between the West and "the rest of us." Instead, my work focuses on culturally specific notions of identity that exist in spite of enlightenment-based notions of race and identity.[2]

Even more useful, though, has been the changing body of critical studies of Caribbean and African diasporic women's literature. Several important texts have emerged. Among these texts, *Framing the Word: Gender and Genre in Caribbean Women's Writing*, edited by Joan Anim-Addo, is an important critical intervention into the study of Caribbean women's writing internationally. Anim-Addo "frames the words" of Caribbean women writers within the context of feminist theory and praxis, attempting to highlight the ways in which gender has shaped literary history, production, and publication in the field. The essays in this collection add to discussions of the diasporic dimensions of Caribbean women's writing, representing authors throughout Europe including the Netherlands. Myriam J. A. Chancy's work *Framing Silence and Searching for Safe Spaces: Afro-Caribbean Women Writers in Exile* provides an interesting formulation that sits in sharp contrast to the con-

---

2. Paul Gilroy provides useful scholarship in this area. His *"There Ain't No Black in the Union Jack": The Cultural Politics of Race and Nation* offers a helpful analysis of racial politics in England that explores the relationship between race, class, and nation from the 1960s to the late 1980s. In *The Black Atlantic*, Gilroy attempts to move beyond essentialist notions of diasporic identity. However he falls into the trap of centering Europe by arguing that various Black Atlantic thinkers developed critical awareness of themselves as Black intelligentsia as a result of their relationship with Europe. As such, Michael Echeruo has argued that Gilroy's text focuses on a "golden age of nothingness," in which the entire history of Africans and race is elided. Echeruo sees diaspora not as a subjective event but as a nation, a race of people in exile from Africa (see Michael Echeruo, "Black Atlantic or Africanity Regained?"). Colin Palmer submits, "There is no one Black Atlantic. . . . The term runs the risk of defining a people by an ocean. It's sexy, but it doesn't have a lot of intellectual precision" (quoted in Winkler, "Historians Explore Questions"). In spite of its methodological problems and lack of a gendered discussion of diaspora, *Black Atlantic*, includes a discussion of the ways in which diaspora cultures developed by Black people in Britain contain an inherent critique of capitalism.

cept of exile as presented by an earlier generation of Caribbean male writers such as George Lamming. Lamming's *Pleasures of Exile* and Sam Selvon's *The Lonely Londoners* are texts that encapsulate the exile identity of this generation. Chancy reimagines this idea within the context of Caribbean women of African descent in the late twentieth century.

Overtly feminist examinations of Caribbean women's lives have been offered by scholars such as Ramabai Espinet, Caroline Cooper, Patricia Mohammed, and Rhoda Reddock. The foundational work of Boyce-Davies and Elaine Savory-Fido, coeditors of the first critical anthology of Caribbean Women's Writing that located a tradition of feminism within the history of women of the region, has been particularly useful to this study. The critical essays in their collection offer insights into the history of Caribbean women writers in and outside of the region.[3] Although the essays in their volume do not speak directly to the issues my work pursues, they provide historical and cultural context for this literature.[4]

Scholarship on Black women in Britain has identified the ways in which Caribbean women, as part of larger communities of women of

3. Ramabai Espinet, ed., *Creation Fire: A CAFRA Anthology of Caribbean Women's Poetry,* is collection developed out of the pan-Caribbean work of the Caribbean Association for Feminist Research and Action. CAFRA is a grassroots organization that works with both women and men around issues of gender within the Caribbean region, across ethno-linguistic lines. In the introduction, Espinet argues that the text functions to give voice to everyday Caribbean women who write poetry in the margins of their lives. See also Cooper, *Noises;* Patricia Mohammed, *Gendered Realities: Essays in Caribbean Feminist Thought;* Rhoda Reddock, ed., *Interrogating Caribbean Masuclinities: Theoretical and Empirical Analyses;* Boyce Davies and Savory Fido, *Out of the Kumbla;* and Selwyn R. Cudjoe, ed., *Caribbean Women Writers: Essays from the First International Conference.*

4. The epilogue to the collection, Sylvia Wynter's "Beyond Miranda's Meanings: Un/Silencing the 'Demonic Ground' of Caliban's 'Woman,'" takes theorizations beyond imperialistic discussions of the struggle for the theoretical terrain of Caribbean studies and literature as discussed by male Caribbean writers in, for example, the Caliban/Prospero struggle in Shakespeare's *The Tempest,* moving towards an embracing of Sycorax as the erased and disenfranchised Caribbean woman. In so doing, Wynter begins to uncover a Caribbean female identity submerged by both a patriarchal Western literary tradition and a male dominated Caribbean literary canon. Although in referring to this colonial schema by returning to *The Tempest,* Wynter seems to run the risk of reinscribing it, she pushes theorists to move beyond "Miranda's meanings" to create new theoretical frameworks for Caribbean women's writing, as represented by the essays in Boyce Davies and Savory Fido, *Out of the Kumbla.*

color, problematize migration, race, and structural inequalities. Several anthologies identify Blackness as a political category embraced by South Asian women, African women, and women of African descent.[5] The creative work in Rhonda Cobham and Merle Collins's anthology *Watchers and Seekers: Creative Writing by Black Women in Britain* challenges essentialist constructions of culturally and racially diverse Black women's identities in Britain. The emphasis of *Watchers and Seekers* on what the editors call the "cycle of emotional and material interdependence between mother and daughter, grandmother and granddaughter, aunts and nieces, cousins sisters, friends," lends itself well to an examination of the concept of "sucking salt."[6] *Bringing It All Back Home*, by Margaret Prescod-Roberts and Norma Steele, *The Heart of the Race: Black Women's Lives in Britain* by Beverley Bryan, Stella Dadzie, and Suzanne Scafe, and Selma James's collection *Strangers and Sisters: Women, Race and Immigration* have been particularly helpful in providing a context for studying migration and women's encounters with British social, economic, and political institutions.

Inside Babylon: The Caribbean Diaspora in Britain, edited by Winston James and Clive Harris, contains essays that explore the lives of modern Black women in Britain as victims of physical and emotional abuse, police violence, and racism. The essays "Woman Abuse in Black Communities" and "Black Women and the Police: A Place Where the

5. For a discussion of the ways in which the notion of "home" is complicated for Black women migrants to Britain, see Grewal et al., *Charting*. In their introduction, the editors problematize the notion of "home" for Black women whose lives have undergone severe upheaval resulting from a series of migrations, forced and otherwise, to and from various metropolitan centers. A collection of prose, poetry, interviews, essays, and reflections, *Charting* problematizes the homelessness created by centuries of British colonialism and imperialism as it shapes the lives of Black women in Britain of multiple races, sexualities, and from various regions. Lauretta Ngcobo, ed., *Let It Be Told: Essays by Black Women in Britain*, also includes in its introduction a detailed discussion of the overlapping oppressions in the lives of Black British women and the daily and literary confrontation of these oppressions by Black women. She identifies White prejudice, class prejudice, patriarchy, and "the burden of history" as the ideological links that chain Black women to external and internalized misrepresentations of their identities. They break these links in their creative writings as they recreate themselves in their own image, and in so doing, "shake off" "limiting stereotypes" (1).

6. Rhonda Cobham and Merle Collins, eds., *Watchers and Seekers: Creative Writing by Black Women in Britain*, 6.

Law is Not Upheld," both by Amina Mama, contain valuable information on Black women's experiences with state and domestic violence.
Claudette Williams presents a history of Black women's organizations
in Britain. Heidi Safia Mirza's *Young, Female, and Black* explores the
realities of young African Caribbean women in London coming of age
in the light of the racism, police brutality, sexism, and dispossession
that is part and parcel of the experience of young Black "school leavers,"
the factors that influence job opportunities, and choices that these young
women make. These works shed light on the ways in which "sucking
salt" manifests itself in the lives of Black women in Britain.[7]

Kobena Mercer's early work in Black cultural studies is also an important contribution in this area, especially in relationship to discussions of
race and identity for Black British peoples during and subsequent to the
1980s. *Welcome to the Jungle: New Positions in Black Cultural Studies* is
a study of the emergence of "Black British" identity in the wake of
the economic devastation caused by the "Thatcher/Reagan decade" of the
1980s. Mercer examines the simultaneous transnational oppression of
the era and the resulting reconfiguration of identities.[8] Mercer examines
various aspects of Black British cultural production, much of which
comes from a generation of writers and scholars (such as Isaac Julian,
Adrian Piper, Sonia Boyce, and Dorothea Smartt) who, in the wake of a
history of racism and violence within Britain and in her colonies, employ

7. The work of several scholars has provided useful background to my reading
of racial politics in the United Kingdom. Cecil Gutzmore's "Carnival, the State, and
the Black Masses in the United Kingdom" (in James and Harris, *Inside Babylon*,
207–30) provides a perspective on state and institutionalized attempts at cultural
repression and racist oppression as seen during the 1976 Notting Hill Carnival.
James, "Migration, Racism, and Identity Formation" (ibid., 231–87) contributes an
overview of migration to England across generations and the ways in which articulation of Caribbeanness develops over time. Institute of Race Relations, *Policing
against Black People*, a 1987 revision of a 1979 study entitled *Police against Black
People*, chronicles several incidences of police brutality in cases involving Black people
in London.

8. Mercer, *Welcome*, 2. Work on the Caribbean Diaspora in Britain is abundant.
Alrick Cambridge and Stephan Feuchtwang, in their books *Where You Belong: Government and Black Culture* and *Antiracist Strategies*, explore Black cultural, racial,
and racist politics in Britain, examining the strategies utilized by Black people to
mobilize against further abuse. Harry Goulbourne, ed., *Black Politics in Britain*,
anthologizes work that contributes to the ever-increasing literature on Black politics and the politics of Blackness in Britain.

the Du Boisian notion of "art as propaganda"—propaganda in resistance to oppression.[9] Regarding Caribbean women's writing internationally, it is this resistance, and the creation of new cultures and
identities, with which my work is preoccupied.

Ethnographic information obtained in London from January to May
1996 has been instrumental in providing a context for the experiences
and literary production of Caribbean women in England. In an interview
with writer and educator Beryl Gilroy, I received valuable information
on noneconomic motives for migration to London during the 1950s.
Gilroy (the first Black teacher in London) offered insight into the racial
climate confronted by Black professional women and the strategies employed by herself and others to combat them. She also spoke freely to
me about her writing, her literary influences, and her own experience
with migration, and she provided a tremendously useful historical concept for some of the meanings of *sucking salt*.

"Live artist" Dorothea Smartt provided insight into second-generation
migrant experience in London. Actively involved in a community of
Black women writers and poets, Smartt speaks of the experience of coming of age as a Black woman and zami writer in England.[10] She also
speaks to the politics of publication that often excludes Black British

9. See Mercer, *Welcome,* for an elaboration of Black British racial politics and
the development of national identity in twentieth-century Britain: "From Tianan-
men Square and the fall of the Berlin Wall to the collapse of the Soviet Union and
the end of the Cold War, from insurgent Islamic fundamentalism and the Gulf War
to the savage ethnic neonationalisms of Eastern Europe—this was hardly your standard case, 'best of times, worst of times' scenario. Yet I would argue that it is in relation to such global forces of dislocation in the world system as a whole, that Britain
too has been massively reconfigured as a local, even parochial, site in which questions
of 'race,' nation, and ethnicity have brought us to the point where "the possibility
and necessity of creating a new culture ... —that is, new identities—is slowly being
recognized as *the* democratic task of our time" (3).

10. Boyce Davies provides a definition for *zami* in *Black Women, Writing;* Audre
Lorde's revision of the term *lesbian* (of Greek origin) with the term *zami* (of Carib-
bean/creole origin) is an important attempt at redefinition that has not entered the
critical language in any significant way. Lorde was talking in her biomythography
about the way Carriacou women work together as "friends and lovers" (Boyce Davies,
Black Women, Writing, 18). Dorothea Smartt embraces zami identity, rejecting the
dependence on Western definitions on Black women's racial, sexual, political, and
philosophical identity attached to the term *lesbian* (Smartt, interview with the author,
April 17, 1997).

writing, as well as attempts of these writers to build their own literary institutions. The work of community activists and organizers provides a practical dimension to the strategies devised by Caribbean women in Britain to create opportunities and provide young Black women access to necessary educational and financial resources. Sybil Phoenix, founder of the Marsha Phoenix Memorial Trust home for homeless girls in Lewisham, London, argues that the strategy for survival used by her and many other Black people evolved out of their spiritual relationship to God. It is the intensity of faith that provides her and others with the sustenance and moral fortitude to take the initiative to help those in need. Since its founding in 1972, it has been a safe haven and training center for hundreds of girls in London. In *Willing Hands,* Phoenix speaks of her work with the homeless in a narrative that chronicles her early experiences as a migrant from Guyana in the 1950s. Her work ties into my conceptual understandings of *sucking salt* as it provides a practical example of the ways in which Caribbean women strategize through adversity and creatively resist further degradation.

Recent historiographical work in Black migration studies in the United States and in the Atlantic world offer greater insight into the historical meanings of migration for peoples of African descent.[11] Irma Watkins-Owens, *Blood Relations: Caribbean Immigrants and the Harlem Community, 1900–1930,* has been particularly useful. Watkins-Owens explores the noneconomic reasons for the movement of peoples of African descent from the Caribbean to the United States during the first period of the Great Migration. She explores the issues of Caribbean immigrant and migrant African American relations in the context of community formation, relying primarily on personal narratives, letters, interviews, and oral histories. Watkins-Owens uses oral and personal materials as her sources and so marks an important methodological shift in

11. The essays in Joe William Trotter, ed., *The Great Migration in Historical Perspective: New Dimensions in Race, Class, and Gender,* interrogate previous approaches to Black urban history that paid little attention to the "historical dynamics of black migration itself" (2). By framing their research within the context of interracial relations, earlier scholars missed the importance of the intraracial relations that motivated and supported Black migration patterns. The authors in Trotter's collection (including Nell Irvin Painter, Darlene Clark Hine, and Earl Lewis) utilize similar sources.

researching and studying the history of migration. Ramon Grosfougel has also done some important sociological work in the area of Caribbean metropolitan migration to the United States and Europe.[12]

Mary Chamberlain has focused on Barbadian migrants to Britain, particularly on oral histories and transgenerational life stories. Her work resonates with that of Irma Watkins-Owens. In the essay "Family Narratives and Migration Dynamics: Barbadians to Britain," Chamberlain discusses the importance of examining migration not only from the study of metropolitan records but also from the perspective of family dynamics. In moving away from the methodological approach to migration studies, one can see how family history, culture, and the culture of migration determine patterns of movement between home and overseas. Also, it highlights the facts that it was not always the metropole that figured largely in migrants' choices to leave home and that economics was not the only imperative that factored into the decision to migrate. As I found in my interviews with my aunts, Barbadians often left home to seek new opportunities and to broaden their horizons. Chamberlain adds that migration studies must move toward examinations of family history and to the islands of birth instead of to place of destination. "Indeed, once family stories and memories are taken into consideration, then the motives for migration become more complex, ambiguous and culturally specific."[13]

I have found this point to be particularly helpful to my own work. The interviews collected for this study from Caribbean women writers, activists, and relatives provide myriad motivations for migration that, once considered, altered my own understandings of Caribbean migration. For instance, when asked why she left Barbados in 1967, my mother answered, "to see what the world had to offer." She did not leave to escape economic turmoil or adversity. She left to extend her experiences and options beyond the confines of the island. In fact, a few of her cousins who left home at about the same time were all professional people who held civil service posts. They chose to leave Barbados not out of neces-

---

12. Ramon Grosfougel, "Colonial Caribbean Migrations to France, the Netherlands, Great Britain, and the United States."
13. Mary Chamberlain, "Family Narratives and Migration Dynamics: Barbadians to Britain," 154.

sity but out of a desire to see the world, to escape familial restrictions, and to seek more space.

This kind of work on migration is beginning to be pursued more deliberately. The collection *Islands in the City: West Indian Migration to New York,* edited by Nancy Foner, provides an excellent examination of class, gender, and racial politics within Caribbean communities in New York City. Reuel Rogers's essay "'Black Like Who?'" discussed in the introduction, addresses this issue.

Monica Jardine's work is also quite helpful in this area. Her paper "When Women Emigrate: The Immigration of Caribbean Women in the U.S. and Canada" explores the reasons behind migration to these areas, the composition of the migrant populations, and the effects of the experience on Caribbean women. The early work of Dolores Mortimer and Roy S. Bryce-Laporte laid the foundation for studies on immigration of women of color to the United States after 1965; their *Female Immigrants to the United States: Caribbean, Latin American, and African Experiences* is an examination of the "new immigration," or immigration of women after the Immigration Act of 1965.[14] The editors argue that this "new" wave of immigration was predominately female. "This characteristic, plus the legal, ethnic and cultural concomitants of the New Immigration bode serious implications for the United States as a society both on the level of political-diplomatic issues and of sociocultural phenomena.... Along with the American preoccupation with overpopulation, urban and environmental problems, and economic, racial, and international crises, such characteristics help to convert the New Immigration into a persistent though usually subordinated political issue of the times."[15] The feminization of the immigrant population that entered the United States primarily as laborers meant that these

---

14. This act is distinctive from earlier acts because it marks the first time in U.S. history in which immigration legislation sought to balance the numbers of immigrants from both hemispheres, instead of granting entry primarily to Europeans. Its goal was to maintain familial relationships whenever possible. This meant that larger numbers of immigrants from regions previously underrepresented, such as the Caribbean, Latin America, and Africa, were entering the United States, often as illegals.

15. Dolores M. Mortimer and Roy S. Bryce-Laporte, eds., *Female Immigrants to the United States: Caribbean, Latin American, and African Experiences,* viii–xi.

migrants would also be entering into the matrix of racial, gender, and sociocultural relations already existent in the nation. Their experiences would therefore be further complicated by their immigrant status.[16]

Patricia Pessar's collection *Caribbean Circuits: New Directions in the Study of Caribbean Migration* is a more recent study of Caribbean migrants that continues the work begun by Mortimer and Bryce-Laporte, who had argued in 1981 that "the presence of women immigrating to the United States is not new to American history. Women have been migrating to and within the United States from the earliest of recorded movements."[17] The character of post-1965 immigration changes the nature of the experience of women migrants, particularly women of color. Pessar makes the important argument that Caribbean migration is incredibly fluid and is characterized by constant departure and return. She also submits that return has thus far been a neglected dimension of the phenomenon, for scholarship has generally focused on the notion of permanent departure. Pessar and her colleagues have concluded that "the very meaning and utility of the term *return* requires serious rethinking." They identified several stages of return and "very few cases of definitive return."[18]

---

16. Claudia Jones, a Black Communist and international feminist, discusses the specifics of being an African Caribbean female migrant to the United States within the context of racism, sexism, and poverty. Her experience is examined in greater detail in Chapter 3.

17. Mortimer and Bryce-Laporte, *Female Immigrants*, xv.

18. Pessar, *Caribbean Circuits*, 3. Also useful in the early stages of my research was Dawn I. Marshall, *Eastern Caribbean Migration Report*, a two-volume study of outmigration from the Caribbean to the United States and Canada conducted in 1984. Including Barbados and St. Vincent, the reports, conducted by the Institute of Social and Economic Research of the University of the West Indies at Cave Hill, Barbados, was a "longitudinal study of current migration from two of the Eastern Caribbean countries to the U.S.A. [and Canada]" (1:viii). The project is unique among Caribbean migration studies because it followed the migrant from his home country at the time that he received his visa for admission to the United States and Canada and the completion of this first year. Taken together, both volumes are a study of outward migration from the perspective of the sending country. Although they only track migrants to North America for one year and focus primarily on the movements of men from the Eastern Caribbean, these studies provide insight into the economic, political, and social situations in the Caribbean that impelled migration from the post-independence Caribbean.

Stuart Hall argues that Blackness in the British context is a hybridization of identities and experiences that resist any notion of the phenotypic specificity it is subject to in the United States:

> Despite the fact that efforts are made to give this "black" identity a single or unified content, it continues to exist as an identity alongside a wide range of differences. Afro-Caribbean and Indian people continue to maintain different cultural traditions. "Black" is thus an example, not only of the political character of new identities— i.e. the positional and conjunctural character (their formation in and for specific times and places)—but also of the way identity and difference are inextricably articulated or knitted together in different identities, the one never wholly obliterating the other.[19]

Paul Gilroy's discussion of identity also leans on the framework of "cultural hybridity," arguing that "Black diaspora" cultures are anti-essentialist, anti-nationalist, and international. They cannot be subjected to limited post-1980s United States–centered Afrocentrism and instead are dialogically interpolated back and forth across the Atlantic at the level of popular culture. Gilroy, in *There Ain't No Black in the Union Jack,* discusses the context in which Black popular culture in Britain, emerged as a distinct entity in resistance to and as a result of the virulent conservatism of the Thatcher era. Gilroy's *The Black Atlantic* is a continuation of this work, with emphasis on the Black Atlantic intellectual tradition. In Gilroy's conception, Blackness is an internationally constituted identity that is by nature resistant to various systems of oppression, often existing in spite of them.[20]

---

19. Hall, "Question," 309.

20. As previously mentioned, Gilroy's work has come under harsh scrutiny. Another critique of his notion of Black identity is presented by Pnina Werbner in her introduction to Pnina Werbner and Tariq Modood, ed., *Debating Cultural Hybridity: Multi-cultural Identities and the Politics of Anti-Racism.* Werbner contends that Gilroy vilifies nationalism in favor of the cosmopolitanization of culture: "Hybridisation is a politically correct solution to an anti-ethnic or nationalist agenda; yet it is completely remote from the real global, anti-ecumenical processes that the weakening nation-state as a modernist project has precipitated. . . . So while Gilroy recognises that identities have depth and are not totally instrumental and manipulable, he still seems to imply . . . that self-consciously ethnic identities are 'bad,' and nationalism remains the source of all evil" (13–14).

Since 1965, when the International Congress of African Historians convened in Tanzania and included in its program a panel entitled "The African Abroad, or the African Diaspora," the concept of African diaspora has been used by scholars of African history and across disciplines. Joseph E. Harris submits that the use of diaspora as a recurring theme in UNESCO's multivolume *General History of Africa* has ensured that the historical relationship between continental Africans and peoples of African descent worldwide will remain a subject for multidisciplinary research. Challenging Harris's time frame, George Shepperson has argued that *African diaspora* had been used by many writers and thinkers between the middle 1950s and middle 1960s who were concerned with the future of newly independent African states and the status of peoples of African descent.[21]

At the plenary session at the start of the 1999 meeting of the American Historical Association in Washington, D.C., historian Colin Palmer argued that diaspora is a problem that invites a great deal of methodological fuzziness, ahistorical claims, and even romantic condescension. The theme of the conference, "Diasporas and Migrations in History" incited much criticism from many in the historical community, who argue the question of diaspora has become a fad. Despite such criticism, historians such as Palmer continue to grapple with the term, arguing for specificity without essentialism. He ended his presentation by asking scholars to study both the different societies from which diasporic peoples originate and the communities they have established outside of Africa. Prior to the conference, in the fall 1998 issue of *Perspectives,* the A.H.A. newsletter, Palmer had described five distinct diasporas that constitute the African diaspora as we know it. The first three, dating from the movement of people on the African continent some one hundred thousand years ago through the trading communities established by merchants (and some slaves) around the fifth century B.C., were primarily (although not exclusively) voluntary dispersals. The last two African diasporas—the people scattered by the Atlantic slave trade starting in the fifteenth century and the people of African descent who resettled around the world after slavery's demise in the Americas—constitute the

21. Joseph Harris, ed., *Global Dimensions of the African Diaspora,* 2; Shepperson, in ibid., 41.

modern African diaspora. The defining characteristics of those more recent streams have been racial oppression, the struggle against it, and a shared emotional bond with the African continent.[22]

Palmer pointed out that much scholarship on diaspora focuses on the ways in which enslaved people rebuilt their cultures and identities away from home, an example of what he calls "feel good" history. I would argue, however, that there is an intellectual way to discuss the re-creation of culture and identity without eliding the pain and suffering of slavery. In fact, it could be argued that complex discussions of such re-creations that call on a variety of disciplinary contributions to the field of diaspora studies would lead to the comparative approach that he advocates. Also, interdisciplinary approaches can begin to talk about the diaspora cultures that have emerged in spite of this pain and suffering. Palmer expects that clarity in our theoretical and methodological focus in diaspora history will develop in time: "We're going to develop growing pains for a while."[23]

22. Palmer's ideas are discussed in Winkler, "Historians Explore Questions." In her report on the conference, Winkler writes, "Today there are scholarly journals devoted to diaspora studies, conferences, research programs, courses, and a host of books. That development has been spurred by globalization, by the awareness that most cultures are multi-ethnic, and by the apparent decline of nation states. Within the academy, it stems from growing interest in world history, in studying racial and ethnic groups, and in looking at culture and how it is transmitted. But diaspora history is still also very much a concept in search of definition" (A11).

23. Ibid., A12.

Bibliography

Adisa, Opal Palmer. "De Language Reflect Dem Ethos: Some Issues with Nation Language." In *Winds of Change: The Transforming Voices of Caribbean Women Writers and Scholars,* ed. Adele S. Newson and Linda Strong-Leek, 17–29. New York: Peter Lang, 1998.

———. *It Begins with Tears.* Oxford: Heinemann, 1997.

———. "Three Jamaican Women Writers at Home and the Diaspora." Ph.D. diss., University of California, Los Angeles, 1992. Ann Arbor, Mich.: UMI Dissertation Services, 1994.

Adshead, Samuel Adrian Miles. *Salt and Civilization.* New York: St. Martin's Press, 1992.

Allen, Lillian. "Marriage." *Prism International* 22, no. 4 (summer 1984), 33.

Allen, Ray, and Lois Wilcken, eds. *Island Sounds in the Global City: Caribbean Popular Music and Identity in New York.* New York: New York Folklore Society: Institute for Studies in American Music, Brooklyn College, 1998.

Allsopp, Richard. *Dictionary of Caribbean English Usage.* New York: Oxford University Press, 1996.

Alwes, Derek. "The Burden of Liberty: Choice in Toni Morrison's *Jazz* and Toni Cade Bambara's *The Salt Eaters.*" *African American Literature Review* 30, no. 3 (autumn 1996): 353–65.

Anatol, Giselle Liza. "Transforming the Skin-Shedding Soucouyant: Using Folklore to Reclaim Female Agency in the Caribbean." *Small Axe* 7 (March 2000): 44–59.

Anim-Addo, Joan, ed. *Framing the Word: Gender and Genre in Caribbean Women's Writing.* London: Whiting and Birch, 1996.

Ashcroft, Bill, Gareth Griffiths, and Helen Tiffin, eds. *The Postcolonial Studies Reader.* London: Routledge, 1995.

Bambara, Toni Cade. *The Salt Eaters.* New York: Vintage Contemporaries, 1992.

Beckles, Hilary. *Natural Rebels: A Social History of Enslaved Black Women in Barbados.* New Brunswick, N.J.: Rutgers University Press, 1989.

Benitez-Rojo, Antonio. *The Repeating Island: The Caribbean and the Postmodern Perspective.* Durham, N.C.: Duke University Press, 1992.

Bennett, Louise. *Jamaica Labrish.* Kingston, Jamaica: Sangster's Book Stores, 1966.

———. *Louise Bennett: Selected Poems.* Kingston, Jamaica: Sangster's Book Stores, 1982.

Berlin, Ira, and Philip D. Morgan, eds. *Cultivation and Culture: Labor and the Shaping of Slave Life in the Americas.* Charlottesville: University Press of Virginia, 1993.

Besson, Gérard. *Folklore and Legends of Trinidad and Tobago.* Port-of-Spain, Trinidad: Paria Publishing, 1989.

Black Womantalk Collective (Da Choong, Olivette Cole Wilson, Bernardine Evaristo, Gabriela Pearse eds.). *Black Women Talk Poetry.* London: Black Womantalk Publishers, 1987.

Boyce Davies, Carole. *Black Women, Writing, and Identity: Migrations of the Subject.* New York: Routledge, 1994.

———. "Black Women's Journey into Self: A Womanist Reading of Paule Marshall's *Praisesong for the Widow*." *Matatu* 1, no. 1 (1987): 19–34.

———. "Caribbean Women Writers: Imagining Caribbean Space." *Thamyris: Mythmaking from Past to Present* 5, no. 2 (autumn 1998): n.p.

———. "Carnivalised Caribbean Female Bodies: Taking Space/Making Space." *Thamyris: Mythmaking from Past to Present* 5, no. 2 (autumn 1998): 333–46.

————. "The Politics of African Identification in Trinidad Calypso." *Studies in Popular Culture* 8, no. 2 (1985): 77–94.

Boyce Davies, Carole, and Elaine Savory Fido, eds. *Out of the Kumbla: Caribbean Women and Literature.* Trenton, N.J.: Africa World Press, 1990.

Boyce Davies, Carole, Meredith Gadsby, Charles Peterson, and Henrietta Williams, eds. *Decolonizing the Academy: African Diaspora Studies.* Trenton, N.J.: Africa World Press, 2003.

Boyce Davies, Carole, and 'Molara Ogundipe-Leslie, eds. *Moving beyond Boundaries.* Vol. 1, *International Dimensions of Black Women's Writing.* New York: New York University Press, 1995.

————. *Moving beyond Boundaries.* Vol. 2, *Black Women's Diasporas.* New York: New York University Press, 1995.

Brand, Dionne. *"Sans Souci" and Other Stories.* Ithaca, N.Y.: Firebrand Books, 1989.

————. *Bread Out of Stone: Recollections, Sex, Recognitions, Race, Dreaming, Politics.* Toronto: Coach House Press, 1994.

————. *No Language Is Neutral.* Toronto: Coach House Press, 1990.

Brathwaite, Edward Kamau. *History of the Voice: The Development of Nation Language in Anglophone Caribbean Poetry.* London: New Beacon Books, 1984.

Bryan, Beverley, Stella Dadzie, and Suzanne Scafe, eds. *The Heart of the Race: Black Women's Lives in Britain.* London: Virago, 1985.

Busby, Margaret, ed. *Daughters of Africa: An International Anthology of Words and Writings by Women of African Descent from the Ancient Egyptian to the Present.* New York: Ballantine Books, 1994.

Cambridge, Alrick, and Stephan Feuchtwang. *Antiracist Strategies.* Aldershot, England: Avebury, 1990.

Cambridge, Alrick, and Stephan Feuchtwang; with J. Clarke and J. Eade. *Where You Belong: Government and Black Culture.* Aldershot, England: Avebury, 1992.

Cary, Lorene. *Black Ice.* New York: Vintage Books, 1992.

Cassidy, F. G., and R. B. Le Page, eds. *Dictionary of Jamaican English.* 2d ed. Barbados and Jamaica: University of the West Indies Press, 2002.

Chamberlain, Mary. "Family Narratives and Migration Dynamics: Barbadians to Britain." *Immigrants and Minorities* 13, no. 2 (July 1995): 153–69.

———. *Narratives of Exile and Return.* New York: St. Martin's Press, 1997.

Chamberlain, Mary, and Paul Thompson, eds. *Narrative and Genre.* New York: Routledge, 1998.

Chancy, Myriam J. A. *Framing Silence: Revolutionary Novels by Haitian Women.* Piscataway, N.J.: Rutgers University Press, 1997.

———. *Searching for Safe Spaces: Afro-Caribbean Women Writers in Exile.* Philadelphia: Temple University Press, 1997.

Chang, Kevin O'Brien, and Wayne Chen. *Reggae Routes: The Story of Jamaican Music.* Philadelphia: Temple University Press, 1998.

Christian, Barbara. "The Race for Theory." In *The Postcolonial Studies Reader,* ed. Bill Ashcroft, Gareth Griffiths, and Helen Tiffin. London: Routledge, 1995.

Clarke, Austin. *Pig Tails 'n Breadfruit: Rituals of Slave Food.* Kingston, Jamaica: Ian Randle Publishers, 1999.

Cliff, Michelle. *Abeng: A Novel.* Trumansburg, N.Y.: Crossing Press, 1984.

———. *Bodies of Water.* New York: Dutton, 1990.

———. "Caliban's Daughter: The Tempest and the Teapot." *Frontiers* 12, no. 2 (1991): 36–51.

———. *Claiming an Identity They Taught Me to Despise.* Watertown, Mass.: Persephone Press, 1980.

———. *Free Enterprise.* New York: Dutton, 1993.

———. *Land of Look Behind: Prose and Poetry.* Ithaca, N.Y.: Firebrand Books, 1985.

———. *No Telephone to Heaven.* New York: Dutton, 1987.

Cobham, Rhonda, and Merle Collins, eds. *Watchers and Seekers: Creative Writing by Black Women in Britain.* London: Women's Press, 1987.

Conde, Maryse. *Crossing the Mangrove.* Trans. Richard Philcox. New York: Anchor Books, 1995.

Coombs, Orde, ed. *Is Massa Day Dead.* New York: Anchor Books, 1974.

Cooper, Carolyn. *Noises in the Blood: Orality, Gender, and the "Vulgar" Body of Jamaican Popular Culture.* Durham, N.C.: Duke University Press, 1993.

Cowley, John. *Carnival, Canboulay, and Calypso: Traditions in the Making.* Cambridge: Cambridge University Press, 1997.

Crowley, D. "Toward a Definition of Calypso." *Ethnomusicology* 3 (1959): 57–66, 117–24.

Cudjoe, Selwyn R., ed. *Caribbean Women Writers: Essays from the First International Conference.* Wellesley, Mass.: Calaloux Publication; Amherst; Division of the University of Massachusetts Press, 1990.

Curtin, Phillip D. "The Slavery Hypothesis for Hypertension among African Americans: The Historical Evidence." *American Journal of Public Health* 82: 1681–86.

D'Aguiar, Fred. *Feeding the Ghosts.* Hopewell, N.J.: Ecco Press, 1999.

Danticat, Edwidge. *Breath, Eyes, Memory.* 2d ed. New York: Soho, 1994.

———. *The Dew Breaker.* New York: Knopf, 2004.

———. *The Farming of Bones: A Novel.* New York: Soho Press, 1998.

———. *Krik? Krak!* Vintage: New York, 1996.

———. "We Are Ugly, but We Are Here." *Caribbean Writer* 10 (1996): n.p.

Davis, Wade. *The Serpent and the Rainbow.* New York: Vintage, 1995.

Depestre, René. *Change.* Violence II, no. 9, Paris: Seuil, 1971, 20.

Diamond, J. "The Saltshaker's Curse." *Natural History,* October 1991, 20–26.

Dodgson, Elyse. *Motherland: West Indian Women to Britain in the 1950s.* Heinemann: London, 1984.

Douglas, Marcia. *Madame Fate.* New York: Soho Press, 1999.

Du Bois, W. E. B. *The Suppression of the African Slave Trade.* 1896. Reprint, Baton Rouge: Louisiana State University Press, 1969.

Dundes, Allan, ed. *Mother Wit from the Laughing Barrel: Readings in the Interpretation of Afro-American Folklore.* New York: Garland, 1981.

Echeruo, Michael J. C. "An African Diaspora: The Ontological Project." In *The African Diaspora: African Origins and New World Identities,* ed. Isidore Okpewho, Carole Boyce Davies, and Ali A. Mazrui, 3–18. Bloomington: Indiana University Press, 1999.

Edmondson, Belinda. *Making Men: Gender, Literary Authority, and Women's Writing in Caribbean Narrative.* Durham, N.C.: Duke University Press, 1999.

Elder, J. D. "The Calypso." Paper presented at the Seminar on the Calypso, University of the West Indies, St. Augustine, Trinidad, 1973.

———. *The Calypso and Its Morphology.* Port of Spain: National Cultural Council of Trinidad and Tobago, 1973.

———. "The Male/Female Conflict in Calypso." *Caribbean Quarterly* 14, no. 3 (1968): 23–41.

Elder, J. D., ed. *Ma Rose Point: An Anthology of Rare Legends and Folk Tales from Trinidad and Tobago*. Port of Spain: National Cultural Council of Trinidad and Tobago. 1972.

Ellison, Ralph. *Invisible Man*. New York: Vintage International, 1990.

Espinet, Ramabai, ed. *Creation Fire: A CAFRA Anthology of Caribbean Women's Poetry*. Toronto: Sister Vision, 1990.

Fackelmann, K. A. "The African Gene? Searching through History for the Roots of Black Hypertension." *Science News* 140 (October 19, 1991): 254–55.

Fanon, Frantz. *The Wretched of the Earth*. Trans. Constance Farrington. New York: Grove Press, 1963.

Foner, Nancy, ed. *Islands in the City: West Indian Migration to New York*. Berkeley and Los Angeles: University of California Press, 2001.

Forde, G. Addinton. *De Mortar-Pestle: A Collection of Barbadian Proverbs*. Barbados: National Cultural Foundation, 1987.

Frohme, Andrea. "Jean-Michel Basquiat as Heroic Hunter: An Assertion of Identity." Paper presented at "The African Diaspora: African Origins and New World Self-Fashioning," Binghamton University, April 11–13, 1996.

Fryer, Peter. *Staying Power: The History of Black People in Britain*. London: Pluto Press, 1984.

Fugees. *The Score*. Sony Music 67146, CD, 1996.

Gilroy, Beryl. *Black Teacher*. 1976. Reprint, London: Bogle L'Ouverture, 1994.

Gilroy, Paul. *The Black Atlantic*. Cambridge: Harvard University Press, 1993.

———. *Small Acts: Thoughts on the Politics of Black Cultures*. London: Serpent's Tail, 1993.

———. *"There Ain't No Black in the Union Jack": The Cultural Politics of Race and Nation*. London: Hutchinson, 1987.

Glissant, Edouard. *Black Salt*. Ann Arbor: University of Michigan Press, 1999.

Goldsmith, M. F. "African Lineage, Hypertension Linked." *Journal of the American Medical Association* 266, no. 15 (October 16, 1991): 2049.

Goodman, Lizbeth. "Who's Looking at Who(m)? Re-Viewing Medusa." *Modern Drama* 39, no. 1 (spring 1996): 190–210.

Goulbourne, Harry, ed. *Black Politics in Britian.* Aldershot, England: Avebury, 1992.

Grant, Jaime M. "Building Community Based Coalitions from Academe: The Union Institute and the Kitchen Table: Women of Color Press Transition Coalition." *Signs* 21, no. 4 (summer 1976): 1024–33.

Grewal, Shabnam, Jackie Kay, Liliane Landor, Gail Lewis, and Pratibha Parmar. *Charting the Journey: Writings by Black and Third World Women.* London: Sheba Feminist Publishers, 1988.

Griffin, Gabrielle. " 'Writing the Body': Reading Joan Riley, Grace Nichols, and Ntozake Shange." In *Black Women's Writing,* ed. Gina Wisker, 19–42. New York: St. Martin's Press, 1993.

Grosfougel, Ramon. "Colonial Caribbean Migrations to France, the Netherlands, Great Britain, and the United States." *Ethnic and Racial Studies* 20, no. 3 (July 1997): 595–612.

Guy-Sheftall, Beverly, ed. *Words of Fire: An Anthology of African-American Feminist Thought.* New York: New Press, 1995.

Hall, Stuart. "Cultural Identity and Diaspora." In *Colonial Discourse and Postcolonial Theory: A Reader,* ed. Laura Chrisman and Patrick Williams, 392–403. New York: Columbia University Press, 1994.

———. "The Question of Cultural Identity." In *Modernity and Its Futures,* ed. Stuart Hall, David Held, and Tony McGrew, 274–316. Cambridge, U.K.: Polity Press, 1992.

Hanchard, Michael. "Identity, Meaning, and the African-American." *Social Text* 24, no. 8 (1990): 31–42.

Harris, Joseph, ed. *Global Dimensions of the African Diaspora.* 2d ed. Washington, D.C.: Howard University Press, 1993.

Higman, Barry. *Slave Populations of the British Caribbean, 1807–1834.* Baltimore: Johns Hopkins Press, 1984.

Hill, E. "On the Origin of the Term Calypso." *Ethnomusicology* 11:359–67.

Hill, Lauryn. *The Miseducation of Lauryn Hill.* Ruffhouse Records, CK 69035, 1998.

Hill, Patricia Liggins, ed. *Call and Response: The Riverside Anthology of the African American Literary Tradition.* Boston: Houghton Mifflin, 1998.

hooks, bell. *Feminist Theory: From Margin to Center.* Boston: South End Press, 1989.

Hopkinson, Nalo. *The Salt Roads*. New York: Warner Books, 2003.

Hull, Gloria T., Patricia Bell Scott, and Barbara Smith, eds. *All the Women Are White, All the Blacks Are Men, but Some of Us Are Brave: Black Women's Studies*. Old Westbury, N.Y.: Feminist Press, 1982.

Hurston, Zora Neale. "Hoodoo in America: Conjure Stories." *Journal of American Folk Lore* 44 (1931): 317–417.

Institute of Race Relations. *Police against Black People: Evidence Submitted to the Royal Commission on Criminal Procedure*. London: Institute of Race Relations, 1979.

———. *Policing against Black People*. London: Institute of Race Relations, 1987.

James, Selma, ed. *Strangers and Sisters: Women, Race, and Immigration*. Bristol, England: Falling Wall Press, 1985.

James, Winston, and Clive Harris, eds. *Inside Babylon: The Caribbean Diaspora in Britain*. New York: Verso, 1993.

Jardine, Monica. "When Women Emigrate: The Immigration of Caribbean Women in the U.S. and Canada." Paper presented at Twenty-first Century Paradigms in African Studies conference, May 1, 1998, Florida International University.

Johnson, Buzz. *"I Think of My Mother": Notes on the Life and Times of Claudia Jones*. London: Karia Press, 1985.

Jones, Gavin. "'The Sea Ain't Got No Back Door': The Problems of Black Consciousness in Paule Marshall's *Brown Girl, Brownstones*." *African American Review* 32, no. 4 (winter 1998): 597–606.

Jones, Gayle. *Corregidora*. Boston: Beacon Press, 1975.

Keller, Lynn, and Christiane Miller, eds. *Feminist Measures: Soundings in Poetry and Theater*. Ann Arbor: University of Michigan Press, 1994.

Kincaid, Jamaica. *At the Bottom of the River*. New York: Farrar, Straus, Giroux, 1984.

Levine, Lawrence W. *Black Culture and Black Consciousness: Afro-American Folk Thought from Slavery to Freedom*. New York: Oxford University Press, 1978.

Lewis, Gail. "Black Women's Employment and British Economy." In Winston James and Clive Harris, eds., *Inside Babylon: The Caribbean Diaspora in Britain*, 73–96. London: Verso, 1993.

Linebaugh, Peter. "All the Atlantic Mountains Shook." *Labor/Le Travailleur* 10 (autumn 1982): 87–121.

Liverpool, Hollis. *Kaiso and Society.* Diego Martin, Trinidad: Juba Publications, 1990.

Lorde, Audre. *Sister Outsider: Essays and Speeches.* Freedom, Calif.: Crossing Press, 1984.

———. *Zami: A New Spelling of My Name.* Freedom, Calif.: Crossing Press, 1982.

Lovejoy, Paul. *Salt of the Desert Sun: A History of Salt Production and Trade in the Central Sudan.* New York: Cambridge University Press, 1986.

Lovelace, Earl. *Salt: A Novel.* London: Faber and Faber, 1996.

Mahabir, Kumar, ed. *A Dictionary of Common Trinidad Hindi.* 3d ed. Trinidad and Tobago: Chakra Publishing House, 2005.

Maison-Bishop, Carole. "Women in Calypso: Hearing the Voices." Ph.D. diss., University of Alberta, 1994. Ann Arbor, Mich.: UMI Dissertation Services, 1998.

Marley, Bob. "Redemption Song." In *Uprising.* Tuff Gong Records, distributed by Island Records, manufactured for BMG Direct Mktg. (D101682), cat. no. 422–846–211–2. 1980.

Marshall, Dawn I. *Eastern Caribbean Migration Report.* Barbados: University of the West Indies, 1984.

Marshall, Paule. *Brown Girl, Brownstones.* New York: Random House, 1959.

———. *The Chosen Place, the Timeless People.* New York: Harcourt, Brace and World, 1969.

———. *Daughters.* New York: Plume, 1991.

———. "Little Girl of All the Daughters." Interview. *Second Shift,* summer 1993, 20–21.

———. *Merle: A Novella and Other Stories.* London: Virago Press, 1985.

———. *Praisesong for the Widow.* New York: G.P. Putnam and Sons, 1983.

———. *Reena and Other Stories.* New York: Feminist Press, 1983.

———. "Shaping the World of My Art." *New Letters* 40, no. 1 (1973): 97–112.

———. *Soul Clap Hands and Sing.* Washington, D.C.: Howard University Press, 1988.

Marson, Una. *Heights and Depths.* Kingston, Jamaica: Gleaner, 1931.

———. *Tropic Reveries.* Kingston, Jamaica: Una Marson, 1930.

McDaniel, Lorna. *The Big Drum Ritual of Carriacou: Praisesongs in Rememory of Flight.* Gainesville: University Press of Florida, 1998.

McDougall, E. A. "Salts of the Western Sahara: Myths, Mysteries, and Historical Significance." *International Journal of African Historical Studies* 23 (spring 1990): 231–57.

Memmi, Albert. *The Colonizer and the Colonized.* Trans. Howard Greenfeld. New York: Orion Press, 1965.

Mercer, Kobena. *Welcome to the Jungle: New Positions in Black Cultural Studies.* New York: Routledge, 1994.

Mighty Sparrow. "Saltfish (Solfish)." Performed by the Sparrow and the New Troubadours. In *Sparrow Party Classic 4: Survival.* Slinger Francisco for BLS Records, Arrow Records, B00008EOND, CD 1993.

Mintz, Sidney W. *Sweetness and Power: The Place of Sugar in Modern History.* New York: Penguin, 1986.

Mirza, Heidi Safia. *Young, Female, and Black.* London: Routledge, 1992.

Mohammed, Patricia. *Gendered Realities: Essay in Caribbean Feminist Thought.* Kingston, Jamaica: University of the West Indies Press; Mona, Jamaica: Centre for Gender and Development Studies, 2002.

Monarch. "Saltfish Tongue." In *Say What: Double Entendre Soca from Trinidad.* Rounder Select 5042, CD, 1992.

Montano, Machel. "Big Phat Fish." In *Reggae Gold, 1999.* VP Records, 1559, CD, 1999.

Moraga, Cherríe, and Gloria Anzaldúa, eds. *This Bridge Called My Back: Writings by Radical Women of Color.* 2d ed. Latham, N.Y.: Kitchen Table, Women of Color Press, 1983.

Morrison, Toni. *Song of Solomon.* New York: Signet, 1978.

Mortimer, Dolores M., and Roy S. Bryce-Laporte, eds. *Female Immigrants to the United States: Caribbean, Latin American, and African Experiences.* Washington, D.C.: Research Institute on Immigration and Ethnic Studies, Smithsonian Institution, 1981.

Murrell, Nathaniel Samuel, William David Spencer, and Adrian Anthony McFarlane, eds.; Clinton Chisholm, consulting ed. *Chanting Down Babylon: The Rastafari Reader.* Kingston, Jamaica: Ian Randle Publishers, 1998.

Nasta, Susheila, ed. *Motherlands: Black Women's Writing from Africa, the Caribbean, and South Asia.* New Brunswick, N.J.: Rutgers University Press, 1992.

Ngcobo, Lauretta, ed. *Let It Be Told: Essays by Black Women in Britain.* London: Pluto Press, 1987.

Nichols, Grace. *I Is a Long Memoried Woman.* London: Karnak House, 1990.

Ogundipe-Leslie, 'Molara. "Re-creating Ourselves All Over the World: A Conversation with Paule Marshall." In *Moving beyond Boundaries,* vol. 2, *Black Women's Diasporas,* ed. Carole Boyce Davies and 'Molara Ogundipe-Leslie, 20–24. New York: New York University Press, 1995.

Olmstead, Jane. "The Pull to Memory and the Language of Place in Paule Marshall's *The Chosen Place, the Timeless People* and *Praisesong for the Widow.*" *African American Review* 31, no. 2 (summer 1997): 249–68.

Ottley, C. R. *Tall Tales of Trinidad and Tobago.* Port of Spain, Trinidad: Victory Commercial Printers, 1977.

Ottley, Rudolph. *Women in Calypso.* Part 1. Arima, Trinidad: LAL, 1992.

Palmer, Hazelle. *Tales from the Garden and Beyond.* Toronto: Sister Vision, 1995.

Paquet, Sandra Pouchet. *Eric Williams and the Postcolonial Caribbean.* Baltimore: Johns Hopkins Press, 1998.

———. *The Novels of George Lamming.* London: Heinemann, 1982.

Parvisini-Gebert, Lizabeth. "Women Possessed: The Eroticism and Exoticism in the Representation of Woman as Zombie." In *Sacred Possessions: Vodou, Santería, Obeah, and the Caribbean,* ed. Margarite Fernández Olmos and Lizabeth Parvisini-Gebert, 37–58. New Brunswick, N.J.: Rutgers University Press, 1997.

Pearse, Andrew. "Carnival in Nineteenth Century Trinidad." *Caribbean Quarterly* 4, nos. 3,4 (1956): 175–93.

———. "Mitto Sampson on Calypso Legends of the Nineteenth Century." *Caribbean Quarterly* 4, nos. 3, 4 (March–June, 1956): 250–62.

Pepin, Ernest. *L'homme au Baton.* Paris: Gallimard, 1992.

Perinbam, B. Marie. "The Salt-Gold Alchemy in the Eighteenth and Nineteenth Century Mande World: If Men Are Its Salt, Women Are Its Gold." *History in Africa* 23 (1996): 257–78.

Pessar, Patricia. *Caribbean Circuits: New Directions in the Study of Caribbean Migration.* New York: Center for Migration Studies, 1997.

Pettis, Joyce. *Toward Wholeness in Paule Marshall's Fiction.* Charlottesville: University Press of Virginia, 1995.

Philip, Marlene Nourbese. "Dis Place: The Space Between." In *Feminist Measures: Soundings in Poetry and Theater,* ed. Lynn Keller and Christiane Miller, 287–317. Ann Arbor: University of Michigan Press, 1994.

———. *Genealogy of Resistance and Other Essays.* Stratford, Ontario: Mercury Press, 1998.

———. *Looking for Livingstone: An Odyssey of Silence.* Stratford, Ontario: Mercury Press, 1991.

———. *She Tries Her Tongue, Her Silence Softly Breaks.* Charlottetown, Prince Edward Island, Canada: Ragweed Press, 1989.

Phoenix, Sybil. *Willing Hands.* London: Bible Reading Fellowship, 1984.

Pilkington, Edward. *Beyond the Mother Country: West Indians and the Notting Hill White Riots.* London: I. B. Tauris, 1988.

Pollard, Velma. "Cultural Connections in Paule Marshall's *Praisesong for the Widow." World Literature Written in English* 25, no. 2 (1985): 285–98.

———. *Dread Talk: The Language of Rastafari.* Barbados: Canoe Press; Montreal: McGill-Queens University Press, 2000.

Prescod-Roberts, Margaret, and Norma Steele, eds. *Black Women: Bringing It All Back Home.* Bristol, England: Falling Wall Press, 1980.

Prince, Mary. *The History of Mary Prince, a West Indian Slave, Related by Herself.* Ed. Moira Ferguson; preface by Ziggi Alexander. 1831. Reprint, London: Pandora, 1987.

Prince, Nancy. *A Black Woman's Odyssey through Russia and Jamaica: The Narrative of Nancy Prince.* 1850. Reprint, New York: M. Wiener, 1989.

Pryse, Marjorie, and Hortense J. Spillers, eds. *Conjuring: Black Women, Fiction, and Literary Traditon.* Bloomington: Indiana University Press, 1985.

Reddock, Rhoda, ed. *Interrogating Caribbean Masuclinities: Theoretical and Empirical Analyses.* Kingston, Jamaica: University of the West Indies Press, 2004.

Rickford, John R. *African American Vernacular English: Features, Evolution, Educational Implications.* Malden, Mass.: Blackwell Publishers, 1999.

———. *Spoken Soul: The Story of Black English.* New York: John Wiley and Sons, 2000.

Riley, Joan. *A Kindness to the Children.* London: Women's Press, 1992.

———. *Romance.* London: Women's Press, 1988.

———. *The Unbelonging.* London: Women's Press, 1985.

————. *Waiting in the Twilight*. London: Women's Press, 1987.

————. "Writing Reality in a Hostile Environment." *Kunapipi* 16, no. 1 (1994): 547–52.

Riley, Joan, and Briar Wood, eds. *Leave to Stay: Stories of Exile and Belonging*. London: Virago Press, 1996.

Rogers, Reuel. "'Black Like Who?' Afro-Caribbean Immigrants, African Americans, and the Politics of Group Identity." In *Islands in the City: West Indian Migration to New York*, ed. Nancy Foner, 163–92. Berkeley and Los Angeles: University of California Press, 2001.

Rohlehr, Gordon. *Calypso and Society in Pre-Independence Trinidad*. Port of Spain, Trinidad: Gordon Rohlehr, 1990.

Rutherford, Jonathan, ed. *Identity: Community, Culture, Difference*. New York: New York University Press, 1990.

Savannah Unit, Georgia Writers' Project, Work Projects Administration. *Drums and Shadows: Survival Studies among the Georgia Coastal Negroes*. Athens: University of Georgia Press, 1986.

Scott, Patricia Bell, Gloria T. Hull, and Barbara Smith. *All the Women Are White, All the Blacks Are Men, but Some of Us Are Brave*. New York: Feminist Press, 1982.

Schwartz, Meryl F. "An Interview with Michelle Cliff." *Contemporary Literature* 34, no. 4 (1993): 595–619.

Shepherd, Verene, and Hilary Beckles, eds. *Caribbean Slave Society and Economy*. New York: New Press, 1991.

Shinebourne, Janice. *The Last English Plantation*. Leeds, Yorkshire: Peepal Tree Press, 1988.

Silvera, Makeda, ed. *The Other Woman: Women of Colour in Contemporary Canadian Literature*. Toronto: Sister Vision, 1994.

Smartt, Dorothea. *Connecting Medium*. Leeds, Yorkshire: Peepal Tree Press, 2001.

Smitherman, Geneva. *Black Talk: Words and Phrases from the Hood to the Amen Corner*. Boston: Houghton Mifflin, 2000.

————. *Talkin and Testifyin: The Language of Black America*. Detroit: Wayne State University Press, 1986.

————. *Talking That Talk: Language, Culture, and Education in African America*. London: Routledge, 2000.

Spillers, Hortense J. "Chosen Place, Timeless People: Some Figurations on the New World." In *Conjuring: Black Women, Fiction, and Literary*

Tradition, ed. Marjorie Pryse and Hortense J. Spillers, 151–75. Bloomington: Indiana University Press, 1985.

Springfield, Consuelo López, ed. *Daughters of Caliban: Caribbean Women in the Twentieth Century.* Bloomington: Indiana University Press, 1997.

Steady, Filomina Chioma, ed. *The Black Woman Cross-Culturally.* Cambridge, Mass.: Schenkman Publishing, 1981.

Traylor, Eleanor W., Alphonso Frost, and Leota S. Lawrence, eds. *Broad Sympathy: The Howard University Oral Traditions Reader.* Needham Heights, Mass.: Simon and Schuster Custom Publishing, 1997.

Trotter, Joe William, ed. *The Great Migration in Historical Perspective: New Dimensions in Race, Class, and Gender.* Bloomington: Indiana University Press, 1991.

Walker, Alice. *In Search of Our Mothers' Gardens: Womanist Prose.* San Diego: Harcourt Brace Jovanovich, 1983.

Warner, Keith Q. *Kaiso! The Trinidad Calypso: A Study of the Calypso as Oral Culture.* Washington, D.C.: Three Continents Press, 1982.

Warner Lewis, Maureen. *Guinea's Other Suns: The African Dynamic in Trinidad Culture.* Dover, Mass.: Majority Press, 1991.

———. *Trinidad Yoruba: From Mother Tongue to Memory.* Tuscaloosa: University of Alabama Press, 1996.

Waters, Mary C. *Black Identities: West Indian Immigrant Dreams and American Realities.* New York: Russell Sage Foundation; Cambridge: Harvard University Press, 2001.

Watkins-Owens, Irma. *Blood Relations: Caribbean Immigrants and the Harlem Community, 1900–1930.* Bloomington: University of Indiana Press: 1996.

Werbner, Pnina, and Tariq Modood, eds. *Debating Cultural Hybridity: Multi-cultural Identities and the Politics of Anti-Racism.* London: Zed Books, 1997.

Williams, Wilda. "Must-Reads for Fall." *Library Journal,* September 1, 2003, 36.

Wilson, Thomas W. "Africa, Afro-Americans, and Hypertensions: An Hypothesis." *Social Science History* 10 (1986): 489–500.

———. "Salt Supplies in West Africa and Blood Pressures Today." *Lancet* 1, no. 8484 (April 5, 1986): 784–86.

Wilson, Thomas W., and C. E. Grim. "Biohistory of Slavery and Blood Pressure Differences in Blacks Today: A Hypothesis." *Hypertension* 17 (January 1991): 122–28.

Winkler, Karen J. "Historians Explore Questions of How People and Cultures Disperse across the Globe." *Chronicle of Higher Education,* January 22, 1999, A11–A12.

Index

Credits

. . . .

Acknowledgment is made as follows for permission to quote from copyrighted material:

Passages from "Marriage," by Lillian Allen. *Prism International* 22, no. 4 (summer 1984), 33. Reprinted with permission of Lillian Allen.

Passages from "Transforming the Skin-Shedding Soucouyant: Using Folklore to Reclaim Female Agency in the Caribbean," by Giselle Liza Anatol. *Small Axe* 7 (March 2000): 44–59. Bloomington: Indiana University Press.

Passages from "Re-creating Ourselves All Over the World: A Conversation with Paule Marshall," by 'Molara Ogundipe-Leslie. From *Moving Beyond Boundaries,* vol. 2 *Black Women's Diasporas,* ed. Carole Boyce Davies and 'Molara Ogundipe-Leslie, 20–24. New York: New York University Press, 1995. Reprinted by permission of Professor Carole Boyce Davies.

Passages from "Carnivalised Caribbean Female Bodies: Taking Space/ Making Space," by Carole Boyce Davies. *Thamyris* 5, no. 2 (autumn 1998): 341. Reprinted by permission of Najada Press, Amsterdam, and Carole Boyce Davies.

Passages from "The Slavery Hypothesis for Hypertension among African Americans: The Historical Evidence," by Phillip Curtain. *Ameri-*

CPSIA information can be obtained at www.ICGtesting.com
Printed in the USA
LVOW05*0819040913

350863LV00001B/1/P